U.S. Energy Policy

**Errors of the Past,
Proposals for the Future**

U.S. Energy Policy

Errors of the Past,
Proposals for the Future

Edited by

Walter J. Mead
University of California at Santa Barbara

and

Albert E. Utton
NATURAL RESOURCES JOURNAL
University of New Mexico Law School

Ballinger Publishing Company • **Cambridge, Massachusetts**
A Subsidiary of Harper & Row, Publishers, Inc.

Contents

RECENT DEVELOPMENTS

Chapter 1

POLITICAL-ECONOMIC PROBLEMS
OF ENERGY—A SYNTHESIS

WALTER J. MEAD*

Economic research concerned with the "energy crisis" of the 1970's has increasingly indicated that the primary problems of energy are best understood in a long-lost discipline called "political economy." From a purely economic point of view, solutions to the energy crisis are relatively simple—remove government controls and tax subsidies, except in those few instances where large externalities are clearly present. Most of the existing subsidies and regulations were introduced as a result of strong political pressure from beneficiary groups. Economic evidence demonstrating that particular subsidies or regulations waste scarce resources and do not serve the general welfare is not enough. While the beneficiary economic interests and their associated administrative bureaucracy may be limited to a few thousand people, the concentrated power of these beneficiary groups is clearly greater than the dispersed and usually disinterested power of 220 million people who pay the bill. It is increasingly obvious to students of energy economics that the problems are broader than economic analysis and require a broader approach in terms of political economy.

In purely physical terms, there is no energy crisis. While the United States has only 4.5 percent of the world's crude oil reserves and consumes 29.4 percent of world production, this nation is extremely well endowed with fossil fuel resources. United States coal reserves are 28 percent larger than crude oil reserves in the entire world (measured in terms of Btu content). In addition, U.S. oil shale resources[1] are 65 percent greater than world wide crude oil reserves.

The problem of the "energy crisis" is not that this nation lacks fossil fuel resources. Instead, the problems are economic and political. Thus for fully a half-century, the power of government has been used by dominant economic groups to indirectly promote energy consumption. Two tax subsidies, percentage depletion allowance and provisions for expensing intangible drilling costs, have artificially

---

*Dr. Mead is a Professor of Economics at the University of California at Santa Barbara.

1. These energy resources are not currently producible under prevailing price, cost, and technological conditions.

stimulated capital flows into oil and gas exploration and production, thereby increasing supplies and lowering prices. This low price policy has resulted in the well-known American "love affair" with big cars and other forms of wasteful consumption of nonrenewable energy resources. After a half-century of tax subsidies favoring oil and gas production, the nation has virtually exhausted its low cost oil and gas reserves. We may still have large undiscovered resources of oil and gas plus known but currently uneconomic shale oil resources. These future energy sources will not be cheap.

The historic low price policy is not dead. President Carter, in his National Energy Plan (April 1977) noted that under Federal Power Commission price controls, natural gas "is now the nation's most underpriced and oversold fuel." One would expect, following this observation, that the President would have called for decontrol of new natural gas supplies. Instead, for political reasons, he recommended the opposite, namely that wellhead price controls be extended to include intrastate gas. The President correctly noted that both oil and natural gas are "priced domestically below their marginal replacement costs, and, as a result, the nation uses them wastefully, with little regard to their true value." Economists can take pride in the President's comprehension of this important economic principle. However, in the next paragraph of his statement, he yielded to political reality and stated that "the residential sector is sheltered as the Plan would keep natural gas prices to residential users down and provide tax rebates for home oil use." Once again, political expediency nullifies valid economic principles.

The authors who have been asked to contribute to this volume have been selected because of their well established expertise in energy research. Many of them have been involved in economic analysis of energy problems for more than a decade. Most of the important areas of energy policy are covered in the papers contained in this volume. However, because of the limits of space, a comprehensive treatment of all energy policy problems was not possible. For example, there is no specific treatment of nuclear energy economics. The multitude of environmental issues arising out of energy development have not been given systematic treatment. Also, solar power potential plus other exotic energy forms are not evaluated. These gaps notwithstanding, the papers cover a broad spectrum of pressing energy problems.

The purpose of this first chapter is to attempt a synthesis of the several authors' findings and conclusions. The papers have been arranged in such a way that a story emerges.

3

A SYNTHESIS

The major areas of interest in international oil concern: (1) forecasts of future oil supplies available to the United States, (2) the probable world demand for oil in the future, (3) the probable behavior of world oil prices under the impact of both competitive market forces and potential cartel policies of the Organization of Petroleum Exporting Countries (OPEC), and (4) the important issue of oil import dependence. The dependence issue is paramount for reasons of military security and also the potential for economic instability and reduced economic growth due to a boycott or substantial price increases.

Forecasting supply, demand, and price for international oil is both difficult and easy. Based partly on personal experience, McKie acknowledges that the uncertainties in forecasting energy supply and demand and legendary and he confesses that "Ouija boards could hardly have done worse than some of our models." Forecasting future oil prices is said to be difficult, primarily because both demand and supply functions are highly inelastic in the short run. Thus any small shift in the supply function can bring about relatively large changes in price. This fact was clearly demonstrated in the Arab oil embargo.

At the same time, forecasting oil prices is said to be easy because there are relatively long lead-times affecting changes in market supplies. Large new discoveries are known from one to ten years before such supplies reach the market. Similarly, existing oil fields decline under rather precisely known decline rates. Unlike hula hoops and television sets, output cannot be suddenly doubled and redoubled with consequent price effects. And unlike computers and calculators, major technological changes bringing forth significant cost and price reductions are unlikely to occur.

Among the more pessimistic forecasts is one by the U.S. Central Intelligence Agency which foresees world energy demand exceeding supply by the early 1980's, bringing about rapidly rising prices in a crisis atmosphere.[2] Similarly, a recent MIT report concludes that "The supply of oil will fail to meet increasing demand before the year 2000, most probably between 1985 and 1995, even if energy prices rise 50% above current levels in real terms."[3]

A more recent report by Lichtblau and Frank, commissioned by

2. CENTRAL INTELLIGENCE AGENCY, The International Energy Situation: Outlook to 1985, ER 77-1024 OU (April 1977).
3. REPORT ON THE WORKSHOP ON ALTERNATIVE ENERGY STRATEGIES, ENERGY: GLOBAL PROSPECTS 1985-2000, 3, 4 (1977).

4

the Electric Power Research Institute (EPRI), reaches more optimistic conclusions: "An oil shortage before the late 1980's is unlikely, an oil shortage before the end of the century is a possibility but not a probability, and a gradual transition, accompanied by moderate real price increases, over the next 25-35 years from oil to non-oil sources to meet incremental world energy requirements is more likely than an extended oil shortage of crisis proportions."[4]

The Adelman paper concerned with international oil is more in accord with the EPRI report. He classes the CIA forecast as a doomsday scenario and a distorted version of the problem. Adelman concludes that "We can probably look forward to a decade of rising real oil prices. . . ." The idea of a shortage in which oil selling nations are assumed to hold oil prices below market clearing levels is appropriately ridiculed by Adelman. Those who forecast a "shortage" implicitly assume but rarely explain why oil exporting countries would hold oil prices at artificially low levels, thereby creating a shortage. McKie also doubts the CIA scenario. He writes that "The world does not seem to be confronted with early exhaustion of liquid hydrocarbons." Instead, potential supply appears to be "about a 75-year supply at current rates of production. Much additional oil might become available at higher cost horizons consistent with expected OPEC prices. . . ."

As a result of what he calls his "small experiment," Adelman concludes that we cannot possibly explain current and prospective international oil price levels by scarcity, present or foreseen." His explanation instead is in terms of an imperfect cartel system tested in terms of two conventional cartel theories. Adelman sees some characteristics of a conventional cartel in which members control prices through either a market sharing mechanism or a dominant-firm price-leadership model led by Saudi Arabia.

In his "small experiment" he assumes that the nearest alternative to conventional oil supplies could be installed in very large amounts after the year 2000 and could supply apparently unlimited amounts of energy at $16 per barrel of oil equivalent (1975 constant prices). He concludes that the "competitive" price of oil in 1975 should have been about $2.25 per barrel. However, at that time the observed price was around $12.70 per barrel. In reaching this conclusion, Adelman apparently used a ten percent *real* discount rate. This is an inordinately high discount rate, given the real opportunity cost of capital in Saudia Arabia and other leading oil producing countries.

4. J. LICHTBLAU and H. FRANK, The Outlook for World Oil into the 21st Century, With Emphasis on the Period to 1990 S-1, EA-745 SOA-76-328 (May 1978).

Further, the possibility that unlimited supplies of an oil substitute will be available at a real price of $16 after the year 2000 appears to be unduly optimistic.

Following Adelman's methodology, if one uses a three percent real discount rate and a $20 (1975 prices) oil substitute price in the year 2000, the national 1975 price becomes $9.55 per barrel. This is a reasonably close approximation to the observed $12.70 per barrel cited by Adelman.[5]

Some new research by Johany, recently completed as part of a Ph.D. dissertation at the University of California at Santa Barbara has shown that crude oil price movements from approximately $3 per barrel in the early 1970's to approximately $12.50 per barrel in 1974 after the Arab embargo ended are rational in terms of individual oil producing countries maximizing the present value of their resources.[6] Johany has joined two relevant principles of economics, capital theory and property rights theory, to shed new light on rational price behavior for nonrenewable oil resources.

Johany pointed out that during the 1950's and 1960's there was a progressive awareness on the part of international oil companies holding oil concessions in the Middle East that their property rights were in jeopardy. Nationalization, or its euphemism, "participation," was the wave of the future. But as the concessionaire companies became increasingly fearful concerning their property rights, they naturally reacted by raising their discount rates. This means that production was shifted from the future to the present. This fear of loss of property rights resulted in rapid increases in oil production from Middle Eastern sources. From 1950 through 1970 the compound annual growth rate in oil production from the Middle East was 10.9 percent. From 1970 through 1973, the compound annual growth rate was 15.0 percent.

Reflecting these output increases, world crude oil prices were relatively stable during the two decades from 1950 through 1970. Output increases were matched by world-wide growth in demand with only modest increases in nominal prices. Real prices for crude oil in the United States actually declined 6 percent from 1950 through 1970.

By the end of 1973, a complete shift in property rights had, in

5. A much more elaborate experiment was performed by Pindyck which concluded that the rational price for world oil in 1977 was between $12.50 and $13.00 per barrel. PINDYCK, *Gains to Producers from the Cartelization of Exhaustible Resources,* Rev. Econ. Stat. (May 1978).

6. Ali D. Johany, OPEC is not a Cartel: A Property Rights Explanation of the Rise in Crude Oil Prices, (unpublished dissertation, University of California, Santa Barbara) (1978).

fact, occurred. Host countries were in complete control of output within their borders by year-end 1973, and they were either unilaterally determining the terms of sale for their crude, or nationalizaton had been completed.

With property rights shifted from companies to host countries, security of property rights was reestablished. The relevant discount rate became that of the host country rather than the concessionaire company. Discount rates declined not only because property rights became secure in the hands of the host country, but also because the opportunity cost of money for the host country was relatively low. Investment opportunities for large sums of money in Saudi Arabia are relatively unattractive. Investments abroad yield only competitive rates of return, but were further jeopardized by exchange rate losses. With secure property rights, the most attractive investment for some countries was simply leaving their oil in the ground. The oil minister for Kuwait has stated that, "We have the capacity to produce 5 million barrels daily but are producing at a maximum rate of only 2 billion barrels daily and are endeavoring to spread our oil resources evenly over 80 years."[7] This policy is rational for Kuwait given (1) secure property rights and (2) relatively low discount rates. It is a rational policy independent of a cartel. Oil producing countries with the exception of Saudi Arabia appear to take the price of oil in the long-run as market determined and unaffected by their own behavior.

Given firmly established property rights and lower discount rates, one would expect reduced output growth rates and sharply higher prices. The record shows that from 1973 to 1977 Middle Eastern oil output increased at a compound annual rate of only 0.7 percent. This is in contrast to an 11.4 percent compound annual rate from 1950 through 1973 under insecure property rights and correspondingly high discount rates. As a consequence, crude oil prices in world markets rose sharply, from 1970 to d⌐te, a fact which can be explained without the aid of a cartel theory.

The Johany thesis stands in sharp contrast to the conventional wisdom which explicitly or implicitly assumes that the world price of oil is fixed by an effectively collusive OPEC cartel. Adelman clearly shares this latter viewpoint, and other authors in this volume refer to cartel pricing. McKie asks whether the U.S. energy economy should adjust to the world price of oil as if it were a competitive price or should the government intervene to offset the monopoly element in the cartel price? In discussing oil shale, McDonald asserts that "[shale

---

7. Vol. XX Middle East Econ. Survey No. 42, at 2 (August 1977).

oil's] price is effectively set by OPEC. . . ." Hudson and Jorgenson refer to "the establishment of the OPEC oil cartel in late 1973 and early 1974" without claiming that OPEC is an effective cartel today. However, in another recent paper, Jorgenson says that "Although the OPEC cartel is not a perfect monopoly, it comes sufficiently close. . . ."[8]

In the international area the import dependence issue is dealt with specifically by McKie and peripherally by several other authors. Continuation of the present U.S. consumption pattern requires a high level of oil imports. McKie estimates that oil imports in the mid-1980's will exceed nine million barrels per day. In 1977, imports amounted to 8.7 million barrels per day. He notes that "national security is ostensibly the overriding objective of import policy." Economic impact is an important but secondary consideration. Given important external effects of oil imports, he concludes that "the free market is an inadequate instrument for handling questions of national security. . . ." Brannon concurs and argues on behalf of an import tax to internalize security costs.

The import dependence issue has been an important element of U.S. policy for approximately two decades and was used as a rationale for the oil import quota program instituted by President Eisenhower in 1959. But this program collapsed largely of its own weight in 1973. This country, having produced more domestic oil as a result of tax subsidies and import quotas was even more vulnerable than it would have been in the absence of such interference with market forces.

In McKie's view, optimum policies for solving the national security issues of oil and import dependence are fairly obvious. He holds that the most important step is one currently being taken by the U.S. government, that of establishing a Strategic Petroleum Reserve System (SPRS). This System would provide protection against short-run interruptions with obvious benefits for consumers. Brannon proposes that the costs of the petroleum reserves system should be financed by import taxes. His argument rests on the proposition that consumers of imported oil are the beneficiaries and should bear the cost of reducing import dependency hazards.

McKie suggests that the SPRS might be supplemented by greater reliance on relatively secure import sources. He might have recommended another policy, that of nourishing mutually interdependent and lasting relations with crude rich nations. This approach unfor-

---

8. JORGENSON, The Role of Energy in the U.S. Economy (a paper presented at the National Tax Association—Tax Institute of America, Symposium on Energy Taxation, Washington, D.C., May 17, 1978) (forthcoming in National Tax Journal).

tunately involves conflicting alliances between the United States and Israel, on one hand, and Arab oil producing nations, on the other hand.

Moyer points out that the national commitment to reduce import dependence "must necessarily favor coal, at least for the remainder of the 20th Century." United States coal reserves are vast and constitute a secure energy source. However, as the nation learned in the winter of 1977-78 energy supply interruptions are not limited to imported sources. At its worst, the prolonged bituminous coal strike reduced domestic coal production to one third of its normal level. This reduction in Btu supplies was greater than occurred during the Arab oil embargo, but its consequences were relatively minor.

Given the import dependence problem, consideration must be given to policies for finding new domestic oil and gas reserves as well as for use of other energy sources including our abundant coal and oil shale resources. Concerning federal oil and gas leasing policies, McDonald offers a valuable contribution in his identification of appropriate objectives from an economic analysis point of view. Where more than one land management objective is established, the possibility of conflicting goals immediately arises. The present law states three objectives: (1) to assure orderly and timely resource development, (2) to protect the environment, and (3) to insure the public a fair return on the disposition of its resources. The law provides no standard by which conflicts between these objectives are to be resolved. Given this obvious confusion, land administrators have wide latitude in reacting to political pressures brought to bear on them. The history of U.S. leasing policy suggests that the stated goals are secondary and mitigating political pressure is primary. The annual volume of oil and gas leasing will be accelerated under pressure from the petroleum industry (and occasionally out of government budgetary considerations), or will be reduced under pressure from environmentalists. This is a serious problem for the nation inasmuch as the Federal government owns most of the remaining potential oil and gas resources.

McDonald proposes a single decision rule for allocating scarce resources over time. He proposes that the government seek to "capture a maximum of the present value of pure economic rent arising from mineral production on its lands." This rule gives paramount consideration to the economic meaning of conservation. If future generations "need" oil and gas resources more than present generations, then research will show the *in situ* value of such resources increasing faster than the opportunity cost of money. Under Mc-

Donald's proposed decision rule, administrators would be required to reduce their rate of leasing in favor of future generations.

Having determined a single land management objective, McDonald reviews alternative leasing methods. He concludes that given the extent of competition for oil and gas leases and the character of the market, sealed bidding is preferable to oral auction bidding. Further, he finds the existing method of cash bonus bidding is more efficient than any alternative systems.

The United States alone, among the nations of the world, has elected to use a pure competitive system for leasing its mineral lands. Other nations appear to believe that competition for leases would be inadequate and therefore they resort to a variety of forms of administrative discretion.

The Jones-Mead-Sorensen paper reports on a study of competition for Federal oil and gas leases over the period 1954 through 1962. Analysis of this record shows that competition under the cash bonus bidding system has been overly effective. In 839 lease sales, bidding has been sufficiently intense that the internal rate of return earned by lessees has been driven down to 9.5 percent *before taxes.* This rate of return is less than a competitive norm. It indicates that the government has received more than fair market value for its leases.

McDonald wisely sets forth the objective of maximizing the present value of pure economic rent. An inefficient bidding system causes dissipation of economic rent even though competition for such leases may be effective. Thus, under a royalty bidding system an additional marginal cost (payment of the royalty) is imposed on each additional barrel of oil produced under the lease. Because the royalty is a transfer payment and not a social cost, this leads to premature abandonment of a lease. Socially valuable oil or gas is left in the ground and may never be recovered. Further, with high royalty payments, cost-justified investments in secondary and tertiary recovery will be discouraged, again leading to a loss of socially valuable resources.

Similarly, profit share bidding introduces inefficiencies. Profit share payments are approximately the same as additional income taxes (depending on how profits are defined). The higher the profit share bid, the lower the incentive for an operator to manage his lease efficiently. The nation has experience with high corporate income taxes under the excess profits tax system prevailing during the Korean War and World War II. The decision-making structure under very high marginal tax rates leads to wasteful expenditures and underinvestment. In addition, the nation has experience with profit share bidding in Long Beach, California leases. This experience shows that efficiency incentives are lacking and that litigation costs are excessive. Both factors cause a dissipation in available economic rents.

Despite convincing evidence of the effectiveness of the present system of leasing Outer Continental Shelf oil and gas lands (as shown in the Jones, Mead and Sorensen paper), Congress is proposing to move the nation away from the present system of cash bonus bidding with a small fixed royalty, and toward the use of other bidding systems which McDonald shows to be inferior.

In addition to developing new oil and gas reserves from lands not yet explored, the nation must consider developing energy from alternative domestic sources. Moyer presents (in his Table 2) estimates of recoverable energy reserves from alternative energy sources. This table shows that 79 percent of the estimated recoverable energy reserves in the United States are in the form of coal.[9]

In 1920 "King Coal" accounted for 78 percent of the primary energy used in the United States. But oil and natural gas were cheaper, easier to handle and cleaner to use. By the early 1950's, rising oil production replaced coal as the nation's primary energy source. The decline of coal in percentage contribution to U.S. energy supply has been virtually uninterrupted from 1920 to date. After discussing the comparative disadvantages of coal, Moyer concludes that "the intrusive hand of government" overwhelms all other burdens which cloud coal's future. Government restraint comes in the form of legislation, regulations, and court interpretations. But government is both pushing and pulling on coal. The Carter National Energy Plan proposes forced conversion to coal by industry and utilities through both regulation and the imposition of new taxes on the use of oil and natural gas.

In the absence of any government interference either to restrain coal or to encourage it, the fourfold increase in the price of crude oil since 1973 should have restored some of coal's past glory. Moyer's Table 3 shows the Btu cost advantage of coal relative to oil and gas in all regions of the United States except the South Atlantic.

The loss of coal markets in transportation (railroad locomotives) and in home heating is probably permanent. The growth market for

9. The next largest energy source according to this listing is oil shale. The estimate is made by the National Coal Association, which includes only oil shale reserves that are "considered recoverable by demonstrated methods and include oil recoverable from higher-grade oil shale in Utah and Colorado, in beds 25 ft. or more thick, yielding about 30 gals. of oil per ton of rock and lying at depths less than 1,000 ft. below the surface. Assumed recovery is 60 percent of the oil content of the shale in place." This definition is more restrictive than the one drawn upon by the present writer in an earlier paragraph.

coal in the foreseeable future appears to be in electric power generation. The Federal government is moving in the direction of mandating natural gas out of electric power production, and residual fuel oil already appears to be priced out of this market. This leaves the field of new large-scale electric power production available almost exclusively to coal and nuclear. According to a Federal Energy Administration study based on 1975 dollars, the fuel cost alone at $13 per barrel was more than the total cost of electricity generation by nuclear power (and nearly as high as the total costs of coal, without scrubbers). The FEA estimates are as follows:

Base Load Electricity Generation Costs (mills/kwh, 1975 dollars)

	Nuclear	Coal w/o scrubbers	Coal w/scrubbers	Oil
Capital	13.45	9.30	11.74	7.58
Fuel	1.80	10.11	6.85	20.70
Other	3.00	2.00	3.50	1.88
Total	18.25	21.41	22.09	30.16

Source: F.E.A., National Energy Outlook, 1976 pp. 187, 191.

Moyer points out that amendments to the Clean Air Act of 1977 require that new manufacturing plants as well as utilities using coal must use the "best available control technology" to reduce SOx emissions. This legislation not only reduces the advantage of low sulfur western coal relative to eastern coal but also impairs the ability of coal to compete with nuclear power. A more recent study based on mid-1976 costs shows that if scrubbers are required on coal fired generating plants, the generating cost is five percent higher than without scrubbers and 19 percent above the cost of generating electricity from nuclear power. The data are as follows:

Midwestern U.S. Base Load Electricity Generation
Cost (mills/kwh, 1976 dollars)

	Nuclear	Coal w/o scrubbers	Coal w/scrubbers
Total Cost	23.9	27.2	28.5

Source: Report of the Nuclear Energy Policy Study Group, *Nuclear Power Issues and Choices* (1977).

Moyer reviews the problems facing coal in the form of water pollution, conflicts concerning the allocation of water resources, environmental and other lawsuits over the implementation of the Energy Supply and Environmental Coordination Act, Surface Mining Control and Reclamation Act of 1977, and the Federal Coal Mine Health and Safety Act of 1969, and the breakdown of authority of the United Mine Workers Union. He concludes that the future of coal depends as much on "actions in the legislative halls and court rooms as it does on decisions flowing from coal company boardrooms."

Shale oil, unlike coal, has never reigned. Instead it seems to be a perpetual threshold industry. In 1973 spokesmen for the Oil Shale Corporation (TOSCO) informed the Ford Foundation Energy Policy Project that their company was ready to proceed with production of oil from shale. Their calculations indicated that a $250 million capital investment would produce 50,000 barrels per day of oil which, when upgraded, would sell in California markets as virtually zero sulfur content fuel oil at about $5.30 per barrel, yielding the company a 13 percent rate of return on its investment. Since 1973 the price of low sulfur fuel oil has increased nearly fivefold and there is no oil shale industry.[10]

The cost data presented by Schanz and Perry in their Table 3 both confirm the threshhold character of the oil shale industry and also help to explain the cost problems encountered by the industry. Companies may have persistently underestimated the capital costs of plant construction. However, Schanz and Perry point out that environmental contraints enforced by Federal and State governments added substantially to both capital and operating costs. Direct and indirect costs of investments in community support facilities were also factored into capital requirements. Environmental roadblocks thrown in the path of oil shale development also added both procedural and legal problems requiring from two to three additional years for the construction process. The authors estimate that a two year delay is equivalent to a 20 percent increase in the price required for an oil shale plant to be deemed economic. According to Schanz and Perry the price of oil in 1976 would have had to equal $18.30 per barrel in order to yield an acceptable minimum rate of return on an investment in oil shale production. However in 1976, the price of oil was about $13 per barrel. They conclude that current uncertain-

---

10. The history of oil shale in the United States is partly folklore. According to one story, a pioneer Colorado settler by the name of Mike Callahan built a log house in Rio Blanco County in Colorado, then invited friends in for a housewarming. The fireplace was built of an attractive grey stone later known as marlstone. According to legend, when Callahan built his first fire, the fireplace and the house burned down. MONROE, *Introduction* to H. SAVAGE, THE ROCK THAT BURNS (1967).

ties do not justify the required investment for oil shale production and therefore "shale oil production continues to be a game of watchful waiting."

The distant future for oil shale is probably more easily predicted than its near term prospects. Oil shale suffers from high production costs but its basic problem is competition from crude oil. As long as abundant reserves of crude oil exist in the world, the U.S. oil shale industry will probably remain on the threshhold, except for pilot plant production. When crude oil production declines sharply under pressure of economic exhaustion and its price permanently rises to new high levels, only then will large scale U.S. shale oil production begin. But that point is probably at least a half-century away. At lower levels of crude oil production, present members of OPEC will probably reserve their own crude oil for high valued uses, primarily petrochemical production, within their own borders. At that time, perhaps 75 years from now, there is likely to be only one surviving member of OPEC. That survivor is likely to be the United States, producing and exporting oil from its immense resources in oil shale, supplemented perhaps by synthetic crude oil from its large coal reserves.

Erickson, Peters, Spann and Tese have presented a case study of the dominant present form of regulation prevailing in the U.S. oil industry—crude oil price controls. The authors attempt to provide an economic rationale for multi-tier crude oil controls based upon the concept of "regulatory monopsonization" of U.S. crude oil producers. Under this concept the regulatory power of the Federal government might conceivably be used to create monopsony results thereby capturing monopsony profit.

A decision-making rule to accomplish this result would be deceptively simple. Controlled prices for categories of U.S. crude oil production must be set such that the marginal cost of each source is equal to the price of imported oil. The authors identify the necessary conditions for such a system to be efficient in both a static and a dynamic framework. They then find that these conditions are sufficiently formidable and perplexing that efficient monopsonization by the government is unlikely to occur.

While the rationale for crude oil price controls is weak, the fact that controls have reduced prices of some classes of crude oil cannot be denied. Erickson *et al.* conclude that the long term effect of this erosion of incentives to produce oil has been to reduce domestic crude oil supply. The authors give two reasons for this conclusion. Lower prices than would occur in the absence of control lead to a reduction in investments in oil recovery and thus to sub-optimal levels of oil production. Second, in the absence of normal investment incentives, the decline rate in old oil production will be higher than normal. Since the regulated crude oil price is a weighted average of lower and upper tier crude prices, a more rapidly declining volume of lower tier oil necessarily reduces upper tier prices. The authors conclude that "The result, under composite price controls, is to reduce the price incentive for discovering and developing new oil resources."

Erickson and his colleagues also provide a short analysis of how crude oil price controls might affect petroleum product prices. Their analysis indicates that crude oil decontrol would cause product prices to increase approximately 5 cents per gallon for gasoline.

In sum, Erickson *et al.,* like McKie, find that U.S. crude oil price controls have contributed to lower domestic crude oil production, to higher consumption, and to increased U.S. dependence upon imported oil. A phase-out of price controls in May of 1979, as provided by the Energy Policy and Conservation Act of 1975, would "simplify the regulatory environment in which the U.S. petroleum industry operates, increase domestic supplies of oil and reduce reliance upon imports." The economic effects are relatively clear. All that remains is a political question as to whether this economic policy is acceptable at all, and if so, how price controls are to be phased out.

Deacon conducts a more detailed analysis of the effect of price controls on motor gasoline. This paper reports on two hypotheses. First, based on a study of imported versus domestic wholesale gasoline prices under price controls, the author finds that in the two year period 1975-1976 U.S. price controls resulted in domestic gasoline prices significantly lower than would be expected on the basis of uncontrolled gasoline imports. However, for the year 1977 he finds no significant differences and no evidence that price controls were effective in reducing U.S. gasoline prices.

Deacon's second hypothesis examines the increase in wholesale gasoline prices in the U.S. and the Netherlands between 1970-71 and 1977, after adjustments for taxes, transportation, import duties, and the present entitlements subsidy to imports. He finds results "inconsistent with the proposition that U.S. price increases (as of 1977) have been abnormally low when judged against an uncontrolled foreign situation." Again, he finds that price controls resulted in lower U.S. prices only through the year 1976. As a consequence of his analysis, he concludes that "competition, not regulation, is enforcing the current structure of gasoline prices in the U.S." Further, "it is difficult to see why controls should continue; they appear to do little more than impose an administrative burden on government and industry."

Part of the argument in favor of price controls and other forms of regulation in the energy sector is based on an assumption that competition is not effective in this industry. The Jones-Mead-Sorensen paper is based on the theory that free access to crude oil and an effectively competitive crude oil lease sale market makes monopolizaton in downstream sectors of this market impossible in the long run. This paper examines the extent of competition at various levels of the oil industry. Evidence is presented showing that the structure of the crude oil lease market is competitive and that concentration ratios in lease acquisition are relatively low for big-four and big-eight firms. Entry into the lease market is shown to be relatively free. An analysis of performance in the Outer Continental Shelf lease sale market shows no evidence of monopsony profits. To the contrary, the rate of return earned by lessees on 839 leases issued between 1954 and 1962 is less than a competitive norm. Free entry into crude oil lease markets, plus demonstrated low concentration ratios in oil refining and marketing, lead the authors to conclude that collusive behavior to restrain output and increase prices is unworkable in the long-run. "Successful collusion would require either (1) storage of crude oil or products, or (2) control over access to crude oil supplies. The former is prohibitively expensive; the latter does not exist."

Kneese joins Brannon in pointing out that in the energy and environmental areas there may be important externalities resulting in resource misallocation where decisions are made purely on the basis of private costs and benefits. Kneese believes that the market introduces a "systematic bias" and this bias leads to excessive rates of resource use. In his examination of the evidence he considers only the well-known instances of external costs and gives no consideration to the possibility of offsetting external benefits. There is probably widespread agreement in the economics profession that market failures exist and, as a consequence, there is a distortion of resource flows. But a *systematic* distortion has not been demonstrated and probably is not subject to widespread agreement.

Kneese specifically refuses in his paper to define the term "conservation" and examines instead the economic justification for slowing down the use of natural resources by means of deliberate public policies and their implementation instruments. The implementation instruments cited by Kneese are (1) economic incentives in the form of taxes or fees on certain activities or release of controlled prices, and (2) administratively enforced standards, e.g., prohibitions on certain acts.

After criticizing a "systematic bias" in the unregulated market, Kneese notes that past public policies have aggravated the problem of excessive resource usage. His solution to the problem is to "replace [bad policies] with better ones."

It is not clear from the Kneese paper why future public policies utilizing taxes, fees and direct regulations would be an improvement over the past record. The paper by political scientist Daniel Ogden suggests that the principles of national policy making have not changed and that the "power clusters" which dominate policy making and the administrative agencies which guard their "turf" will continue to be successful in constraining and modifying legislation.

Economists are receptive to the idea advanced by Kneese of correcting for market failures by internalizing externalities. However, attempts to apply this principle are confronted with difficult problems.

First, where fees or taxes are levied to offset net external costs, the externality must be evaluated. Once evaluated, legislation must be enacted by Congress. Second, where Ogden's "market clusters" and administrative agencies exercise their customary rights to be heard, any similarity between what economists conclude is an appropriate fee to internalize externalities, or a proposed regulation as a means of avoiding external costs, may be only coincidental. Third, the cost of administering taxes, fees, and regulations must be considered. If the social costs of administration exceed the social costs of the net externality, then society is worse off than in the presence of the net externality. Fourth, once legislation emerges it must then be administered. The process by which a regulatory agency is captured by the group to be regulated has been well documented by political scientists and is well known. As Bernstein has said, "The history of [regulatory] commissions indicates that they may have survived to the extent that they served the interests of the regulated groups."[11] Thus what economists may agree is desirable and what they may collectively urge upon Congress is not necessarily what Congress will legislate. What is administered is a further modification. The record of administering oil import quotas provides an excellent example of the progressive deterioration and ultimate collapse of a program that from the beginning never advanced the general welfare.[12] Fifth, legislation is notoriously inflexible, but the real world is dynamic. Regulation once introduced is extremely difficult to

11. M. BERNSTEIN, REGULATING BUSINESS BY INDEPENDENT COMMISSIONS, 73 (1975).

12. For a description of the oil import program and its operation, see D. BOHI & M. RUSSELL, LIMITING OIL IMPORTS: AN ECONOMIC HISTORY AND ANALYSIS (1978).

change or remove even though conditions prevailing at the time of its introduction may have changed radically.

The Kneese paper discusses several of "the greatest possibilities" for reducing the rate of growth of *energy* usage without drastic reduction of the quality or quantity of production and consumption services which would otherwise occur. All three of the author's illustrations speak of measures which improve *energy* usage. But surely any economic definition of conservation would emphasize not a single resource but conservation of all resources. It would indeed be simple to introduce fees, taxes and regulations which would reduce energy usage, but at the expense of accelerated consumption of other resources. Buildings can in fact be constructed to reduce the energy needed for space heating and air conditioning, but at the expense of more insulation, labor and other resource usage. Reducing consumption of a particular resource or even reducing consumption of all resources at one point in time should not be the objective of a national policy which seeks both static and dynamic efficiency in resource use.[13]

Having argued that the market has a "systematic bias" and under-prices energy resources leading to accelerated energy usage, and then having noted that past public policy has aggravated the problem, Kneese's faith that new public policies can correct this situation should be severely shaken. Several observations will support charges of failure of past and present policy. Price controls still exist on both natural gas and petroleum. Thus, after nearly a decade of the well publicized energy crisis, Federal policy is still aggravating the situation. The Carter National Energy Plan calls for a continuation and extension of natural gas price controls while price controls over oil are to be made permanent in the Carter plan. Regarding tax incentives, percentage depletion allowance is still accorded to all but a handful of integrated oil companies and provisions for expensing intangible drilling costs remain intact.

Brannon in his review of the use of taxation to correct for externalities in the energy sector, takes a broad view of the public choice problem, viewing it as a matter of both politics and economics. While conceding the presence of net externalities, he asserts that "a great deal, but not all, of an efficient solution for allocating energy re-

---

13. In another context and with a co-author, Kneese and Herfindahl wrote, *"The optimum sequence of outputs will reflect the impossibility of increasing the present value of total revenue minus outlays by transferring a unit of output from one period to another. This will be the case only if the present value of price minus long-run marginal cost is equal in all periods of production." See,* O. HERFINDAHL and A. KNEESE, Economic Theory of Natural Resources, 117 (1974).

sources could be achieved by simply letting markets work, which means that the market prices for energy resources would rise sharply in the U.S." This process would of course immediately raise the political problem of burdens on consumers and windfalls for energy producers and resource owners.

The policy maker must contend with the political realities, the power of those who gain versus that of those who lose by removing old tax subsidies or introducing new taxes. Brannon points out that Congress "bought off" some opposition to continued crude oil price controls by the simple expedient of exempting a multitude of oil producers—the stripper well producers (those wells producing less than 10 barrels of oil per day). Also, opposition to price controls was reduced by creating a substantial beneficiary interest. Small refiners are largely exempt from the cost of price control but share in the benefits. Refiners that receive less than an average input of price controlled old oil are entitled to receive cash payments from other refiners receiving more than the average share of old oil.

Brannon evaluates a number of energy tax systems in terms of their economic rationale (resource allocation efficiency) and in terms of political feasibility. He concludes that the energy crisis itself is a political crisis which cannot be resolved through economic policy instruments. In another recent paper evaluating the record of tax policy in dealing with energy issues, Brannon wrote that "the whole collection of income tax incentives [relating to energy] must be written off as failures."[14] The Brannon evaluation of the use of taxes to correct for market failure stands in sharp contrast with the more optimistic view of Kneese.

Ogden's view of the problems encountered by government as it attempts to deal with the energy crisis is quite similar to those of Brannon, although Ogden writes from the perspective of a political scientist. He reminds us that policy must pass through a system of "power clusters" representing various interest groups. Further, administrative agencies jealously guard their turf and yield jurisdiction only after a major struggle and only in the face of overwhelming political force.

The progress of legislation creating the new Department of Energy (DOE) is used by Ogden to illustrate his point. The politically naive among us might have assumed that the DOE would be *the* government agency exercising the lawful power of government in the energy area. Ogden cites a large number of illustrations to show that "more of energy is left out of the new Department than is included," and further that "the Department of Energy emerges as a paper tiger to wrestle with the foremost problems besetting the United States today. It has virtually no authority to conserve energy. ... It is virtually powerless to expand the nation's production of domestic energy . . . and several other agencies have the authority to check or stall energy development."

The shortcomings of DOE authority do not reflect Congressional failure to respond to the President's wishes. As Ogden puts it, "the stark truth is, the President did not ask for a Department of Energy which would assemble all Federal responsibilities under one roof. He really asked for very little more than he got." This apparent anomaly is explained in terms of political reality. Ogden observed that the President utilized a task force of experienced natural resource administrators who wrote "the strongest bill they thought could be passed." Being well aware of the strength of the power clusters and of the propensity of all agencies to protect their turf, they wrote a bill which would avoid antagonizing the most effective of these clusters." For those readers who might still believe that government could legislate a "comprehensive national energy policy" which would alleviate or solve the energy crisis, the Ogden paper should come as an enlightening lesson in political reality.

An unrestrained free market suffers from its well known externalities. But governmental attempts to correct for these market failures introduce their own shortcomings. What is in the interest of the general welfare but in conflict with dominant power clusters and administrative agencies is not likely to become public policy. The political approach to economic problems obviously has its own externalities. Political decision-makers rarely bear the costs of their collective decisions. Costs are borne by taxpayers and consumers, present and future. This is the classic externality case.

The final chapter by Hudson and Jorgenson is an empirical study showing the adjustments in energy inputs in production, changes in the composition of final demand, and reductions in economic activity as a result of increased energy prices occurring between 1972 and 1976. The authors utilize a dynamic general equilibrium model which they initially developed for the Ford Foundation Energy Policy Project. Using their revised model, they simulate two economic growth paths over the 1972-1976 period. In the first simulation, actual values of the exogenous variables, including world oil prices, are employed as the price basis for the growth path. In the second simulation, 1972 energy prices are used in order to determine the growth path which would have occurred in the absence of the actual higher energy prices.

The results measured by Hudson and Jorgenson reflect the combined forces of the market and government intervention. The authors assume that increases in energy prices were the principal forces leading to moderated growth rates in energy consumption. They note that non-price energy conservation measures were not of overwhelming importance up to 1976.

The authors find that higher energy prices have caused energy use to decline from a projected level of 81 quadrillion Btu's (quads) based upon historical growth patterns, to an actual 74 quads in 1976, a reduction amounting to 8.6 percent. This reduction in energy use is accounted for by a redirection of final demand—consumption, investment, government, and export purchases—away from energy and energy-intensive goods and services, restructuring of patterns of inputs into production that is not energy intensive, and by a reduced scale of economic activity.

Interesting patterns of change in economic activity are revealed by the analysis. With higher energy prices, the demand for capital is reduced leading to a reduction in investment levels and a slower rate of growth of capital stock and productive capacity. Higher energy prices also lead to increased demand for labor as consumers shift spending toward labor intensive services, with labor substituting for energy as an input in production. But greater demand for labor is more than offset by the adverse employment impacts of the reduced scale of economic activity. As a result, actual 1976 employment is estimated to be adversely affected by higher energy prices to the extent of 500,000 jobs (0.6 percent of the labor force) and real GNP in 1976 is estimated to be 3.2 percent lower than would have been the case under a continuation of 1972 energy prices. In sum, Hudson and Jorgenson conclude that the oil price rise "imposed a significant and continuing cost on the U.S. economy."

It is clear that market forces performed their expected function of moderating energy demand. One might further infer from this study that in the absence of oil and gas price controls, the consequent higher energy prices would have led to even further reductions in demand growth rates. This would have resulted in lower oil imports and moderated balance of payment pressures in 1976 and after.

This synthesis has attempted to relate the twelve papers and to emphasize broad areas of agreement and disagreement. If one general view pervades among most of these authors, it is that resource conservation would be better served and the nation would be better off if markets had been allowed to allocate energy resources and if past government intervention had been avoided. On the other hand, some of the writers express confidence in the ability of government, through new and better regulatory policies, to improve society's welfare in areas relating to energy. The reader is now urged to determine by means of a careful reading of all of the papers, whether the analysis and evidence supports either of these positions.

Chapter 2

INTERNATIONAL OIL

M. A. ADELMAN*

If all deposits of oil in the earth's crust were known, the cheaper ones would be exploited first, and within each deposit cost would be higher the more intensively the oil was exploited. Thus at the intensive and the extensive margin the cost would rise over time. When marginal cost (which exceeded average cost, thus affording a royalty) equaled the cost of the cheapest available alternative, there would be no new investment in oil, and mankind would gradually switch over to the alternative energy source as existing deposits were run down.

Since prices in this ideal scenario are expected to rise over time, the royalty on a given deposit would also rise. Hence, the owner of a low cost deposit, whether a public or private holder, would have a problem of timing: should he hold off for the higher price later, or take the lower price sooner? Depending on what he thought was the appropriate interest rate, which may include a large element of risk, he would try to arrange depletion so that the present value of exploiting the oil deposit at any given moment was equal to the present value of doing so at any other moment. Thus a market process levies a tax on premature use of low cost minerals, including oil.

The ideal process just described is logically sound, but does not quite match what happens in the real world: mineral prices have not generally risen (in relation to the general price level). However, few today will heed the warning of Richard L. Gordon that firms in the mineral industries have acted as though their reserves were inexhaustible and even renewable, and they have usually been proven right. For purposes of this paper, we too will disregard this possibility in the particular case of oil. Some time ago I did a small experiment by assuming that the nearest alternative energy source to conventional oil would cost $16 per barrel in 1975 prices, about $18 in 1977 prices, and could be installed to produce very large amounts after the year 2000 A.D. Mr. Ait Laoussine of Algeria recently estimated the cost of alternative energy sources in the range of $15.30 to $18.80 per barrel in 1977 dollars.[1] I assumed that costs increased relatively

*Department of Economics, Massachusetts Institute of Technology. This paper is part of a research project of the M.I.T. Energy Laboratory, NSF SIA 75-00739.

1. N. Ait Laoussine, Marketing of Oil and Gas: Sonatrach Case 9 (at OPEC seminar on The Present and Future Role of the National Oil Companies, Vienna, October 10-12, 1977).

little as one went from better to poorer deposits so that the royalty increased almost as much as the price. In addition, some rather conservative assumptions about demand, risky interest rates, and above all, assuming that ultimate oil reserves were indeed as estimated in 1975 and that gas reserves were to be ignored, the competitive price of oil in 1977, making full allowance for its nonrenewable character, was about $2.25 per barrel in 1977 prices. Since the price was around $12.70 per barrel it is clear that we cannot possibly explain the current and prospective international oil price levels by scarcity, present or foreseen.[2]

A different industry supplies a cautionary tale. Airline capital and operating costs have increased in recent years, yet domestic and international fares were substantially reduced because of the loss of official support for fixing rates far above competitive levels. Cost changes were less important than the strength of the monopoly. Since the oil price is also far above cost (including the present value of assumed future scarcity) only a continuing monopoly can sustain it.

Assuming that the optimal monopoly price is higher than the current price (a consensus view, which I personally share but some respected observers do not) we will try to indicate why the monopoly will move slowly and gradually. To a first approximation, we can think of the oil nations as a single seller. If they were selling tin or coffee for example, and knew the optimal price, they would charge it forthwith. But oil is so large a part of the world flow of payments that it would be reckless to disregard the effects of large sudden changes in that flow. The actions of the Organization of Petroleum Exporting Countries (OPEC), as distinguished from their rhetoric, have always been sober and cautious. The big price increases of 1973 and of 1974 (over 50 percent from January 1 to mid-October) have played a significant part in the world recession and stagnation of later years. The direct results of the price increases were not nearly as important as the secondary effects arising from the consuming nations' attempts to restrain inflation and prevent excessive balance of payments deficits. The oil sellers are much better off with higher prices and world stagnation. However, yet higher prices and worse recession would not be good for them. One should not expect higher prices until world monetary and trading systems are in better shape than they are at the time of this writing, January 1978.

---

2. ADELMAN, The World Oil Cartel: Scarcity, Politics, and Economics, 16 Quarterly Review of Economics & Business (Summer 1976).

There is a more particular reason for caution in price raising. The consuming nations, far from offering any resistance to the higher oil prices, have talked only of "cooperation, not confrontation," and have suited the action to the word. The official truth in the United States is that OPEC actions are good for us. One alleged benefit, incidentally, is a stronger dollar.[3] The consuming nations ought not to be goaded into seeing things as they are, and seeing OPEC as a burden to be lessened. The consuming nations could, if they wished, tax away the great bulk of OPEC revenues into their own pockets if price were in the neighborhood of the "natural limit," the same prices as an alternative energy source. The nations could also keep the price from increasing, as has been demonstrated elsewhere, by levying a progressive tariff or excise tax whose rate increases with the price.[4] A sensible monopoly ought to sacrifice considerable revenues, and stay well below the "natural limit" to lessen the risk of such a catastrophe for them. Consuming governments might never deliberately choose this policy, but if they struggled year after year with balance of payments difficulties and revenue needs, they might slowly increase taxes on oil products. Since they are closest to the final consumer, they have the power to preempt much or most of the stream of payments from ever getting to the producing governments.

There is a particular version of this weapon which an individual government could use. I have suggested an auction of American import entitlements, which would not lower consumer prices but would divert much or most monopoly revenues to the U.S. Treasury.[5] This would enable any OPEC nation to cheat, and make additional sales, or prevent loss of sales, thereby increasing its revenue, by rebating to our government for the right to export to this country. A number of OPEC governments now sell from one third to over half of their oil to the United States, and such a system would require an immediate decision between sticking with OPEC principles, boycotting the auction, and dumping oil on the world market; or bidding competitively and secretly for sales enough to keep the industry going at capacity.

The proposal for auctioning oil import rights was approved by the Economic Task Force of the then President-elect Carter.[6] Sub-

3. *Huge OPEC Oil Price Rise Benefited U.S.*, Washington Post, July 10, 1977 (an excellent paraphrase of the official view, which has ruled since at least mid-1970, when the State Department supported Libyan demands).

4. For a formal proof, see my *Constraints on the World Monopoly Price* (forthcoming in vol. 1 *Resources and Energy*, (1978).

5. *See* Adelman, *Oil Import Quota Auctions*, 17-22 January/February, 1976.

6. Oil & Gas J., January 10, 1977.

sequently his energy chief agreed that the plan would work if the United States dared to let it work.[7] But the Carter Administration is, in its own language, "grovelling for Arab oil,"[8] for reasons not explained. One cannot see much with his forehead to the ground.

At any rate, the oil selling nations ought not to change the fixed belief by the consuming nations that producing nations will, for some never stated and hence irrefutable reason, hold the world oil price below the market-clearing level. (If they did so, the shortage of oil products would make product prices soar, with huge windfall gains to refiners and marketers. These gains would be appropriated by higher crude prices.) Therefore, there will always be a "gap," with more oil demanded than is offered. Oil will then be distributed by favor and influence. Hence arises the irresistible ego trip for the statesmen in declaring that they have succeeded in getting the producers, particularly Saudi Arabia, to produce "enough to meet our needs." Of course, no matter what price is set, the amount demanded at that price will equal the amount supplied. Conversely, no matter what the Saudis produce, the price will rise high enough to where anybody paying it can have all he wants. So the Saudis will produce "enough to meet our needs" no matter how much they produce and sell, at whatever price. The longer we believe in the nonsensical gap, the better for the cartel. Anything but a slow upward price adjustment might shock us into clarity.

We now relax the assumption that there is a single monopolist, and recognize that the oil exporting nations are really a group of sellers of unequal size, of whom Saudi Arabia is by far the biggest in terms of current and potential oil capacity. It is often asserted that the Saudis are in effect monopolists of any residual supply, letting everyone else currently produce at full tilt. So far, this theory does violence to the facts. The Saudis increased output by 23 percent between 1973 and 1977, while OPEC output was static. One could argue persuasively that their ability to be the residual supplier or restrictor of last resort strengthens the cartel. But if they did become the residual suppliers, their interests would diverge radically from those of the rest of the cartel. Others would benefit from a present price increase, and they would bear the cost. Higher prices would, in the long run, lessen the market and penalize those with the largest reserves and longest perspective. Assume that long run elasticity of demand for OPEC oil is around an improbably low −0.3. Allow Saudi Arabia to initially produce nearly a third of OPEC output and absorb

---

7. Washington Post, July 10, 1977.
8. Wall Street Journal, October 20, 1977.

the total impact of the increased price and lower consumption. Then a price increase would pay the cartel handsomely but Saudi Arabia miserably and perhaps not at all. If prices doubled, revenues for OPEC as a whole would be 62 percent higher, but for Saudi Arabia they would be only 8 percent higher.

Stagnant revenues are unacceptable to a residual supplier in a market as uncertain as the world oil market. Net demand is not predictable with any accuracy. Even mild percentage changes in the world demand for oil become magnified into large changes in the demand for OPEC oil, and still larger changes in the demand for the residual suppliers' oil. Assume that consumption expected in the non-Communist world in the early 1980's was about 60 million barrels daily, but turned out really lower by 5 percent, or 3 million barrels less daily. Nobody would be surprised. But if all the reduction were borne by Saudi Arabia, then the unexpected cut coming atop an expected cut would be intolerable.

Thus the overall notion of the producing nations as *either* a conventional cartel with a market sharing mechanism, *or* as a dominant firm monopoly or a residual-supplier monopoly, are both too simple. In truth both concepts are included. We can now understand why price fixing without allocation of markets has made for haphazard fluctuations in market shares of the OPEC governments. The over-publicized squabble in early 1977 over the "two tier" system only hides the real problem. The relative value of various crude oils keeps changing incessantly because markets change. Hence, without a system of prompt corresponding adjustments in oil prices, buyers move from one supplier government to another in search of a better deal. There was a time when the margins of the operating companies were so wide that they could accept reductions in net realizations from one or another country, without switching from one supplier to another. But their margins are now so low that while it would be an exaggeration to call them mere buyers, like independent refiners, their incentives to change from one supplier to the other are many times as great as they used to be. In the current over-supply of light crudes, North Sea production is maximized at the expense of everyone else.

Thus we have three problems which must be solved simultaneously or not at all: crude oil price differentials, company producing margins, and governments' market shares. There is no solution in sight, and the cartel has gone from one ad hoc arrangement to another. The OPEC members must from time to time somehow reach an accommodation to allow all of them to share to some extent in the benefit of a higher price. The Saudis will veto the higher price unless there is something in it for them.

With all of these complex problems we really have no need for the phantoms of "gaps" and "crunches." Nor shall we be distracted by the alleged political objectives of the oil producing nations, which are served perfectly by economic gain. There is no sacrifice or trade off of one or the other. The more money one has, the better position one is in to make friends and put down enemies.

The last useless distraction involved is the notion that the Saudis keep oil in the ground for conservation or for its future value. Given their reserve position, if they produced 10 million barrels daily, a barrel produced today would sacrifice a barrel in fifty or more years. The future value of that barrel must be liberally discounted because of risks: technical, economic, political, and military. At a discount rate as recklessly low as 5 percent real, $12 from a barrel of oil sold today is better than $120 from a sale in 2025 A.D. The Saudis restrain output today to maintain the price today—a good reason, and the only one which makes sense.

CONCLUSION

We can probably look forward to a decade of rising real oil prices, slowed economic growth, chronic surpluses and increasingly strident eventual-shortage rhetoric. By 1985, the OPEC cartel may be in no worse shape than it is now, but this writer is not inclined to make any bets on any particular scenario, even his own. The world oil project at M.I.T. is working out a simulation model where many variant assumptions can be tried, but that is another story, which will not be dealt with here.

Chapter 3

OIL IMPORTS: IS ANY POLICY POSSIBLE?

JAMES W. McKIE*

A tone of fatalism seems to intrude upon any discussion of petroleum imports into the United States. By now everyone should be aware of our predicament since a surfeit of information on the "energy crisis" has been available during the last few years. Yet the public gives few signs of heeding, and policy has exhibited a delayed and uncertain response.

RECENT INITIATIVES

Project Independence of 1974 and the National Energy Plan of 1977 did formulate goals on oil imports. Project Independence, in a hurried response to the crisis, offered a set of recommendations that under a combination of favorable circumstances could reduce oil imports to zero by 1985. The Project Independence Report went on to make some pertinent observations:

> Over the next few years it will be difficult to reduce or even maintain our current level of imports. Hence, our vulnerability may well increase. By 1985, however, just the opposite will be true. The United States has a tremendous range of alternatives which can reduce or eliminate our domestic vulnerability to import disruptions. . . .
> While zero imports is achievable, it is simply not warranted economically or politically. Some imports are from secure sources. Others are from insecure sources but they can be insured against through emergency demand curtailment measures or standby storage. . . .
> It is clear from the analysis that at high world prices import vulnerability will almost take care of itself, but at lower prices our situation will worsen without new policy initiatives. . . .[1]

Four years later, we appear no closer to the goal of low import vulnerability, let alone zero imports. The government has done very little to accelerate supply or conservation. Prices of imported oil in the U.S. have stayed near $11.00 (1973 dollars), but prices on do-

---

*Dr. McKie is a Professor of Economics at the University of Texas at Austin.
1. FEDERAL ENERGY ADMINISTRATION, PROJECT INDEPENDENCE REPORT 34, 43-44 (1974).

mestic output have been held at considerably lower ceilings. Domestic production of crude oil and liquids fell to 9.7 million barrels per day (b/d) in 1976, down from 11.2 million b/d in 1971. Production increased slightly in 1977 because of the new output from Elk Hills and Alaska's Prudhoe Bay, but no long-term reversal of the decline in U.S. production was yet evident. Meanwhile, domestic demand had recovered from its slump of 1974-75 and was again bounding upwards, to 18.3 million b/d. Imports of crude and products in 1977 averaged 8.5 million b/d and in some months were running above 9 million.[2]

President Carter's National Energy Plan of April 1977 (NEP) advocated a number of policies similar to those in Project Independence. It also called for "relative" invulnerability, but not for elimination of imports.[3]

The continued difficulties with oil import policies are due partly to lack of reliable knowledge about the underlying facts. The energy system is exceedingly complex. Critical mechanisms and relationships in the system are very imperfectly known, notwithstanding the intense efforts in physical and economic research since the energy crisis began to threaten us. Choices—or "policy"—must probe into the future and make present firm, long-term commitments on the basis of unknown future facts. We have to "overdrive our headlights." The uncertainties far exceed those affecting ordinary economic decisions, whether by business firms or governments. Some of the vectors determining the future will, in fact, be governmental acts and decisions for which no "model" seems possible.

The uncertainties in forecasting energy supply and demand are legendary. Most forecasts look ridiculous within a short time after they are made. Ouija boards could hardly have done worse than some of our models.[4] Aside from difficulties with unknown data and mechanisms, they are affected by prevailing moods of optimism and pessimism.[5] The pessimistic phase now so evident certainly seems

---

2. BP Statistical Review of the World Oil Industry, 1972 and 1976; Oil & Gas J., January 11, 1978.

3. EXECUTIVE OFFICE OF THE PRESIDENT, THE NATIONAL ENERGY PLAN, 27 (1977).

4. One of the worst forecasts was the author's own, in CABINET TASK FORCE ON OIL IMPORT CONTROLS, THE OIL IMPORT QUESTION, Appendix D (1970).

5. Without this influence it would hardly be possible to account for the drastic changes made between 1970 and 1975 by the U.S. Geological Survey in its estimates of recoverable petroleum reserves in the United States, amounting to a downward revision of over 50 percent in some components. The laws of physics and geological science do not change that abruptly. See Geological Survey Circular 725, especially Figure 37, at 46 (1975). See also infra, note 16.

justified by events, but so did the optimism of the 1950's and 60's about energy and economic growth.

Alterations in the set of assumptions or projections made from the various constraints and decision variables in a model generate different "scenarios." The amount of oil imports forecast for some date such as 1985 is usually quite sensitive to changes in the assumptions since imports are the residual item in the domestic balance. Table 1 lists a number of different forecasts of future oil imports based on differing assumptions.

Most sources agree that demand for imported oil will rise sharply after 1990, especially if depletion of domestic supply is accelerated in the 1980's, unless demand is deflected onto other sources of energy. The 1980's are the critical period for transition, and the decisions that will affect events in the 1980's must be taken very soon; but the premises for those decisions are still unsettled.

SECURITY AND ECONOMIC CONSTRAINTS

Policy toward imports has not clearly defined its objectives, nor has it decided what weight to give national security. It has been beset by conflicts and uncertainties about means as well as ends—principally concerning the role of prices in energy policy.

Ends and Means

National security is ostensibly the overriding objective of import policy; but import policy is part of energy policy as a whole, which has other goals as well. One is the efficient operation and growth of the economy, including its energy inputs, subject to a security constraint. Another is equity, or ensuring that whatever policies are directed toward the ends of security and efficiency will not drastically alter the distribution of income or confer large windfall losses or gains on the wrong people. Intermingled with these public goals are a host of private and particular interests which make their influence on policy felt in special ways.

The security objective cannot really be disentangled from the others; policy affects them all. Security policy would be much simpler if the government could merely assess the degree to which petroleum imports are reasonably safe and limit imports to that percentage of domestic demand, allowing all of the other elements in the energy balance to adjust to the import constraint. But that kind of policy is no longer feasible. In the 1960's a simple policy of restricting imports of oil to a fixed percentage of domestic production was workable but only because imports were not needed to meet

TABLE 1

VARIOUS RECENT ESTIMATES OF U.S. OIL IMPORTS IN 1985

Source	Conditions	Imports, 1985 million barrels/day
Ford Foundation Energy Policy Project, *A Time to Choose*, 166-172 (1974)	Historical Growth Scenario:	
	Domestic oil and gas option	4.0
	High nuclear option	6.0
	High import option	11.0
	Technical Fix Scenario	2.0
	Zero Energy Growth Scenario	2.0
Federal Energy Administration, *Project Independence Report*, 34 (1974)	Base Case:	
	$ 7/bbl $11/bbl (constant 1974 dollars)	12.4 3.3
	Accelerated Supply and Conservation:	
	$ 7/bbl	5.6
	$11/bbl	0
Sherman H. Clark Associates, *Projection of Use of Crude Oil Handling Facilities of Seadock, Inc.*, 11 (1975)	Base Case (Comprehensive energy model)	9.2
Federal Energy Administration, *National Energy Outlook*, 41 (1976)	P.I.E.S. Reference Scenario:	
	$13/bbl $16/bbl (constant dollars)	5.9 3.3
	Accelerated supply and conservation, $13/bbl	1.7
	Price control and supply pessimism, $13/bbl world price	12.6
Central Intelligence Agency, *The International Energy Situation, Outlook to 1985*, 15 (1977)	Maximum production, minimum demand	11.2
	Minimum production, maximum demand	15.6
Exxon Corporation, *World Energy Outlook*, 29 (1977)	Historic finding rates, "favorable" government policies	12.5
National Energy Plan, 59 (April 29, 1977)	Current trends	11.5
	Security and economic policies in NEP	7.0
Council on Energy Resources, University of Texas, *National Energy Policy: A Continuing Assessment* (1978)	NEP prices and demand projections; production model for oil, gas and coal: Median case.	16.5

demand.[6] At stake then were only the degree of price protection for domestic producers and the fraction of domestic producing capacity that was to be held idle.

For the present and future, oil imports are a dependent variable for policy. The nation can have a goal of reducing imports, but policy must address the numerous primary elements in the energy balance, such as those that determine domestic oil and gas supply, supply and substitution of other domestic sources, domestic energy demand and conservation, and new energy technologies. Import quotas would start at the wrong end of the process, damming up the inflow without attending to the consequences for the energy system. Quotas would inflict a permanent embargo on ourselves.

If policy is to work on the basic elements of the energy balance, it must make clear how much control and coercion should be imposed and how much reliance should be placed on price incentives and markets. Price movements involve troublesome conflicts among criteria for policy as recent history demonstrates. When excess capacity finally disappeared from the U.S. oil industry in 1972, continued maintenance of rigorous import controls would have resulted in rapid escalation of domestic oil prices; the government chose instead (in April 1973) to remove the limits on imports. It had meanwhile imposed price controls on domestic production from already-discovered oil ("old" oil) to prevent windfall gains. Since then it has maintained ceilings on domestic oil lower than the price of imported oil.

Under these circumstances, of course, proposals to restrict imports by imposing high tariffs in order to raise import prices seem misplaced. They would deflect more demand onto domestic sources without creating any new incentives for domestic production and would necessitate even more elaborate arrangements than we have now for equitable averaging of high-priced import costs and price-controlled domestic oil. If the aim is merely a higher average price, that could be achieved by removing price controls on domestic oil; the world price seems quite high enough already to afford strong price incentives to produce and to conserve.

Policy toward natural gas, a strategically significant substitute for oil, illustrates the influence of distributional goals still more vividly: instead of allowing prices to rise, stimulating more supply and allocating gas through the market to the most valuable uses, the govern-

---

6. East of the Rockies imports were at first limited to 12.2% of eastern domestic production; west of the Rockies to the amount necessary to meet demand, at current prices, after all western production was absorbed. As the decade wore on, certain exceptions were added which raised the import percentage to over 20% of U.S. consumption by 1970.

ment has continued price controls imposed in the 1950's and has allowed shortages to develop which it can ultimately manage only by end-use controls.

The same conflicts, and the same inclination to give predominant weight to equitable distribution over efficiency and security, are illustrated in President Carter's National Energy Plan proposals. The President's message says of the Plan:

> Above all it is fair. Our guiding principle, as we developed the Plan, was that none of our people should be asked to bear an unfair burden, and none should reap an unfair advantage.[7]

The debate over these policies has not ended. But it is clear that the government has not chosen to optimize security, or efficiency: its policy choices have weakened both, and at the same time have opted for more and more centralized authority and direct controls in lieu of market allocation and free prices.[8]

The free market is an inadequate instrument for handling questions of national security, and it is indifferent to some questions of equity; but can it deal with all other aspects of oil imports? Leaving goals of security and equity aside, would uncontrolled U.S. energy markets, including petroleum imports, fail to meet the criteria of economic efficiency?

Market Failure?

Economists have little difficulty with the economic anatomy of energy. For the near and middle term, it resolves itself into costs, prices, and investment. If domestic oil is seen to be running out, its value will reflect that fact; uses of lowest value will convert to alternatives; relative prices will determine the rate of expansion of alternative energy sources; emergent profit opportunities responding to price movements will call forth investment in the requisite sectors. In a free market, oil and gas will be imported if they are cheaper than the domestic articles. Energy will tend to be valued at replacement cost from the relevant source. Would this machinery generate any problems that require the intervention of "policy"?

The U.S. balance of payments and the international monetary system

We need not dwell on elementary economics: imports exchange

---

7. The National Energy Plan, *supra,* note 3, at iii.

8. Here, and elsewhere, I am indebted to Milton Russel and Douglas R. Bohi for valuable insights on energy security policy, especially in U.S. ENERGY POLICY: ALTERNATIVES FOR SECURITY (1975) and LIMITING OIL IMPORTS (1978).

for exports, and if it is cheaper to use resources to produce other goods and exchange them for oil than to use those same resources to produce domestic energy, it is economically better to do so. The effect on the balance of payments is a special problem in the short run only because of the size of the expected outlays on oil imports (which could reach $85 billion per year in 1985 if imports were running at 12 million b/d at a price of, say, $20 per barrel) and because of the abruptness of change in the terms of trade on this critically important commodity.[9] The difficulties in absorbing the changes into a new, moving equilibrium of trade for the U.S. could be regarded as temporary market malaise. But it must be remembered that West Germany and Switzerland import *all* of their oil, and have been subject to the full force of escalating world prices; yet their currencies have been climbing relative to the dollar and their international balance of payments are not in trouble. The dollar is, of course, a reserve currency, and a protracted crisis of liquidation would undoubtedly lead to government intervention of some sort; but limiting oil imports would be a poor option.

The technology of energy source development

A market economy relies on the response of technology to prices and investment opportunities, given an underlying autonomous rate of advance in scientific knowledge. If the energy economy is to reduce dependence on petroleum, including imported petroleum, in the future the pace of technology might have to be forced if the period of conversion were to last no more than fifteen or twenty years. Unfortunately, the uncertainties are very great, and the outlays required for development of coal liquefaction, nuclear waste disposal technologies, shale oil, hydrogen technology, nuclear fusion, solar energy, etc. are prodigious. Private firms might not respond adequately to price signals without government help—subsidization, tax incentives, risk-bearing. This type of government intervention need not be motivated directly by the goal of reducing oil imports. If, however, there were no reason to doubt *either* the security *or* the availability of oil in abundant quantities in the world for the indefinite future, the government would probably see little need for such policies on any large scale. That was the viewpoint of the 1950's on energy technology: no market failure was evident.

---

9. Oil imports in 1977 involved outlays of about $40 billion. The 1977 trade deficit overall was about $27 billion, up from $6 billion in 1976. Total imports in 1977 exceeded $150 billion.

OPEC prices

An effectively functioning price system depends on competition. Should the domestic U.S. energy economy adjust itself to the world price of oil as if it were a competitive price? Or should the government intervene to offset the monopoly element in the cartel price by limiting imports for economic reasons, as a weapon in countervailing trade policy? Or should the government buffer the impact on the domestic energy economy with subsidies and controls? So far the government had acquiesced in the cartel price increases, and has even appeared to welcome them as a means to the end of reducing imports. The import-reducing effect of these price increases has unfortunately been nullified by other policies. Whether one does or does not think that the OPEC price is an exorbitantly monopolistic price to be actively resisted depends on one's view of the future world supply situation.

THE LONG RUN: DIFFERING VIEWS

For present purposes we shall assume that recoverable supplies of conventional liquid hydrocarbons in the United States are limited: production will probably not rise appreciably above 10-12 million b/d before 1985 and will follow a decline curve thereafter into the middle of the next century. We also assume that domestic "backstops" are available in the U.S. These backstops are alternative energy sources more abundant than oil but having higher costs to users, perhaps accessible only after further technological development, and with higher elasticities of supply after the threshold is passed. They could include, successively, (1) coal and synthetics from coal, (2) the breeder reactor, shale oil, geothermal energy, and geopressured gas, and (3) ultimately fusion and solar technologies.

Now let us consider the implications of two different states of the world oil economy outside the United States. The first scenario is world depletion. In this view, demand is rapidly overtaking supply. One such pessimistic view is that of the CIA. By 1985, according to its recent Report, total oil demand on the OPEC producers (after absorption of all non-OPEC supply) will be from 47 to 51 million b/d, including the net import demands of the U.S. on OPEC countries. The Report asserts that OPEC countries will have difficulty meeting this demand. Saudi Arabia alone would have to supply 19-23 million b/d, whereas its planned maximum capacity in 1985 is said to be about 18 million. Excess capacity in the world would be gone; excess demand would cause prices to break substantially upward; and thereafter the world demand for oil would press against a decline curve as the world supply was depleted.[10] In short, the rest of the world would track the U.S. oil trajectory with a lag of about 15 to 20 years. After 1985 and on into the next century, the world would increasingly make the transition to alternative energy sources.

Under these circumstances, U.S. "import policy" in the long run would derive naturally from general energy economics. Petroleum policy would be an end game. If the private markets for energy correctly foresaw and discounted future prices and costs, the economy would embark on massive development and substitution of other energy sources for oil and of other inputs for energy, as relative prices changed. Development of the backstops would become profitable against the projection of world oil prices, though the government might have to bear some of the uncertainties of research and development, as pointed out above. Policy might also set up some incentives to overcome lags in conversion. In the long run, security and economics would tend to run in tandem: imports would tend to phase out after 1985 for economic reasons.

In the short run (e.g. to 1985), however, the U.S. would remain highly vulnerable to interruptions of imports. If the government chose to force the rate of reduction of dependence on oil imports beyond what higher oil prices would produce, it could also speed up development of domestic oil and gas supply by providing special incentives for high-cost sources and phase out low-value consumption more rapidly with tax incentives.

The assumptions of the world depletion scenario also imply that prices of the magnitude of OPEC oil prices, which will rise in the future, may be justified by the long-run conditions of the oil industry in the world.[11] In other words, they reflect the scarcity value of a depleting resource and are not pure monopoly rents; the low marginal cost of development and production in the Middle East is not the "competitive" standard for world oil prices.[12]

This implication would be sharply opposed, however, to the price

---

10. U.S. Central Intelligence Agency, THE INTERNATIONAL ENERGY SITUATION: OUTLOOK TO 1985, E. R. 77-10230 U (April, 1977).

11. Professor Robert Pindyck of MIT has calculated the optimum OPEC price with the aid of a computer model that includes world oil demand, income growth, price changes, non-OPEC supply, depletion of world oil resources, and different rates of time discount among OPEC members. He finds that OPEC's best price today is between $12 and $13 per barrel—slightly below the actual posted price—and that it will rise in real terms no more than 2% per year over the next 10 years. *The Economics of Oil Pricing*, Wall St. J. December 20, 1977.

12. This viewpoint would discourage confrontations with OPEC, and so would contradict the recent (January 1978) recommendations of the General Accounting Office: to prohibit importation of crude oil acquired under a contract that gives OPEC the authority to set prices, and to use the threat of counter-boycott to bring world prices down.

implications of the alternative scenario: indefinite renewal of world supply with low and relatively constant real marginal resource costs. If domestic oil supply elasticity were still as low as in the first case, availability of abundant supplies outside the United States for the indefinite future would create additional difficulties for U.S. energy policy. In this case, OPEC looks more like a true cartel monopoly, and the U.S. would have a better economic reason to participate in a buyers' campaign to break up the OPEC price. If world supplies were rapidly expandable at low cost from a number of different sources, the usual instabilities would probably arise in the cartel anyway. In this situation a buyers' countervailing strategy would have a good chance of success. In the long run, there would be far less economic need for the U.S. and other countries to shift to alternative energy sources. We assume that flexible prices would help to cure the world balance-of-payment problems.

Abundant Middle Eastern supplies and low world prices would not, however, help to solve the security problem for the U.S.[13] If it chose to pursue the goals of (approximate) energy independence—sharply reduced imports, from secure sources only—it would isolate itself from the world energy economy. High domestic prices and price guarantees, additional conservation controls, and accelerated development of alternatives, would produce major anomalies between the U.S. economy and the rest of the world, which would in all probability operate on a cheaper and more abundant energy base. Increased reliance on domestic oil and accelerated internal oil supply development in the near future would give some substance to the derisive description, "drain America first," which some critics have attached to Project Independence policies. It would make development of energy alternatives imperative to prevent future vulnerability. Security and economics in the long run would diverge rather than converge. The mix of depleting domestic U.S. petroleum supplies, abundant world supplies, and an acute threat to security assumed in this scenario is almost the worst case, designed to produce maximum strain on U.S. energy policy.

These are not the only scenarios.[14] A number of different as-

---

13. My only point of disagreement with the excellent analysis of Arthur W. Wright, *Energy Independence: Insuring Against Disruptions of Supply,* OPTIONS FOR U.S. ENERGY POLICY 41-59 (1977) is his implication that a concerted effort by oil importing countries to weaken or break the power of the cartel over price is an integral part of U.S. security policy (46). That could be an appropriate economic policy under some circumstances, but it is not evident how it could strengthen security.

14. It will be apparent that both of the cases hypothesized here would be "hard path" alternatives in the view of Lovins, *Energy Strategy, The Road Not Taken?*, FOREIGN AFF. 65-96 (October 1976).

sumptions are possible about domestic petroleum supply, which many energy producers vehemently assert is much more elastic than Federal energy planners usually assume. Different assumptions about the positioning of energy backstops, secure and insecure sources of imports, etc. are possible. It makes a great deal of difference to the environment of U.S. import policy whether oil supplies in the rest of the world will be substantially depleted within the next 30 to 50 years, or whether the supply can be replaced indefinitely at low incremental cost. Which vision of the future is more nearly correct?

If we knew the answer to such questions, we would have been spared much of the recent agony of energy policy formation. During the *last* 50 or 60 years the fundamental outlook on the energy future has changed at least twice, from pessimism to optimism and back to pessimism.[15] Prevailing opinion leans toward the pessimistic view. The CIA compendium, the USGS projections, and King Hubbert's famous decline curves were referred to above.[16]

Not every expert agrees. M. A. Adelman, for one, thinks that oil could probably be developed for a considerable time at low incremental costs in sufficient quantities to keep pace with growth in world demand, at correspondingly low prices. In 1938, he notes, world production was 5.9 percent of reported world "reserves" and 2.9 percent in 1974. But reserves are only a working inventory. Ultimately recoverable reserves are systematically underestimated and underreported. Already-discovered oil in Saudi Arabia could support a production rate of 20 million b/d for 50 years, which would cast doubt on the CIA "maximum" estimate for 1985.

> The low [production/reserve ratio] of 3 percent or less at the Persian Gulf is one of the great historic constants in the world oil industry. *There has always been a huge potential surplus* of productive capacity—occasionally an actual surplus— . . . and never greater than today.[17]

The current estimates of potential supply of conventional oil in the world seem to converge at about two trillion barrels, of which only one-fifth has already been produced. Almost two-fifths is yet to

15. Walt W. Rostow has argued that periods of scarcity and abundance in foodstuffs and raw materials—signalled by rises and declines in real or relative prices—have alternated during the last two centuries in the world to form irregular cycles: a "Kontratieff" long wave, whose last upswing began about 1972. *Kontratieff, Schumpeter and Kuznets: Trend Periods Revisited,* 35 J. ECON. HIST. 719 (1975).

16. See also the Ford Foundation Energy Policy Project Report, A TIME TO CHOOSE (1974); and the findings of the Workshop on Alternative Energy Strategies (W.A.E.S.) in C. Wilson, ENERGY: GLOBAL PROSPECTS, 1985-2000 (1977).

17. Adelman, *U.S. Energy Policy,* in NO TIME TO CONFUSE at 32.

be "discovered."[18] Although we do not know what the marginal costs of all this oil might be, that estimate was already circulated before the 1974 price escalation. It amounts to about a 75-year supply at *current* rates of production. Much additional oil might become available at higher cost horizons consistent with expected OPEC prices such as the two trillion barrels in Western Hemisphere tar sands. The increase in recovery ratios made possible by high prices would itself increase producible reserves of conventional oil.[19] These figures do not decisively support either scenario, but they probably understate rather than overstate supply elasticity. In any event, the world does not seem to be confronted with early exhaustion of liquid hydrocarbon.

FURTHER OBSERVATIONS ON SECURITY

Security and economic efficiency seldom coincide. It was argued above that policies to promote security may also be appropriate for economic goals in the long run if the state of the world corresponds to the depletion model, but not in the face of abundant low-cost supply outside the United States. In the short run, the two aims conflict in most respects, whatever the state of the world in the 21st Century.

During the next five to eight years, there will probably be a short-run surplus in the world at current OPEC prices. Excess capacity reported at the beginning of 1978 was between four and five million b/d.[20] Up to the present, OPEC has successfully maintained high prices, largely because Saudi Arabia has been willing to act as the supply balancer, but it is not impossible for short-run competition to break out and the world price to fall to much lower levels for an extended period. In a system geared to price incentives, this competition would set the process of conversion back several years and extend the critical period of vulnerability unless the economy were assured that the long-run incentives would be unaffected. Guarantees of minimum price or insurance of major investments might be ways of doing that, though these are not very palatable politically.

The pure security policies are fairly obvious. The most important is a storage policy for protection against short-run interruptions. At long last the United States has begun to construct a Strategic Petroleum Reserve System. The National Energy Plan of 1977 stipulates a

18. Schneider, *Common Sense About Energy, Part One*, WORKING PAPERS January-February, 1978, at 38.

19. Singer, *Living With Imports*, THE NEW REPUBLIC, February 25, 1978, at 33.

20. Saudi Arabia alone had most of this excess capacity: in December, Aramco was producing 8 million b/d but its capacity was rated at 12 million. Wall St. J., Dec. 15, 1977.

reserve of one billion barrels (up from 500 million planned earlier) which when ready would replace three million b/d lost from imports for ten months.

Is this enough? In an emergency, of course, consumption can also be reduced by controls and rationing. We are sanguine enough to hope that the government has some efficient plans for short-run allocation in lieu of what it did in 1972-74—refuse to use any of the available rationing systems, including rationing by price. It might also be possible to increase domestic production while the emergency lasts, especially if oil storage gives us a lead time of 6 to 12 months, although the present decline of U.S. producing capacity does not encourage the belief that a major program of developing "reserve producing capacity" is now feasible.

A primary difficulty is in modeling the threats. Is another Arab embargo the only serious threat? Is it wise to plan on nothing longer than ten months? If imports from Arab lands rise to, say, six million b/d by the early 1980's, and if the Arabs' expressed determination to force any future embargo to the bitter end can be taken at face value,[21] what is the fallback position for the U.S. when the storage runs out? We are no longer talking about "import policy" when matters reach that pass.

Security policy can also promote greater reliance on relatively more secure sources of oil, *if* it can identify them by such means as differential tariffs or bilateral agreements, which have economic costs. It can also plan to switch supply sources in a partial embargo if the U.S. is the only target. No one knows with certainty what the international political problems of the mid-1980's will be. It is uncertain whether the U.S. will be trying to extricate itself from dependence on Latin American sources and increase imports from our staunch friends in Libya and Algeria; so planning has to be flexible.

A preference policy for imports of liquified natural gas (LNG) is struggling to be born. This paper has said little about gas imports because they have not been an important factor in energy security up to recently. Most gas imports have come from Canada, which evidently intends to honor past commitments while prohibiting future growth in exports from the developed gas provinces in the Western Sedimentary Basin.[22] LNG from outside North America is a dif-

---

21. *Cf.* Sheikh Yamani's several recent statements to the press. In 1976, U.S. imports from Arab countries were about 2 million b/d.

22. Canada has declared its intention of cutting back on export commitments if a domestic gas shortage actually becomes likely. Minister of Energy, Mines, and Resources, *An Energy Strategy for Canada* 15 (1976). Exports of gas from Canada to the U.S. have recently been a bit less than one trillion cubic feet (TCF) per year.

ferent proposition. As plans to import LNG neared maturity, the government in 1976 first declared that the U.S. could import one trillion cubic feet (TCF) of LNG annually by 1985 (less than five percent of expected consumption) without endangering national security. Later, the limit was changed to two TCF per year so long as no more than one TCF came from any one country. In 1977, the Carter administration announced that approval of LNG import proposals would be *ad hoc*. If all such proposals currently under consideration were approved, LNG would account for 1.8 TCF, or nearly ten percent of U.S. consumption, by 1985.[23] This would be enough to elevate LNG imports above the threshold of security problems.

Rational choice in natural gas policy (as in oil policy) is muddled by price control. LNG imported from Indonesia will be priced at $3.42 per MCF, although the NEP called for a price ceiling on domestic gas of $1.75 (plus price-level escalation). Algerian gas will also have a much higher price than the ceiling on gas produced in the lower 48 states,[24] as will conventional Canadian gas and Mexican gas once an agreement to import it has been reached.[25] The exceptions to the price ceiling will encourage development of a new, relatively "secure" supply in the Canadian and Alaskan Arctic, and will permit construction of a pipeline to deliver gas from those regions to the U.S. (and Canadian) markets.[26] But the ceiling holds back the development of new conventional supplies in the lower 48 states and encourages prolongation of low-value use there. Both of these effects conflict with security policy. The National Energy Plan of 1977, in effect, assumes for gas as it does for oil that no additional major conventional supplies remain to be developed in the U.S. outside Alaska. As noted above, it elevates equitable income transfer above

---

23. Wall St. J., Jan. 3, 1978.

24. The first contract for Algerian gas, with El Paso Natural Gas, called for a price of $3.37 per MCF; a more recent one with Tenneco provides for a price of $4.50 plus escalation. Washington Post, Nov. 12, 1977. However, the prospective opening of European markets for LNG will probably deflect additional North African supplies toward that, their "natural" market.

25. Gas imported from Mexico is expected to supply another .7 trillion cubic feet annually to the U.S. market once the pipeline is completed. Mexico has proposed an initial price of $2.60 per MCF—somewhat above the current U.S. intrastate (free market) price in Texas. The U.S. government appears willing to agree to a price higher than the domestic price ceiling of $1.75 proposed in the NEP, but not above the current free market price.

26. The Alcan Pipeline Route was approved by both the U.S. and Canadian governments in 1977. Arctic gas is expected to supply still another trillion cubic feet annually to the U.S. market by the mid-1980's. The National Energy Plan proposes individual exceptions to the $1.75 ceiling for high-cost supply such as Arctic gas, geopressured gas, gas from "tight" sands and very deep horizons, etc.

efficient allocation as a goal of energy policy, while losing sight of security in this part of the Plan.

A Western hemisphere preference policy for oil imports looks good as a security option. The prospect of large new supplies from Mexico (even at OPEC prices) is encouraging news for the U.S. On the other hand, we must remember that Canada, once regarded as the most secure source of oil to the United States, is the only producing country in the world to have imposed a permanent embargo on it.[27] True, Canada intended only to promote her own security and economic self-sufficiency, not to injure the U.S., but the decision is a reminder that even friendly countries will always put their own interests first. Other examples of this tendency are the difficulties that the oil importing countries who participate in the International Energy Agency have encountered in planning for another embargo. While IEA is certainly a better medium than the *sauve qui peut* displayed by the Western countries during the 1973-74 embargo, IEA has not been able to elicit agreement on a comprehensive sharing plan for all supplies—only for imports. Each country undoubtedly will trust its own resources and provisions more than the IEA plan.[28]

The outlook is not encouraging. Little can be done to lessen the degree of dependence on foreign oil before the mid-1980's, but the immediate future may be the period of maximum danger. For that period and beyond it, present policy choices have to be made on the basis of partially unknown facts and uncertain developments. Policy toward imports is likewise beset by differing views on priorities and criteria for government action; the current debate gives lip service to national energy security as a paramount aim, but actually shoves it into the background.

Oil imports in the mid-1980's and beyond are very likely to exceed nine million barrels per day. If we cannot protect the economy against embargoes by developing adequate reserves and deflecting energy requirements toward secure sources, notwithstanding the high costs of doing so, those energy requirements are likely to have an undue influence on U.S. foreign policy.

---

27. Canada decided in 1973 to reduce exports of oil to the United States. They have been reduced by 60 percent since 1972, and will phase out altogether by 1981. Though Canada is not a member of OPEC, she collected the high OPEC prices from the U.S. after 1973 by imposing a rising export tax. Mexican exports of crude oil to the United States, currently negligible, are expected to reach one million b/d by 1982—again at the world price for oil, though Mexico is likewise not a member of OPEC.

28. *See* Wright, *supra,* note 14, at 51.

Chapter 4

FEDERAL ENERGY RESOURCE LEASING POLICY*

STEPHEN L. McDONALD**

It is generally believed that the greater part of this country's re-maining undeveloped energy resources—oil and gas, coal, and oil shale—is to be found on lands subject to federal jurisdiction.[1] Such lands are normally made available to private persons for possible discovery and production of mineral fuels by means of leases, the terms and conditions of which are prescribed by responsible federal agencies, chiefly the Bureau of Land Management and the Geological Survey of the Department of the Interior. In addition to conditions included in lease contracts, the federal government, chiefly through the Geological Survey, imposes operating regulations designed to pro-tect the environment and conserve natural resources. It is obvious that the policies followed by the government in leasing lands for mineral fuels production have an important bearing on the future of the nation's energy economy.

In this article we shall discuss a number of issues relating to leasing policy, from the basic objective(s) in leasing to the incidental regula-tion of oil production for conservation purposes. Some issues, such as the manner of bidding in lease sales and regulation for environ-mental protection, we shall barely touch upon for reasons of space. We shall devote most of our attention to the basis of bids (e.g., lease bonus vs. royalty rate), the rate of leasing, and conservation regula-tion in the case of oil. We begin with a discussion of what ought to be the objective in federal land leasing.

THE BASIC OBJECTIVE(S)

As present law is officially interpreted, the major objectives in the management of publicly owned mineral resources are: "(1) to assure orderly and timely resource development; (2) to protect the environ-ment; (3) to insure the public a fair market value return on the

*The research underlying this article was made possible by a generous grant from Re-sources for the Future, Inc.

**Dr. McDonald is a Professor of Economics at the University of Texas at Austin.

1. *Federal Leasing and Disposal Policies,* hearings on S. 2727 Before the Senate Commit-tee on Interior and Insular Affairs, 92d Cong., 1st Sess. 35-37 (1972) (statement of Harrison Loesch).

disposition of its resources."[2] No one of these objectives dominates the others, and it is not clear from the law or official pronouncements how they are to be reconciled if they conflict in application, as they may. For instance, sufficiently strong measures to protect the environment may delay development and may also unduly reduce the value of resources to prospective lessees. Sufficiently rapid offering of leases may result in less than fair market value being received. It is not clear in any case just what "orderly and timely" development means in practice. On the other hand, these three objectives may be mutually consistent if we can integrate them into a single decision rule, such as the one we shall now propose.

We suggest that the federal government should seek to capture a maximum of the present value of pure economic rent arising from minerals production on its lands, where "pure economic rent" is the income which tends to accrue in the long run, under conditions of perfect competition and the absence of externalities, to the owners of raw natural resources.

There are several reasons for this proposed rule. First, it gives a concrete meaning to "orderly and timely" resource development and "fair market value," while recognizing the need to internalize externalities such as environmental damages. Second, it is equivalent, in effect, to the rule that the government should seek to maximize the present value of resources to society; assuming the labor and capital employed in minerals extraction have alternative uses, the present value of pure economic rent as defined *is* the present value of the mineral resources to society. Third, pure economic rent is an economic surplus, the capture of which by the government does not affect output, the price level or relative prices, and the allocation of resources. Fourth, as a form of governmental revenue, economic rent received substitutes for taxes which *would* affect output, prices, and resource allocation. Thus, following the rule would promote economic efficiency and tend to maximize the value of resources to society.

Of course, the government cannot measure pure economic rent *a priori* and set the price of leases accordingly. Rather, to follow the rule it must create conditions conducive to its satisfaction in the normal process of marketing leases. Thus, conditions which reduce uncertainty, increase competition, promote the optimum rate of extraction of minerals, internalize externalities, and relate the rate of leasing to the capacity of the affected industries all tend to satisfy the rule. Note that the rule is not the same as that of maximizing the

---

2. *Id.* at 38.

present value of land revenues, for the latter would call for the disregard of environmental costs and lead to the exploitation of some minerals whose social cost exceeded their social value. Let us now see what the rule implies in regard to the several issues noted earlier.

THE MANNER OF LEASE BIDDING

Present law requires that bidding for oil and gas leases on the outer continental shelf be in the form of sealed bids, but it allows either sealed bids or oral auction, or a combination, in the competition for coal or oil and gas leases on the onshore public lands.[3] In the only sale of oil shale leases sealed bids were required.[4]

Under conditions of uncertainty, which typify especially the leasing of lands for oil and gas production, sealed bids are to be preferred to oral bids. In contrast to oral bidding, sealed bidding is characterized by (1) the absence of certain knowledge by any bidder at the time he commits himself as to the number and identities of his competitors for a given tract; (2) the inability of bidders to react to competitive bids; and (3) by the inability of bidders to give implicit signals or to engage in punitive bidding. Lacking knowledge of either the lessor's reservation price or the size of others' bids, the bidder with the highest valuation cannot tailor his bid to be just above the reservation price or the second highest valuation, but is motivated to bid his actual valuation. When bidders are uncertain of the underlying quality of mineral deposits, valuations tend to differ widely. Consequently, the winning sealed bid is likely to be substantially higher than the winning oral bid would be.[5] If uncertainty causes bidders to bid conservatively anyway, the government tends to capture a larger proportion of the pure economic rent available if sealed bids are required.

One disadvantage of sealed bidding as presently practiced relative to oral bidding arises from the fact that, for a given set of tracts in a sale, all bidding is closed before any individual bids are opened. The result is that a bidder of limited capital must select a few tracts to bid upon and, if he fails to be a winner on one or more tracts, has no opportunity to use the freed funds to bid on other tracts in the same sale. (Note that the very large bidder may be able to bid on every

3. Onshore oil and gas leases on lands not overlying a known geological structure of a producing oil or gas field are granted noncompetitively to the first qualified applicant. Where there are two or more simultaneous applicants, the winner is determined by a drawing.

4. Interview with H. Roy McBroom, Bureau of Land Management, Denver, June 27, 1975.

5. The definitive discussion of this subject is Mead, *Natural Resource Disposal Policy— Oral Auction versus Sealed Bids,* 7 NAT. RES. J. 194 (1967).

tract put up for lease.) Consequently, (1) small bidders are at a disadvantage in securing leases and (2) the average number of bids per tract in a sale is less than it might be. In short, the present system limits competition in both the short and and the long run. The remedy is to permit what may be called sequential bidding. After a tentative closing of bidding in a sale, bids would be opened for individual tracts in the order of the number of bids per tract. Drawings would be held in the case of ties. The winning bid for each tract would be announced, but not the identity of the winner; the losers (or winner) would be permitted to submit new bids on other tracts in the sale before bids on the latter were opened. This system would increase the cumbersomeness of a large lease sale, but it would increase the average number of bids per tract and tend to result in higher winning bids under uncertainty, to say nothing of increasing the scope of opportunity for relatively small firms.[6] The effective increase in competition would make it more likely that the government captures all the pure economic rent available.

When there is greater certainty as to the underlying value of mineral deposits, as is usually the case in coal leasing, sealed bidding offers less relative advantage. Where all parties, including the lessor, are knowledgeable, the reservation price, the second-highest valuation, and the highest valuation cannot differ much; and the government may lose nothing from truly competitive oral bidding. But it would gain nothing either, relative to truly competitive sealed bidding with sequential bidding allowed.

THE BASIS OF BIDS

At present mineral leases on federal lands are granted to the highest bidder of a lease bonus, the royalty rate being specified in advance by the lessor.[7] The law covering outer continental shelf leasing allows royalty bidding also, the lease bonus being specified in advance; there have been a few experimental sales of oil and gas leases on this basis. Pending legislation would permit bonus bidding, royalty bidding, profit share bidding and work commitment bidding based on a dollar amount for exploration.[8]

---

6. The advantage to small firms is two-fold: it allows them to bid on more tracts and this makes fuller use of available capital; and it reduces pressure on such firms to over-commit themselves on a few key tracts in a desperate attempt to win at least some.

7. Note the exception given in footnote 2.

8. S. 9, 95th Cong., 1st Sess. (1977) *Outer Continental Shelf Lands Act Amendments of 1977.* This bill was passed by the Senate July 15, 1977; the corresponding bill in the House failed to be reported out of committee in the 1977 session.

The essential characteristics of bonus bidding are (1) it gives rise to an often large front-end payment; (2) it settles a heavy burden of risk and uncertainty on the lessee rather than the lessor; and (3) the bonus, once paid, becomes a sunk cost that is irrelevant to exploration, development, production and abandonment decisions—except that the immediate tax write-off of a bonus on surrendered leases tends to bias decisions in the direction of abandonment of marginal properties. Only the sunk cost characteristic is favorable to the objective of maximizing the capture of pure economic rent.

Pure economic rent is the surplus of value over labor and capital costs. Since no rent is paid by the marginal activity, pure economic rent does not affect the margin of exploration, development and production. A lease bonus has precisely these characteristics (abstracting from the noted inducement to abandon marginal tracts to secure an immediate tax write-off of the lease bonus). With certainty and perfect capital markets, it would be the ideal form in which to capture all pure economic rent.

But, of course, there is great uncertainty facing minerals producers at the point of leasing. The lessee's exposure to this uncertainty is maximized by bonus bidding. Uncertainty means, among other things, that operators cannot finance the proving of deposits exclusively with borrowed funds, e.g., from banks. A substantial proportion of equity capital is required, and given an imperfect equity capital market, small firms cannot raise such capital on equal terms with large firms. Small firms must depend more than large firms on retained earnings. Thus the often large front-end payment associated with bonus bidding is a barrier to entry and a restraint on competition in bidding.

This barrier and restraint is reduced by the practice of joint bidding, under which two or more potential lessees submit a single, common bid for a given tract. Joint bidding allows the smaller operator to tailor the size of his front-end commitment to his means. It allows him to spread uncertainty by bidding on a larger number of prospects. It allows a group to assemble sufficient capital to participate in the bidding for the most promising, and hence most valuable, leases.

The question is whether joint bidding increases or decreases the number of independent bids on the typical tract. It could do either, of course. Span and Erickson have recently tested several hypotheses concerning the competitive effects of joint bidding for outer continental shelf (OCS) oil and gas leases over the period 1954-1973, during which joint bids rose from about 10 percent to about 85 percent of bids cast.[9] They found that (1) the average number of bidders per tract increased substantially over the period; (2) shares of the larger companies in leases acquired varied widely from sale to sale, contraindicating collusion designed to fix market shares; (3) the percentage of winning bids in joint ventures involving nonmajor companies substantially exceeded that involving major companies; (4) the percentage of winning groups containing no major companies increased significantly, while the percentage of winning groups containing only majors declined over the period; and (5) there were few cases of nearly identical bids, and in no such cases were groups involved containing major producers. The authors interpret these findings as supporting the view that joint bidding has increased, not decreased competition. We know of no conflicting findings by other students of the problem. Accordingly, we have reason to believe that joint bidding significantly reduces the disadvantages of bonus bidding.

The disadvantages are further reduced when bonus bidding is combined with a modest specified royalty, as is the present practice. A required royalty tends to shift some uncertainty from the lessee to the lessor. It reduces the associated lease bonus and lowers the barrier to entry by smaller firms. In these ways it tends to increase the capture of pure economic rent. In other ways it has contrary effects, however, as we shall discuss in our analysis of the question of royalty bidding.

For reasons just suggested, royalty bidding tends to reduce uncertainty borne by the lessee and otherwise facilitates entry and competition in comparison with bonus bidding. It has the major disadvantage, however, of adversely affecting the margin of development and production. Unlike a bonus, a royalty is a variable operating cost. The higher it is, the more likely it will result in some discoveries not being developed and in the early abandonment of all. This is because a royalty represents a negative cash flow in the evaluation of expected proceeds from development and production. The higher the royalty rate, the lower the present value of expected net cash flow, *cet. par.;* thus the fewer discoveries that can be economically developed, and the less complete the exhaustion of deposits when they can no longer sustain economical production.[10]

In defense of royalty bidding it may be argued (1) that the government has the authority under existing law to reduce royalty rates

9. Spann and Erickson, *Energy, Risk Sharing and Competition in Joint Ventures for Offshore Petroleum Exploration,* unpublished manuscript (1977).

10. Note that where there is salvageable equipment abandonment occurs when the present value of expected cash flow from operation falls below net salvage value.

that are too high to permit economical development and production of mineral deposits, and (2) that contractual rates established in royalty bidding are unlikely to be so high as to make early abandonment a problem.

With regard to the first point, if the government were to adjust freely royalty rates that turned out to be too high, then the competitive system of establishing the winning bidder would tend to break down. As a record of "appropriate" adjustments was established, prospective lessees would tend to bid higher and higher, regardless of their expected costs, and winners would not necessarily be the most efficient operators. Moreover, the government would have to go into the business of systematically measuring the costs of winning bidders, a task that would be costly and would invite charges of favoritism.

With regard to the second point, the winning royalty bids in the experimental oil and gas sale of October 1974 were quite high.[11] They ranged from a low of 51.8 percent to a high of 82.2 percent of the value of production. The bids by tract were consistent also with great bidder uncertainty. On the tract valued most highly by the Geological Survey the bids ranged from 0.5 percent to 82.2 percent. Such uncertainty is often likely to lead to bids so high as to make ultimate discoveries uneconomical to develop without readjustment by the lessor.

Profit share bidding is similar in effects to royalty bidding. It involves no front-end payment and it reduces the uncertainty borne by the lessee relative to the bonus bidding system. In the same relative sense it encourages entry and competition and avoids discrimination against small firms. In these respects it tends to result in the full capture of economic rent generated. But also like royalty bidding, it may preclude the development of socially economical discoveries, and it may lead to the premature abandonment of producing properties. With a profit share as a negative cash flow, fewer discoveries would be economical to develop than under bonus bidding; similarly, the present value of expected cash flow from continued operation of a producing property would sooner fall below the net salvage value of equipment than under a bonus bidding system.

The importance of these last effects would, of course, depend in part on the definition of profit employed in the profit share system. They are likely to be most adverse if the IRS definition of profit were employed, for a normal return on investment would in no way

11. OSC Sale No. 36. The results of the sale are given in *An Analysis of the Royalty Bidding Experiment in OSC Sale No. 36,* U.S. Department of the Interior (mimeo.) (1975).

be sheltered. They are likely to be least adverse if the British definition were employed. Under the British system, the lessor shares in gross revenue less operating costs, but only after the total capital investment times some factor greater than one has been recovered from operating profits. In any case, the early abandonment effect would be less severe than under royalty bidding, for a profit share acts rather like a diminishing royalty as depletion occurs and operating profits per unit decline.

Work commitment bidding, under which the bidder commits himself to a specified dollar value of exploration effort, could only lead to waste. With effective competition, bidders tend to bid away to the lessor all of the pure economic rent in a prospect. Pure economic rent, in turn, is a surplus of value over the labor and capital costs of efficient exploration, development and production. Consequently, on the typical prospect where there is such a surplus, winning bidders will tend to commit themselves to more than the efficient amount of exploration effort; that is, the amount such that marginal cost equals the marginal value of information acquired. Since operators must either spend their commitment or forfeit the unspent balance to the government, they are led to push exploration beyond the point where marginal cost equals marginal value of information.

All of the above considerations lead the present writer to conclude that the present system of bonus bidding, with joint bidding and sequential bidding allowed, and with a modest royalty of 1/8 or 1/6 specified, is preferable. Profit shring, using the British definition of profit, is a close second best. Royalty bidding is next, and work commitment bidding least acceptable.

THE RATE OF LEASING

Aside from the strategy of reducing dependence on foreign sources of energy in the intermediate run, the present value of pure economic rent should be maximized by pushing the rate of leasing to the point where the marginal gain from earlier receipts equals the marginal loss from increased uncertainty and reduced competition. In practice such a rule would be imprecise, of course. Alternatively, consider the issue in this way: assuming the government has unduly restrained the rate of mineral leasing in the past, to what degree should the rate of offering lands for lease be accelerated? With regard to oil and gas leases on the OCS, we conclude that after a gradual transition period, during which plans are fully publicized, the final sustained rate should be that which exhausts leasable lands over a long enough period of time to justify increasing proportionately the capacity in the affected industries. As for coal and oil shale leases on the public domain, we conclude that the rate of leasing should be governed by the number of and trend in nominations by extractor firms. Before giving our reasons for these conclusions, let us explain why sudden "dumping" of leases would be inappropriate.

If the government accelerated the leasing of mineral lands sharply and unexpectedly, we could expect several short-run effects that would tend to depress realized rents below the pure economic rent available. First, with additional lands to explore and develop, short-run marginal costs in the lessee industries and supply industries would tend to rise above long-run marginal costs. Second, except where an effective price floor exists, as in the case of oil, short-run demand inelasticities would tend to depress mineral prices with a faster growth of output.[12] Third, due to imperfect equity capital markets and the necessity of small firms to rely heavily upon internally generated equity capital, such firms might be unable to generate equity capital at a rate corresponding to the rate of leasing. As a result, competitiveness of bidding for leases would be lessened. Fourth, the mineral industries in question might be unable at first to perform desired predrilling exploration on all lands put up for lease. Consequently, uncertainty in bidding would be increased. Fifth, short primary lease terms might reduce the expected thoroughness of exploration, thus increasing uncertainty at the time of leasing. All of these considerations suggest a gradual build-up of the rate of leasing toward a new higher sustainable rate, with perhaps a transitional increase in primary lease terms.

Aside from the considerations just given, there are relatively few factors to hamper accelerated leasing of oil and gas lands on the OCS. Except along the interface with state lands, where oil and gas reservoirs may overlap the border, all the lands involved are federal lands; there is no checkerboarding with state or private lands, as is frequently encountered in the onshore public domain. There is no serious problem of competing or multiple uses of the lands, since shipping and fishing are scarcely impaired, if at all, by oil and gas operations. The price of oil cannot be depressed by accelerated leasing; additional production simply displaces imports at the going world price set by OPEC. The situation is similar in the case of gas. Additional production simply reduces shortages at the regulated price. The only significant impediment is environmental considera-

---

12. The demand for domestic oil is perfectly elastic at the OPEC price so long as some part of domestic consumption is supplied from foreign sources. It is unlikely, therefore, that accelerated leasing of oil lands would depress prices.

tions and resistance to leasing in new areas on these grounds. Subject to this restraint, the government has great freedom to determine rate of leasing.

The key to capturing a maximum of pure economic rent in the long run for the OCS is an increase in the capacity of the lessee and supply industries along with the increase in the rate of leasing. The industries affected would willingly increase capacity appropriately if the target rate of leasing were certain, and if that rate could be sustained long enough that a normal rate of return could be earned on the additional capacity without artificially depressing rents. Hence, we conclude that the target rate of leasing should be that rate which would exhaust leasable lands in such a period.

Accelerated leasing of coal lands in the public domain presents a number of problems not present in the case of OCS oil and gas lands. The federally owned lands are often checkerboarded with state or private lands; the willingness of potential lessees to bid for federal lands, and the size of their bids, may depend upon the ownership of or terms of securing extraction rights on adjacent nonfederal lands. This problem is intensified where the blocking up of an economical mining unit requires rights on both federal and adjacent nonfederal lands. The lands in question often have several alternative uses (e.g., forestry, grazing, recreation), not all of which would fit into a multiple-use plan that includes coal mining. In many cases the federal government has only mineral rights, having disposed of the surface rights to private interests. Where it is necessary to use or alter the surface in extracting coal, especially in the case of strip mining, the necessity to acquire surface rights separately from and in addition to sub-surface mineral rights may impede competitive bidding for the latter. Due to environmental restraints on coal use, bottlenecks in transportation, fixed investments in oil or gas burning equipment, the short-run price elasticity of demand for coal is low. Consequently, accelerated leasing of coal lands accompanied by similarly accelerated mining might unduly depress coal prices and rents. Finally, privately owned coal resources, in the East as well as the West where federally owned resources are concentrated, are relatively more abundant than privately owned oil and gas resources. Federal restraint in leasing need not "starve" the economy for coal.

All these considerations argue against the approach to accelerated leasing suggested for OCS oil and gas lands. Instead, we suggest a rate of leasing that (1) allows the coal mining industry to secure rights to federal coal deposits when the latter are richer (yield higher rents) than alternative state or private deposits; (2) entails no sacrifice of competition in the bidding for leases; and (3) reserves federal lands for that use or combination of uses that promises the greatest present value of economic rent. The first condition would tend to assure efficient development and use of the nation's total coal resources: utilization of deposits in the order of their rent-yielding capacity. The second condition tends to assure receipt of fair market value for coal lands, while the third tends to assure that all federal lands are allocated to their most valuable uses.

To make such an approach operational, we believe the government should rely primarily upon nominations in selecting the lands for lease and choosing a rate of leasing. The more nominations for a particular tract, *cet. par.*, the more valuable the tract is likely to be, and the more competitive the prospective bidding. The more nominations for federal lands in the aggregate, *cet. par.*, the more attractive such lands would seem to be relative to alternative state or private lands. A trend of increasing nominations in the aggregate would suggest undue restraint in leasing; decreasing nominations would suggest the reverse.

Of course it is not necessary to offer for lease all lands nominated. Considerations of competition may suggest that only those tracts receiving, for example, three or more nominations should be offered for lease. Even if offered and bid upon, leases need not be granted when, in the judgment of lessor officials, bidding is not sufficiently competitive or the high bid falls substantially below independently estimated fair market value. (Note that it is usually easier for the government to determine fair market value in the case of coal than in the case of oil and gas.)

As with coal, we believe that the numbers and trend in nominations should guide the pace of future oil shale leasing. It is highly uncertain that the existing leases, resulting from the single 1974 sale, will lead to profitable production of shale oil in the near future. Given this uncertainty, it is doubtful that the government could secure as much present value of economic rent if new leases were offered "now," as if it waited until profitable production is demonstrated and the extractive industry shows renewed interest in the form of nominations. When given tracts receive a sufficient number of nominations to assure competition in bidding—for example, in the order of three or four, given the government's ability to make an independent determination of a fair market value reservation price—such tracts may be offered for lease without loss to the lessor. An upward trend in nominations, per tract and in the aggregate, may be taken as a signal to increase the rate of leasing. As with conventional oil, there is no danger of "unduly" decreasing the price of shale oil by too rapid leasing. Since shale oil is a close substitute for conventional oil, its price is effectively set by OPEC, and additional domestic output would only displace imports.

ENVIRONMENTAL PROTECTION

The capture of pure economic rent through competition assumes an identity of private and social costs. This in turn implies that externalities in the form of environmental damage should be internalized. Otherwise, the rents received by the government would include an element which would be the equivalent of a tax on environmental amenities, and the government's leasing program would not maximize the value to society of the mineral resources.

The ideal way to internalize environmental externalities would be to levy fees corresponding to environmental damage at each level of output and allow mineral operators to choose that combination of prevention, correction or compensation which maximizes profits. This would assure efficiency of resource use in environmental protection while causing mineral prices to reflect full social costs. It is recognized that in some instances a second-best approach may be required. Without the knowledge that would allow us to equate marginal cost with marginal benefit, standards that are more or less arbitrary and that require preventive or corrective actions could be imposed.

CONSERVATION REGULATION IN OIL PRODUCTION

The fact that unregulated competition among multiple operators in a common oil reservoir leads to wasteful exploitation of the resource is familiar enough. It results from the rule of capture as the effective law of ownership, the ability to attract oil and gas across property lines by accelerating the rate of extraction on a given property, and the negative dependence of ultimate recovery on the overall rate of extraction. Almost as familiar is the standard remedy: regulatory restriction of the rate of extraction from an oil or gas reservoir to the "maximum efficient rate," or MER. In current OCS regulations MER is defined as "the maximum sustainable daily oil or gas withdrawal rate from a reservoir which will permit economic development and depletion of that reservoir without detriment to ultimate recovery."[13] This has been officially interpreted to mean the rate of withdrawal that maximizes ultimate recovery, subject to an acceptable rate of return on the total investment.[14]

13. Geological Survey, Conservation Division, Gulf of Mexico Area, *OCS Order No. 11* at 2.

14. *Petroleum Industry,* hearings before the Subcommittee on Antitrust and Monopoly, Senate Committee on the Judiciary, 94th Cong., 1st Sess. 75-78 (1975) (statement of Jack W. Carlson).

While this definition is distinctly superior to that typically employed by state conservation authorities, which runs in terms of maximizing ultimate recovery without reference to economics, its application in practice does not assure that operators would be able to maximize the value of the resource in question and thus maximize pure economic rent. To do this, operators should be permitted to increase the rate of withdrawal from a reservoir to the point where incremental value is zero, that is, where the rate of return on the *incremental* outlay is just acceptable, regardless of the possible loss of ultimate recovery and regardless of the overall rate of return. Redefinition of MER as the *optimum* rate of withdrawal, or that which maximizes the value of the reservoir, would further the objective of maximizing the economic rent generated and, being anticipated, bid by prospective lessees for federal leases.

But if this principle is recognized, there is a superior alternative to regulation based on redefined MER. That alternative is compulsory unitization of oil and gas reservoirs, with operator freedom as to the rate of extraction. If left free, operators would choose that extraction rate and associated investment which promised to maximize the value of the reservoir. Since under unitization their costs would coincide with social costs, they would in their own interest tend to maximize the value of the resource to society and hence maximize pure economic rent. Anticipating freedom to maximize value, prospective lessees would tend to bid away the available pure economic rent in competitive bidding. Thus the objective of maximizing the capture of pure economic rent would be served by requiring all reservoirs on federal lands to be unitized, and by giving operators in each reservoir freedom to select the extraction rate. No new legislation is required; the federal authorities have the power under existing law to compel reservoir unitization of federal leases.[15]

SUMMARY

In summary, we submit that the federal objective in mineral leasing should be to capture a maximum of the present value of pure economic rent. This objective would best be served by sealed bidding in competition for leases; by granting leases on the basis of bonus bidding, with joint and sequential bidding allowed, and with provision for a modest royalty; by offering leases on the OCS at the highest rate sustainable for a period long enough to induce a corresponding capacity in the affected industries; by offering leases on the public domain in response to nominations; by internalizing the costs

---

15. 30 U.S.C. § 226(j) (1976) and 43 U.S.C. § 1334(a)(1) (Supp. V. 1975).

of environmental damage, preferably by means of taxes that measure damage; and by compelling the unitization of all oil and gas reservoirs discovered on federal lands, while granting operators freedom to select the rate of extraction.

Chapter 5

THE ROLE OF COAL: PROBLEMS AND POLICIES

REED MOYER*

The coal industry is caught up in powerful undercurrents of change that are profoundly affecting its course. Some of the developments are new; others represent a continuation or acceleration of previously existing trends. These developments include the following:

(1) a movement in the locus of coal production from the eastern coal districts to the west;
(2) a breakdown in the authority of the United Mine Workers and a corresponding increased dependence on coal produced by labor not affiliated with U.M.W.A.;
(3) the entry of large firms (especially petroleum) into an industry composed mostly of small firms; and
(4) the increased influence of court cases, legislation and government regulations on the welfare of the industry.

Although each of these factors potentially affects coal's future, the last element, the intrusive hand of government, overwhelms the others in importance. The unpredictability of future governmental moves makes forecasting in this area hazardous. Much of this article deals with the effect on coal's future of the major developments listed above.

President Carter's National Energy Plan (NEP), assigns an important and growing role to coal in the country's energy picture.[1] But coal has occupied a favored position in the nation's economy several times in the past. Coal's golden era occurred in the first two decades of the 20th century when output rose steadily, and coal accounted for 67% of the United States' energy consumption. The next several decades witnessed a steady decline in coal's fortunes. Not until 1947 was the 1920 level of dollar sales surpassed. The World War II coal boom carried over for several post-war years, but the industry soon lapsed into an era of relative decline. Accounting for 47.9 percent of total U.S. energy consumption in 1947, coal's share of consumption

*Dr. Moyer is a Professor of Business Administration at the University of California at Berkeley.
1. EXECUTIVE OFFICE OF THE PRESIDENT, THE NATIONAL ENERGY PLAN (1977).

declined to 17.3 percent by 1972.[2] The oil embargo, sharply higher oil prices, and concern for future energy supplies have contributed to renewed interest in coal as a major energy supplier. The question remains, however, whether coal will achieve the position of prominence that the National Energy Plan envisions.

Coal's future is marked by bright prospects and nagging problems. The favorable prospects are discussed first.

PROSPECTS

Among coal's greatest assets is the Administration's commitment to encourage coal consumption through a combination of legislative proposals that directly or indirectly promote the use of coal. Note that the emphasis is on consumption and not on production. Implicit in the Carter energy program is the belief that increased latent demand will call forth corresponding supplies. But critics of Administration policies argue that consumption will fall short of targeted levels unless the government modifies other policies that hamper coal production and consumption.

What are the elements of the Administration's program to encourage coal use? What the President wants and what Congress delivers may be widely divergent. But the NEP addresses the issue on several fronts. It seeks to encourage coal consumption by taxing oil and natural gas use by utilities and industrial firms, and by banning these alternate fuels in new electric utility plants and new large industrial installations. Allowing investment tax credits for the installation of new coal equipment is another part of the program aimed at increasing coal's relative share of total energy production.

A pro-coal policy by the Administration may enhance coal's position, but underlying forces favor coal in the near term even in the absence of legislative stimulants. The Administration's program calls for the consumption of 1.2 billion tons of coal by 1985, an increase of 565 million tons over the 1975 level. Without the plan coal consumption ought to rise to 1 billion tons in the same year. Coal benefits from two powerful forces: its strong reserve position and its relative cheapness, despite sharp price increases in recent years.

Determining the quantity of available U.S. coal reserves is at the same time, an easy and difficult task.[3] This phenomenon is true of other energy sources as well. Uncertainty exists in the estimation of

---

2. W. DUPREE & J. WEST, UNITED STATES ENERGY THROUGH THE YEAR 2000 (1972).

3. I have used the term "reserves" losely. Technically there is a distinction between "resources" that includes coal *in situ* and "reserves" that takes account of recovery losses.

oil and gas reserves because we have thus far failed to locate large quantities of potential reserves. This condition does not obtain with coal. Existing coal reserves are fairly well known even though they are mapped imperfectly. The uncertainty arises over determining the extent of economically recoverable reserves given the economic, technological, and environmental forces that limit the availability of known reserves.

Table 1 illustrates only a few of the possible measures of potential coal reserves. The largest total includes all identified and inferred reserves and makes no allowance for coal recovery losses. It also includes reserves at depths and with seam thicknesses that render them unmineable under current economic conditions. The 432 million ton reserve base figure eliminates inaccessible coal and reserves that cannot be mined under existing economic conditions. But it neglects recovery losses from the mining process which may run from 20 to 70 percent depending on mining conditions and the mining technology utilized. The 132 to 150 billion ton figure makes this adjustment. This figure is also deficient since it considers neither the varying heat content of coals, nor their sulphur content which may

TABLE 1

DIFFERENT MEASURES OF U.S. BITUMINOUS COAL
RESERVE ESTIMATES

	billion tons
1. U.S.G.S. estimate of total coal resources, identified and hypothetical	3968
2. U.S.G.S. identified resources, 3000' depth maximum	1560
3. U.S. Bureau of Mines estimate of demonstrated coal reserve base	432
4. Recoverable coal reserves under existing economic conditions	132-150
5. Recoverable coal reserves with sulphur content <0.7 lbs/mm BTU	42

Sources: 1 and 2: Paul Averitt, *Coal Resources of the United States, January 1, 1974,* U.S. Geological Survey Bulletin 1412 (Washington: U.S. Government Printing Office, 1975), p. 5.

3: U.S. Bureau of Mines, *Reserve Base of U.S. Coal by Sulphur Content,* 2 vols. (Washington, U.S. Government Printing Office, 1975).

4: William C. Helt, "Coal Resources Available for Power Generation" in *Illinois Coal,* Proceedings of the Fourth Annual Illinois Energy Conference, September 16-17, 1976 p. 31, and National Petroleum Council, *U.S. Energy Outlook Coal Availability* (Washington, 1973), p. 22.

5: Helt, p. 35.

affect their ability to comply with EPA air quality control standards. The 42 billion ton figure represents a rough approximation of the reserve tonnage meeting minimum sulphur content standards.[4] Since the standard used to arrive at this figure is expressed as sulphur content per million Btu's, the reserve totals are far less than those indicated by data published by the Bureau of Mines on reserves by sulphur content, which are unadjusted for the coal's heat content. Normalizing the 42 billion ton figure to adjust for the subaverage Btu content of the majority of the reserves comprising the total would reduce this reserve calculation even more.

Table 1 expresses some of the ways coal reserves data may be calculated. The highest and lowest figures represent the range of probable reserve estimates. It is distressing to note that the maximum figure is 100 times larger than the lowest. How much coal will be eventually mined depends on so many variables that an accurate forecast is impractical. For example, a relaxation of the Clean Air Act's SO_2 standards or improvement in flue gas desulphurization technology would bring enormous quantities of higher sulphur coal into compliance with the Act. Similarly, increased prices for competitive fuels and improved coal mining technology would make certain coal reserves economical that were previously economically unattractive. Also, account must be taken of the likelihood of future conversion of coal to synthetic fuels through utilizing above ground plants or in situ methods that would make use of coals that are marginal by today's standards.

Coal's advocates point to the several hundred years supply of coal; the doomsayers emphasize the minimum reserve figures. The "correct" figure lies somewhere between the minimum and maximum, but probably enough above the minimum to let coal fill the role expected of it in the foreseeable future.

Table 2 reveals coal's strategic position in the total energy reserve picture. Given a national commitment to reduce relative dependence on foreign oil, and given eventual dwindling supplies both of domestic and imported oil and gas, United States' energy policy must necessarily favor coal, at least for the remainder of the 20th century. Table 2 is based upon known and fairly conservative estimates of energy reserves. Allowing for new discoveries and exploitation of marginal reserves would raise the totals considerably, but this dis-

4. The EPA specific-source standard calls for a maximum of 0.6 pounds of sulphur emissions per million Btus for new electric utility installations. This is equivalent to 0.5 percent sulphur content by weight for coal with a heat content of 16 million Btus per ton. Large quantities of so-called low sulphur western coal fail to meet that standard.

TABLE 2

U.S. RECOVERABLE ENERGY RESERVES

Energy Source	Quadrillion BTU	%
Coal	4557	79.5
Petroleum	197	3.4
Natural Gas	258	4.5
Natural Gas Liquids	26	0.5
Oil in Bituminous Rocks	7	0.1
Shale Oil	450	7.9
Uranium Oxide	234	4.1
Total	5729	100.0

Source: National Coal Association, *Coal Facts, 1974-75*, p. 7.

tribution among the sources listed would remain fairly constant. Coal still stands out as the dominant energy source for as long as it is feasible to project in the planning horizon.

Coal's cost advantage over competitive fuels is borne out in the Table 3 data. The cost figures cover the electric utility market which accounts for 72 percent of coal consumption, but excludes nuclear power costs. Comparing coal and uranium costs in this market is difficult for several reasons, not the least of which is the existence of regional cost differences. Overall, coal appears to have an edge over other energy sources as evidenced by a projection for planned additions to electric power plant capacity for the period 1976-1980 broken down as follows: 44 percent for coal, 29.7 percent for nuclear, and 17.7 percent for oil or gas-fired plants or combustion turbines.[5] The final package of energy legislation may well stimulate an even greater use of coal-fired plants in the 1980s.

Table 3 reveals that in some regions coal use lags despite its lower delivered price per million Btus. Added costs and the inconvenience involved in burning coal coupled with non-fuel cost differentials partly counterbalance coal's delivered cost advantage. But coal's improved competitive position vis à vis oil and gas has led to higher market shares for coal in the electric utility market, and has stemmed the long term downward trend in coal's share of the total energy market. The combination of favorable relative prices, abundant reserves and a national commitment to reduce our dependence on foreign oil bodes well for coal. On the other hand, a combination of new and continuing problems block the road to unfettered progress.

5. Coal News, February 27, 1976.

64

TABLE 3

NATIONAL PRIMARY ENERGY PURCHASE DATA
12 MONTHS ENDING APRIL, 1977
FOR STEAM ELECTRIC PLANTS

Geographic Region	% of Total BTU			Avg. Price, Cents/MM BTU		
	Coal	Oil	Gas	Coal	Oil	Gas
New England	5.8	93.5	0.6	126.4	196.8	157.1
Middle Atlantic	58.8	40.8	0.4	102.5	207.0	125.8
East North Central	93.8	4.8	1.4	90.5	238.5	151.3
West North Central	82.6	4.6	12.8	68.8	201.8	81.4
South Atlantic	66.6	29.5	4.0	104.5	195.7	88.2
East South Central	92.2	5.7	2.1	89.2	180.9	143.9
West South Central	8.3	7.9	83.9	48.4	190.7	104.4
Mountain	81.2	4.3	14.4	38.0	225.8	107.1
Pacific	5.6	62.8	31.6	75.4	231.9	166.2
United States Total	61.2	20.5	18.3	86.9	207.7	111.1

Source: Federal Power Commission, *FPC News* (Week Ended August 20, 1977).

PROBLEMS

What are some of these problems? Several have plagued coal since the inception of the industry. Coal is a dirty commodity. It is dirty to handle; its combustion adds to air pollution; mining contributes to water pollution and especially in the case of strip mining, to the despoliation of the land.

Air Quality

Increased social concern for air quality and passage of the Clean Air Act have had profound effects on the coal industry in addition to introducing an element of uncertainty that adds to the industry's woes. Coal users face a congeries of federal and state air quality standards and variances that influence both investment decisions and fuel choices. The primary restriction affecting coal is regulation of sulphur oxide emissions; however, implementation of the federal and state standards have affected consumers unequally. Hence, the impact on coal producers is also uneven.

A result of this development has been increased dependence on the low sulphur western coals at the expense of eastern and midwestern producers. Thus coal output in the west has increased at a much faster rate than in the east. From 1970 through the first six months of 1977 the share of total coal production from mines west of the Mississippi River increased from 7.3 percent to 23.5 percent. Output from western mines during that period rose almost fourfold, while output from eastern mines declined slightly. The next decade should witness an acceleration of that trend. A Federal Energy Administration forecast calls for western coal output to increase from 107 to 378 million tons between 1975 and 1985 and to account for 36.3 percent of total coal output in the latter year.[6] The coal consumption figures parallel the coal production trends. Coal consumption in states west of the Mississippi totaled 102.8 million tons in 1975. It is projected to increase to 289.2 million tons in 1985, a 181 percent increase as opposed to a 79 percent increase for the rest of the country.[7] This development is a function both of the increased demand for low sulphur coal (at the expense of higher sulphur midwestern and eastern coals) and of the switch to coal use and away from oil and gas.

There are, however, elements in the western coal situation that threaten the industry's potential. Amendments to the Clean Air Act of 1977 mandate that new manufacturing plants and utilities use the "best available control technology" to reduce SOx emissions. The failure to distinguish between the use of high or low sulphur coals neutralizes the natural advantage of western coal. Pressure on several fronts is growing in the mining states themselves to thwart the expansion of western coal output. Environmentalists express concern over the ecological threat posed by the disturbance of the fragile surface by strip mining operations in areas with limited rainfall. They fear that inadequate moisture will prevent the revegetation of disturbed strip land to the detriment of the mined-out areas for generations to come. Concern has also been raised about the social and economic problems created by the explosive growth of the once placid mining communities that have been swept up in the expansion of western coal output.

The net effect of enforcement of environmental legislation on both total coal production and its location is conjectural. The General Accounting Office's evaluation of the NEP concluded "that the expanded use of coal, even to the administration's base case level of 1 billion tons, will not take place if all current and proposed air quality policies are strictly enforced."[8] But the fact remains that no

6. FEDERAL ENERGY ADMINISTRATION, 1976 NATIONAL ENERGY OUTLOOK (1976).

7. U.S. BUREAU OF MINES, BITUMINOUS COAL AND LIGNITE DISTRIBUTION, CALENDAR YEAR 1975, U.S. BUREAU OF MINES MINERAL INDUSTRY SURVEY, April 12, 1976 and G. Larwood and D. Benson, COAL TRANSPORTATION PRACTICES AND EQUIPMENT REQUIREMENTS TO 1985, U.S. Bureau of Mines Information Circular 8706.

8. General Accounting Office, AN EVALUATION OF THE NATIONAL ENERGY PLAN 520 (1977).

one can be certain (1) whether and to what extent the policies will be enforced, (2) whether variances and delays will impede their implementation, and (3) what effect on the air quality situation developments both in scrubber technology and the commercialization of coal gasification will have. Much of the coal research effort today is directed at the discovery of ways to reduce SOx emissions either by "scrubbing" the deleterious gases from the smokestack before they are emitted into the atmosphere, or by removing the harmful sulphur before combustion through gasification or intensive coal cleaning.

The results of this uncertainty are fuzzy coal forecasts and a reluctance by coal users and coal producers to press full speed ahead on the development of new coal capacity. An eastern coal operator controlling high sulphur reserves will think twice about investing in a mine whose output may be banned by air quality regulations. The same uncertainty exists for the coal user although he has a possible escape value—a switch to low sulphur western coal. This move often results in increased fuel costs which eventually translate into higher electricity rates. Critics of this condition call for a reform which will spur utilities to seek lower fuel costs. The present approach diminishes the incentive to perfect scrubber technology. Thus, failure to develop effective and economical ways to deal with the SOx problem enhances the prospects for western coal development at the expense of eastern coal development. Conversely, breakthroughs in this area could reverse the fortunes of these two major coal producing regions. If there is not enough uncertainty surrounding the air quality issue, an added concern is the potential for carbon dioxide buildup from coal combustion, which some feel may threaten to significantly alter the ecosystem.

LEASING RESTRICTIONS

Another restriction on the free development of coal reserves is the government's policy concerning the leasing of western coal lands. The federal and state governments are the principal owners of coal deposits in the western states. Fifty four and a half million tons of coal were produced from federal leases in 1976 but this represented a tiny fraction of the 16.2 billion tons of coal controlled by private interests under federal leases.[9] Since most of these leases were entered into when the prospect for western coal development was dim, they create relatively little revenue for the government and in-

9. United States Geological Survey, FEDERAL AND INDIAN LANDS COAL, PHOSPHATE, POTASH AND OTHER MINERAL PRODUCTION, ROYALTY INCOME AND RELATED STATISTICS (1977).

adequate incentive to develop the reserves. Government policy-makers, realizing the shortcomings of the leasing policies, placed a moratorium on leasing to allow development of a new program to encourage production, enhance competition and increase royalty revenue. Meanwhile, a lawsuit instituted by the Natural Resources Defense Council, *NRDC v. Hughes,* prevents implementation of the revised leasing regulations.[10] The need for Environmental Impact Statements hampered development of western coal under the old program and will continue to impinge upon it under the revised policy.

DECLINING PRODUCTIVITY

One of the most pervasive and important influences on the coal industry has been the consistent reduction in productivity both in strip and underground mining, since 1969. The decline can be attributed to several factors including provisions in the 1974 U.M.W.A. labor contract calling for added personnel for safety purposes, increased absenteeism and wildcat strikes, and an alleged weakening of the work ethic among miners. The latter factor lacks substantiation, although it is an article of faith among some coal operators. The absenteeism and wildcat strike charge also cannot stand up to scrutiny since a productivity measure is a ratio of an input (e.g., man hours worked) to output (coal tonnage), and absenteeism reducing coal output affects the ratio's numerator and denominator equally. Absenteeism undoubtedly reduces *production,* but its effect on productivity is probably minimal. The labor contract changes undoubtedly reduced output per man day, although here too, the effect is undetermined.

The biggest factor accounting for coal's productivity slide has been passage and implementation of the Federal Coal Mine Health and Safety Act of 1969. The industry witnessed a decline in productivity of 24 percent from 1969 to 1975 affecting both strip and underground mines.[11] The national average data suggest that underground mines have been affected more than strip. In the 1969-75 period output per man day declined 38 percent for deep mines and 22 percent for strip, but the totals mark the underlying trend.[12] Except for Pennsylvania, where strip mining productivity increased slightly,

---

10. 437 F. Supp. 981 (D.D.C. 1977).

11. U.S. BUREAU OF MINES, MINERALS YEARBOOK (various issues).

12. Two factors account for the apparent discrepancy caused by a decline of 38% for deep mine productivity, 22% for strip and 24% for the two combined: the relative shift in output toward strip during the period and the use of man days and not tonnage as the weighting factor in deriving a national average.

the major eastern strip mining states suffered reductions in productivity of from 19.8 to 48.7 percent.[13] The factor saving strip mine productivity from a decline as sharp as that experienced by underground mines was the growth of strip mining in the west where in the five major producing states output per man day averaged 71.0 tons in 1975, compared with 19.0 tons for the rest of the strip mining sector.[14]

How likely is coal productivity to resume the pace of growth exhibited in the post World War II period when output per man day increased at a compound annual rate of 5.3 percent until the Coal Mine Health and Safety Act took effect in 1970? The answer depends partly on the severity of the Act's enforcement which is another unknown variable facing coal company management. Some operators fear that transfer of the Mining Enforcement and Safety Administration from Interior to the Labor Department will stiffen enforcement of health and safety standards in response to organized labor's pressure. Others expect that adjustment to the Act's enforcement provisions both by management and enforcement personnel will eventually stem the productivity decline.

Other factors ought to aid the total productivity picture. We have already noted the enormous productivity advantage accruing to western strip mines compared to both the eastern underground and strip operations. The changing mix of total production, involving more output from the west and relatively less from the east, will boost overall productivity figures. Additional improvement should flow from the sharply increased research and development expenditures undertaken both by the government and by operating companies. This condition is in stark contrast to the parsimonious research and development outlays that characterized the industry until recently. The increases trace in part to the entry of richly capitalized petroleum companies into coal mining. The infusion of oil industry management talent should also improve productivity.

Another unknown in the productivity equation is the extent to which the coal industry may have reached a cyclical plateau in the introduction of labor-machines and techniques. Much of the steady and substantial improvements in output per man day in the three decades following World War II stemmed from three factors—(1) the growth of strip mining output, with its relatively high inherent productivity, at the expense of the inefficient underground sector; (2) introduction of ever larger machines in strip mining that allowed

---

13. *Id.*
14. *Id.*

strip operators to overcome increasing stripping ratios; and (3) the replacement of hand loading with machine cutting and loading in underground mines. There is still room for productivity growth from the first of these three factors (although probably not in the east and midwest where desirable strip properties are scarce), but the other two forces may have essentially run their course. In the absence of major technological breakthroughs or the introduction of revolutionary mining techniques (e.g., remote control mining or improved underground haulage), productivity growth may fail to resume the growth trend broken by enforcement of the Health and Safety Act.

LABOR UNCERTAINTY

In few industries have labor conditions been as volatile as they have been in the coal industry. A combination of fiercely independent workers often laboring under dangerous conditions in a traditionally competitive industry has contributed to unsettled labor conditions in coal mining. Looming over the labor landscape has been the United Mine Workers of America, a union whose record has been as checkered as the industry whose workers it represents. It has never succeeded in fully capturing the allegiance of the industry's work force. From a fairly strong position around World War I, the union's position deteriorated throughout the 1920's and was not completely resuscitated until after passage of the National Industrial Recovery Act in 1933. Union membership grew from 100,000 to 400,000, wage rates were stabilized and, though labor strife persisted, it took the form of national strikes. The strong leadership of John L. Lewis maintained discipline at the local level and minimized the non-union threat that had magnified the industry chaos for 15 years following World War I. Moreover, Lewis encouraged the introduction of labor saving machinery and techniques.

Today the cycle is turning against the union, and both they and the operators are suffering as a result. We noted earlier the spate of absenteeism and wildcat strikes that has burdened the industry in recent years. Man-days lost from wildcat strikes stood at 2.3 million for the first eight months of 1977, almost seven times above the level five years ago and ten times the average for all industries.[15]

The union suffers from weak leadership and the debilitating effect of internal dissension. Tonnage from U.M.W. mines stands at around 50 percent of national output as the coal union movement weakens

---

15. BUSINESS WEEK, November 28, 1977, at 88. National Coal Association, IMPLICATIONS OF INVESTMENTS IN THE COAL INDUSTRY BY FIRMS FROM OTHER ENERGY INDUSTRIES 9 (1977).

in the eastern coal fields and western miners opt for representation by the Operating Engineers. Achievement of targeted goals for coal production in the National Energy Plan will depend in part on the creation of more stable labor relations. The protracted U.M.W. strike in 1978 dampened the prospects for improved labor conditions. It also strengthened the belief of coal's critics that coal cannot be relied on as a dependable energy source as long as labor relations in the regions organized by the U.M.W. remain in the present chaotic state.

DIVESTITURE

Another cloud over the industry is the prospect of legislative or administrative action mandating horizontal divestiture to reduce the economic power of emerging energy companies. Recent legislative sessions have witnessed bills designed to prohibit energy firms from engaging in the production of more than one energy source. They are aimed primarily at the petroleum companies which have moved vigorously into reserve acquisition and production of coal and uranium.

The divestiture argument is intuitively appealing. It recognizes that the long run substitutability of coal for oil strengthens the oil companies' alleged market power in energy markets. Proponents of divestiture argue that oil companies controlling coal deposits will weaken energy competition by refusing to compete with themselves in markets where coal and oil are ready substitutes. The corollary of this argument is that the growth of energy market power will manifest itself in restrictions on coal production and new capital investment in the monopolist's time-honored tradition. Advocates of divestiture also fear that the oil industry will be reluctant to invest in the development of alternate energy sources since to do so would make obsolete their huge investments in petroleum.[16]

Interest in the possibility of horizontal divestiture has spawned Congressional hearings, symposia, and scholarly research on the subject. The result is a better balanced perspective on the problems and potential of divestiture. Space limitations prevent a complete analysis of the problem. The author's analysis of the issue leads to the following tentative conclusions:

(1) Concentration ratios at the 4, 8, and 20-firm level in the coal

---

16. For a variety of viewpoints on the issue of horizontal divestiture see: D. Norman, Diversification and Competition in the Energy Industry (paper delivered at Annual Meeting of the Southwestern Economics Association, April, 1977). W. Adams, Horizontal Divestiture in the Petroleum Industry: An Affirmative Case (paper delivered at the American Enterprise Institute, January 27, 1977); J. Markham, A. Hourihan and F. Sterling, HORIZONTAL DIVESTITURE AND THE PETROLEUM INDUSTRY (1977).

industry have declined slightly in the last decade and, compared to other American industries, appear to offer no immediate anti-competitive threat.

(2) The share of total coal output controlled by petroleum firms fell in the 1968-76 period from 19.2 percent to 17.5 percent.[17]

(3) The foregoing would seem to bear out the "withholding production" argument, but an analysis of output levels for the oil companies' coal affiliates fails to support it. Comparing average coal output figures for the four major coal-oil companies for the five years before and after the coal companies' acquisition reveals that they increased coal output from 16.8 percent to 73.9 percent.[18]

(4) The percent of economically recoverable coal reserves controlled by oil companies, and the share of announced tonnage of coal mine developments exceeds the oil firms' share of present coal output, suggesting that their share of future output will increase.

(5) None of the price behavior studies in coal have traced elevated coal prices and profits to the entry of the oil industry into coal, although the charge is frequently made. The confluence of the oil industry's entry into coal and an upsurge in the average price of coal seems to support the charge, but the causes run deeper. The combination of increased prices of competitives fuels, sharply higher coal mining costs, a tight spot coal market, and a robust export market, rather than the entry of the oil industry into coal, account for most of coal's higher price level.

(6) Far from deterring research, the oil industry's invasion into the coal industry appears to have enhanced research and development expenditures.

The effect of these conclusions plus recognition of the administrative complexity of divestiture have temporarily blunted the legislative move toward this antitrust remedy. Underlying suspicion of the oil industry's alleged market power, however, keeps the divestiture issue alive. The continuing threat of its implementation forces energy companies to factor it into their planning processes.

CONCLUSION

This article has balanced a few of the coal industry's favorable prospects against some of its major problems. It would be easy to expand the potential problem areas (water pollution, potential manpower shortages, conflict concerning the allocation of precious western water sources, environmental lawsuits over implementation of the Energy Supply and Environmental Coordination Act, and adjust-

17. KEYSTONE COAL INDUSTRY MANUAL (various years).
18. *Id.*

ing to the Surface Mining Control and Reclamation Act of 1977). Some potential entrants into the industry, having assessed the pros and cons, have felt that the disadvantages outweigh the advantages, and have elected to stay out of the industry. Nonetheless, a large number of American industry's biggest firms have chosen to enter the industry via coal company acquisitions or through purchase of coal reserves, some of which are currently under development. They apparently visualize the potential for profitable investment in an industry which offers the prospect rarely afforded American industry —the opportunity for rebirth and expansion after suffering stagnation and decline. Whether the industry meets the goals envisioned for it depends as much on actions in the legislative halls and courtrooms as it does on decisions flowing from coal company boardrooms.

Chapter 6

OIL SHALE—A NEW SET OF UNCERTAINTIES

JOHN J. SCHANZ, JR.* and HARRY PERRY**

INTRODUCTION

A British Petroleum pipeline finds its way across the sea floor from the Forties Field, comes ashore alongside a venerable Scottish golf course, and proceeds southward, broaching ancient Roman walls enroute. At the terminus, within sight of the Firth of Forth, the North Sea oil is held awaiting further shipment by tanker. The tanks are cleverly hidden from casual view by the rolling green terrain. The spoil banks of a bygone Scottish oil shale era now provide a pleasant camouflage for the resource industry that replaced it.

Mining and retorting of oil shale has been practiced for over 100 years in many different countries. However, with the discovery of petroleum reserves the industry declined rapidly in size, and shale oil was used in decreasing amounts. Ever since this development, the intriguing question has been whether shale oil can once again become a major source of liquid hydrocarbons.

One of the periodic revivals in oil shale enthusiasm appeared in the mid-1960's, but by 1969 this enthusiasm had begun to wane. The Oil Shale Corporation's (TOSCO) estimates of operating costs at $1.55 per barrel appeared bullish, but the Cabinet Task Force on Oil Import Policy was considering removal of oil import quotas and world oil was in abundant supply and selling at under $2.00 per barrel.[1] Perhaps most discouraging were the difficulties being encountered by the Sun Oil Company at its Great Canadian Oil Sands venture in Alberta.[2] Reports of Sun's continuing losses triggered caution in the board rooms of firms holding oil shale lands.

Ten more years have now passed, and imported oil now arrives at $14.49 per barrel, and new domestic crude brings an upper-tier price of $12.29.[3] Surely shale oil, which was nearly economic at $4.00 to $5.00 per barrel, must now be ready to burst upon the energy scene. Or is it?

---

*Fellow, Resources for the Future.
**Consultant, Resources for the Future.
1. Schanz, *The Outlook for Synthetic Liquid Hydrocarbons*, 65 Q. Colo. Sch. Mines 13 (Oct. 1970).
2. New York Times, May 12, 1969, at 69.
3. CHASE MANHATTAN BANK, 2 The Petroleum Situation 4 (Table 1) (April 1978).

BOOM AND BUST IN THE SEVENTIES

Among the nation's major oil firms, not all are equally fortunate in having access to crude oil to meet their refinery needs. Thus firms such as Ashland Oil, Atlantic Richfield, or Standard Oil of Ohio have always been on the alert for any turn of events that could improve the outlook for new feedstock sources. Then embargo of the Organization of Petroleum Exporting Countries (OPEC) and the subsequent drastic change in world oil prices was certain to stimulate these firms and others to reexamine their position with regard to oil shale. Atlantic Richfield had already joined the Colony consortium and was engaged in a rigorous technical and economic inquiry into the feasibility of building a plant on private lands.[4] There was revived interest in public land leasing, and it appeared unlikely that there would be a repeat performance of the pitifully small bids that were rejected by Interior in 1968.

Things began to move forward smoothly, with Colony announcing that the first commercial-sized plant would be built at their Parachute Creek site.[5] The bids made for the first two federal tracts in early 1974 surprised the Department of the Interior once again, this time because they were on the high side. Standard Oil Company of Indiana and Gulf Oil Corporation bid $210.3 million for tract C-a in Colorado. Atlantic Richfield, TOSCO, Ashland Oil Company and Shell Oil bid $117.8 million for tract C-b.[6] It appeared that for the first time in the over fifty-year history of the Mineral Leasing Act, there would also be a commercial-sized operation on the public lands. But misfortune does not give up easily on its treatment of oil shale.

Environmental concerns continued to harass and delay the ventures. It was determined that the background levels of certain types of air pollutants exceeded federal clean air standards. There remained uncertainty about the ability to revegetate the surface after mining and the ability to deal properly with the wastes from the retorts. Questions about the adequacy of water supplies and the potential for harming aquifers or causing deterioration in regional water quality could not be answered to everyone's satisfaction.

Problems also appeared with respect to mining itself. The 5,000 acre tracts were not adequate in size for both surface mining and for the disposal of waste rock. Underground mining at the C-b lease, on the other hand, was encountering difficulties related to the strength

---

4. 68 Oil & Gas J. 34, 42 (1970).
5. 184 Science 4143, 1271 (1974).
6. Wall Street Journal, February 13, 1974, at 4.

or competence of the rock to protect the workings. But most alarming was the rapid escalation in the estimates of the capital costs to construct the plants.

While it appeared that higher priced world oil, which was due to OPEC decisions plus the increasing cost of domestic drilling offered an unparalleled opportunity for shale oil development, the financial environment for the capital-intensive shale oil industry was deteriorating rapidly (See Table 1). Although estimates vary among companies and between government and private analyses, there is general agreement about the approximate level of oil shale plant capital costs, operating costs, and the required price, assuming an equivalent rate of return. An examination of the statistical data from a variety of sources shown in Table 1 reveals that, from 1968 to 1973, the capital requirements for a 50,000 barrel per day plant doubled. The estimates then more than tripled between 1973 and 1976. Today on paper the cost of an oil shale plant of a size and degree of processing comparable to those proposed ten years ago has likely passed the $1 billion mark.

Operating costs, given prevailing inflationary conditions, have been somewhat better behaved than capital costs. These costs doubled between 1968 and 1976. This is in reasonable accord with the behavior of the wholesale price index for industrial commodities. Given the 277 percent increase in the value of U.S. crude oil and the 722 percent increase in the posted price of Saudi Arabian oil during this period, the oil shale industry could have improved its relative competitive position if capital costs had stayed in line with other inflationary trends. Unfortunately, the 696 percent increase in the estimated cost of building the shale oil plants totally negated this advantage. By 1976 the required price for shale oil, even at a modest 12 to 13 percent discounted cash flow rate of return, had reached $18 or more a barrel.[7] This was well over the market price of either domestic or foreign oil. So, by 1976, shale oil's competitive picture was perhaps worse than it had been in 1968.

It was already apparent by the end of 1974 that the oil shale bubble had burst once again. In rapid succession, the companies retrenched. By October 1974, Colony announced that it was suspending its plans at Parachute Creek.[8] On the federal leases development was initially delayed, then companies began to withdraw from the ventures. Activity on the leases was replaced by appeals for government assistance of one form or another for shale oil production to be feasible.

---

7. 198 Science 4321, 1023 (1977).
8. J. Comm., November 19, 1974, at 3.

TABLE 1

COMPARATIVE INFLATIONARY TRENDS, SELECTED YEARS

Year	Oil shale plant capital cost (MM $)	Operating cost ($/bbl)	Required price at 12% or 12% DCF	Average value U.S. crude (S/bbl)[a]	Posted price light Saudi Arabian crude[b]	Wholesale price index industrial commodities[c]	Nelson inflation index for refinery cost[d]	Index of payments to drilling contractors[e]
1968	$138[f]	$2.12[f]	$3.60[f]	$2.94	$1.80	102.5	304.1	53.6
1970	250[g]	2.04[g]	4.50[g]	3.18	1.80	110.0	364.9	60.6
1973	280[h]	3.21[h]	5.66[h]	3.89	5.12[i]	125.9	468.0	76.9
1976	960[j]	4.16[j]	18.30[j]	8.14	13.00	182.3	615.7	124.0
% change 1968-76	696	196	508	277	722	178	202	231

Sources of data: (See References for complete citations)

[a] U.S. Bureau of Mines.

[b] American Petroleum Institute.

[c] Bureau of Labor Statistics, base year 1967.

[d] Oil and Gas Journal, base year 1946.

[e] Independent Petroleum Producers Association of America, base year 1974.

[f] U.S. Department of the Interior.

[g] National Petroleum Council.

[h] U.S. Bureau of Mines.

[i] As of November 1, 1973.

[j] The Oil Shale Corporation.

It was apparent to the companies involved that environmental standards were stricter than ever before, that state and local taxes would likely increase, and that the affected communities were very concerned over uncertain socioeconomic impacts rather than being impressed by new employment opportunities. Nonetheless, these problems were probably manageable. The capital costs were the root difficulty. One might be inclined to suspect the calculations themselves, but a comparable quadrupling of capital costs is also found in the estimates made by other firms involved in western coal gasification projects.[9]

There appears to have been a number of circumstances encountered between 1973 and 1976 that caused a multiplicative effect in the cost estimates. Initially, there was the general double digit inflationary trend. To this was added a somewhat faster increase in cost for constructing refineries or similar type plants. These costs were increasing as much as 40 percent per year by 1976.[10] Coupled with these inflationary trends was the fact that oil shale mines and plants had become more expensive in real terms as they were redesigned to meet new and more stringent environmental requirements. The direct and indirect costs of public investments in the communities supporting the plants became apparent and they also had to be factored into the estimates. In many early estimates the cost of the leases had not been included. Procedural and legal matters added two to three years to the time required between the beginning of a project and the time when production could be anticipated. A twenty-four month delay in production commencement is sufficient by itself to require as much as a 20 percent increase in the price required for a plant to be economically feasible. Finally, analysts were making a future inflationary adjustment for all anticipated capital and operating costs. In retrospect, given the above series of events the ratchet effect of these accumulative adjustments is not surprising.

A SHIFT IN TECHNOLOGY

Short of major governmental intervention, it has become apparent that no firm is currently prepared to risk its funds in conventional oil shale mining and surface retorting. Consequently, the search has turned to finding a process that will: reduce total capital costs, permit the project to be built and operated in a series of stages, and

9. GENERAL ACCOUNTING OFFICE, STATUS AND OBSTACLES TO COMMERCIALIZATION OF COAL LIQUEFACTION AND GASIFICATION, Report to U.S. Senate Committee on Interior and Insular Affairs, 27 (1976).
10. *Nelson Cost Indexes,* 76 Oil and Gas Journal 18, 55 (May 1978).

offer a better way to deal with the group of problems involving air and water quality, surface disturbance, and waste disposal.

Since the 1950's a number of surface retorting methods have been developed in the United States, and their technical feasibility has been proven so that there is acceptable technical risk for industry to proceed to commercial scale development. Although there have been some new processes and some refinements in old methods in the last ten years, none have been developed and tested to a point where it has been proven that they would significantly reduce the cost of the plants or the shale oil produced. Some of the more recent designs appear to offer some improvements in surface-type operations and they may actually reduce water consumption and minimize adverse environmental effects. Unfortunately, such processes and plant designs that minimize water requirements and environmental impact tend to be higher in cost than those that do not.

As a result, there has been a recent shift in near-term oil shale development. True in situ retorting (no mining is used) has received sporadic research and development (R&D) efforts by several private companies since the early 1950's. The major difficulty encountered was the inability to create sufficient permeability in the oil shale formation to permit retorting at economic rates. For true in situ mining to become economically attractive, methods must be devised to fracture the shale economically and create enough permeability to permit good contact between the shale and the retorting gases, and to prevent bypassing of unretorted shale so that high recovery of oil is possible.

In true in situ mining, wells are driven from the surface into the shale formation and the shale is then rubblized. The fractured shale is then ignited at a central production well into which air is blown, and combustion takes place underground. The products oil, water, and gas are recovered from a series of production wells driven around the injection well at 35 to 50-foot intervals.

The permeability needed to attain air flow at a reasonable pressure and in the necessary volumes into the oil shale can be attained by hydraulic fracturing, chemical explosive fracturing or a combination of both. In hydraulic fracturing, water or a water base gel containing sand is injected under high pressure into the oil shale. The water pressure fractures the shale and the sand remains in the formation to hold the fracture open in order to remove the oil. In chemical explosive fracturing one of several types of explosives are injected into the borehole and detonated.

Hydraulic fracturing tests have been made at two sites using Wyoming shale, and explosive fracturing experiments have been conducted at three Wyoming sites. On the basis of these experiences it has been concluded that hydraulic fracturing followed by explosive rubblization is relatively difficult to carry out and the bed porosity created is very low. Production efficiencies are expected to be low, and in the tests actually conducted recovery efficiency was less than 5 percent.[11] The explosive fracturing (using a technique known as "well bore springing") is a much simpler system but the dimensions of the retort that is created are limited in total volume, and it is difficult to get sufficient permeability in the shale to sustain combustion. As a result, one can only conclude that at present, true in situ technology is not yet technically proven.

To overcome the difficulties mentioned above and to try to take advantage of the potential benefits of the in situ approach, modified in situ tests have been conducted. Several different methods are being tested. In 1972, Occidental Oil Shale Corporation began a study of its modified in situ process.[12] Since then three research retorts and two commercial-sized retorts have been prepared and combustion tests on them have been conducted.

In modified in situ processing a small part of the oil shale is mined and the balance to be retorted is then fractured and rubblized in the space created by mining, and a permeable zone for retorting is formed. In the Occidental Oil Shale Corporation process approximately 15 percent of the oil shale is mined from the upper and lower levels of the planned retort. After fracturing of the shale between the mined-out areas with explosives that create a rubblized pile, vertical holes are drilled into the fractured chambers. The broken shale is ignited at the top and air is injected downward to maintain combustion. Oil and gas are recovered from the bottom of the retort and part of the gas is recirculated to control the oxygen concentration in the inlet combustion gas.

The Lawrence Livermore Laboratory is also investigating a modified in situ retorting process called Rubble In Situ Extraction (RISE) that is a variation of the Occidental process. The essential difference is in the method of stoping. Where, prior to blasting, the Occidental procedure mines a room above and below the planned retort, the RISE method mines drifts driven the width of the block at multiple levels. Development, fan drilling, and loading after blasting proceed on subsequent sublevels.[13]

In addition to the government-sponsored RISE project, the De-

11. Burwell, Sterner & Carpenter, *Shale Oil Recovery by In Situ Retorting; a Pilot Study,* 22, 12 J. Petroleum Tech. 1520 (Dec. 1970).
12. 71 Oil & Gas J. 39, 94 (1973).
13. A. LEWIS & A. ROTHMAN, *Rubble In-Situ Extraction* (1975).

partment of Energy (DOE) is supporting additional modified in situ projects with Equity Oil Company (modified in situ shale oil solution mining), with Geokinetics, Inc. (horizontal modified in situ), at the Laramie Energy Research Laboratory (horizontal modified in situ), and DOE is providing support for the Occidental process described above.[14] Another government-sponsored project that is designed to develop long-term shale deposits aimed at the production of gas from shale is being conducted by the Dow Chemical Company.

WHITHER NOW?

There has now appeared some optimism, although not universally shared, that modified in situ mining offers a way of getting an oil shale industry under way. Major attention will be focused on two Colorado federal leases. Occidental Petroleum and Ashland Oil Company will be partners using Occidental's modified in situ method at the C-b tract. Concurrently, Gulf Oil and Standard Oil of Indiana have also shifted their Rio Blanco Oil Shale Project on the C-a lease to the RISE modified in situ method (see Table 2). The Rio Blanco project, employing a different approach to preparation of the retorting chamber, is not as well advanced experimentally as Occidental's and will require further small scale investigation before commercial-sized development can be considered.[15]

Numerous advantages are now claimed for modified in situ. Operations will be developed in a series of steps. The projects will require only about one third as many people as the surface plants, minimizing the local socioeconomic adjustments to the new ventures. Water requirements will be reduced to 25 to 33 percent of normal requirements.[16] Spent shale disposal will be sharply reduced by 80 percent.

Government encouragement of commercial oil shale development is now becoming apparent. Colorado's Air Pollution Commission has eased its sulfur emission standards to a level that will make operations feasible. The Environmental Protection Agency has also given its approval for the projects to proceed. Tax credits have been proposed and there will be participation in the "entitlements" program for refinery purchases. Entitlement is a cost allocation program designed to equalize refiners' disparate oil costs from different sources.

14. 75 Oil & Gas J. 42, 65 (1977).
15. Personal communication with Dr. ARTHUR LEWIS, Lawrence Livermore Laboratory, Livermore, California.
16. CONGRESSIONAL RESEARCH SERVICE, ENERGY FROM OIL SHALE, Report to Subcommittee on Energy of the House Committee on Science and Technology, at 18 (Nov. 1973).

TABLE 2

SELECTED MAJOR OIL SHALE DEVELOPMENT ACTIVITIES*

Project and companies	Planned technology	Completed by or 1st test by—	How much shale oil	Expected cost of activity
Prototype of oil shale leasing program tract C-b; Ashland Oil, Inc., Occidental Petroleum Co.	Modified in situ	1983 completed	Planned 57,000 bbl/d	$440,000,000
Department of Energy—Occidental Petroleum Co., cooperative demonstration plant program	Modified in situ	Around 1982	2,500 bbl/d	$60,500,000
Prototype of oil shale leasing program, tract C-a, Rio Blanco oil shale project; Standard Oil Co. of Indiana, Gulf Oil Corp.	Modified in situ	1979 1st test, work towards commercialization after 1981.	Intermittent production of demonstration unit	Planned expenditure of $93,000,000 over the next 5 yr.
Colony Development Operation; Atlantic Richfield Co., TOSCO—formerly Oil Shale Corp.	Above ground retorting, using TOSCO II system.	Commercial plans held in abeyance.	About 47,000 bbl/d	About $1,200,000,000
Union Oil Co. of California	Above ground retorting, using Union's process.	No recent information.	About 7,200 bbl/d pilot plant.	Considering investment of $123,000,000
Paraho Development Corp.; about 17 oil and industrial companies have participated	Above ground retorting, using Paraho process.	Pilot plant tested, semiworks projects operating and producing 180 bbl/d.	4,000 to 5,000 bbl/d modular unit.	Planned investment of $65,000,000
Superior Oil Co.	Above ground retorting, using Superior's 3 mineral process that yields shale oil, alumina, and sodium minerals.	Pilot plant tested, awaiting land exchange deal with Department of the Interior.	13,000 bbl/d	Investment of $300,000,000
Prototype of oil shale leasing program, tracts U-a and U-b, White River oil shale project; Sun Oil Co., Phillips Petroleum Co., Standard Oil Co., of Ohio.	A combination of modified in situ and above ground	Plans suspended pending outcome of legal problems.	100,000 bbld/d	$1,610,000,000

*CONGRESSIONAL RESEARCH SERVICE, LIBRARY OF CONGRESS U.S. ENERGY SUPPLY AND DEMAND 1976-1985 (March 1978).

Further government assistance has been received through the Department of Energy's investments in research on rubblizing techniques and various development projects. The Navy is also becoming involved in sponsoring tests of large scale refining of shale oil.[17]

Occidental has revealed little about the proprietary details of its process, and production costs have been estimated from various sources at anywhere from $8 to $16 per barrel at a 15 percent rate of return on investment. It is currently believed by those developing the technique that the capital costs per barrel of capacity will be significantly less than for surface retorting, but annual operating expenses may be slightly more. There are some questions about how much upgrading of the shale oil is included in these costs, and whether or not the oil can be refined by conventional methods without further processing.

Only the vertical modified in situ process of Occidental has been tested on a scale large enough to assume that it is ready to be demonstrated on a commercial scale. But even the Occidental process is at too early a stage of development to be certain that it will be commercially viable. It is quite apparent that greater technical certainty has been traded for a method of minimizing water needs, environmental problems, and socioeconomic impacts. Thus compared to aboveground retorting which has a much larger R&D history, estimates of technical and economic feasibility are markedly less certain. The estimated costs of producing oil by in situ methods may seem lower than production by surface methods, but the accuracy of the estimates must be considered questionable at this point.

It must also be remembered that the modified in situ approach is not totally free of environmental problems. The impact of a large number of retorting chimneys on water quality and on the alteration of flow through subsurface aquifers is not known. The potential impact of subsidence is another problem. Since some mining has to take place, the eventual disposal or processing of this material must be considered. For the moment, it appears that surface storage is contemplated, but this can only be a temporary answer. Finally, air pollutants are emitted into the atmosphere by in situ combustion. Eventually, if a number of projects gets underway, the question of air quality degradation will have to be faced again.

At the moment, surface retorting will receive additional R&D effort but the modified vertical in situ projects on federal leases still seem to be the "best show in town" (see table 2). However, in addition to being relatively untested, these latter methods are only

---

17. Science, *supra* note 7, at 1026.

usable at certain depths and thicknesses of shale. There has been some reduction in the "front-end" capital burden, but that burden remains sizeable. One must suspect that if tracts C-a and C-b are actually to arrive at production levels of 50,000-plus barrels per day, there is a need for clear-cut federal energy policies and positive financial support. So long as we have no commercially demonstrated technology, the future behavior of domestic and foreign crude oil prices is uncertain, and recalling the past undisciplined and unpredictable policy behavior of both the state and federal governments, it is unlikely that a totally private prototype venture in the $500 million to $1 billion price range will occur.

It will take two or three years before we can begin to assess the current oil shale development strategy. The kind of detailed technical, environmental, and economic information that is required to make a full appraisal apparently will not be in hand until 1983. Thus, as in the past, shale oil production continues to be a game of watchful waiting.

Chapter 7

THE POLITICAL ECONOMY OF
CRUDE OIL PRICE CONTROLS

EDWARD W. ERICKSON,* WILLIAM L. PETERS,**
ROBERT M. SPANN*** and PAUL J. TESE****

INTRODUCTION

Price controls on United States crude oil production and petroleum products are commonly thought of as a unique reaction to the unprecedented increase in the world price of oil associated with the events surrounding the Arab oil embargo. This view is in part true, but it overlooks an important fact: the basic structure of the price controls which are now in force for the U.S. petroleum industry was largely in place and functioning prior to the embargo. The effect of the changes in the price structure of the world oil market, which were being translated into increased U.S. crude oil and oil product prices, was to cause a special set of price controls to be developed and continued for the U.S. petroleum industry.

THE DEVELOPMENT OF CONTROLS

Price controls were imposed on a substantial portion of the U.S. economy during the period August 15, 1971 to April 30, 1974.[1] Until March 6, 1973, the petroleum industry operated under the same general regulations that applied to manufacturing and re-selling industries.[2] Since this date, the petroleum industry has been subject

*Professor of Economics and Business, North Carolina State University.
**Consultant, Washington, D.C.
***Associate Professor of Economics, Virginia Polytechnic Institute and State University.
****Graduate student, NCSU.
The authors are indebted for conversations with Mark J. Frederiksen. All errors remain their own.

1. For a more detailed description of the administrative development of petroleum price controls, see OFFICE OF ECONOMIC STABILIZATION, U.S. DEPARTMENT OF TREASURY, *History of Petroleum Price Controls,* Historical Working Papers of the Economic Stabilization Program, Part II 1227-1340 (Washington: GPO) (hereafter cited as *History*).
2. The specific phases of the general price controls were:

Phase I:	August 15 to November 12, 1971.
	Initial 90 day freeze on wages and prices.
Phase II:	November 12, 1971 to January 10, 1973.
	Mandatory cost pass-through controls.
Phase III:	January 11 to June 12, 1973.
	General price standards applied on voluntary and self-administered basis.
Freeze II:	June 13 to August 12, 1973.
	60 day price freeze.

to special regulations imposed in response to the higher levels of price increases which were occurring in this industry. General price controls on the other sectors of the economy expired on April 30, 1974.

Prior to 1973, petroleum was not viewed as a special inflationary problem. One of the curious, but not surprising, things about the narrative description in *History* is the continued identification of a change in relative prices for a particular industry with the general problem of inflation. For example: "So, as Phase II neared its close at the beginning of 1973 and the administration was preparing to relax inflation controls, the first of a long series of oil price problems was emerging as a major inflationary threat."[3] The initial 90 day price freeze (Phase I) limited prices in all sectors of the economy to their August 15, 1971 levels. Under Phase I, gasoline prices were frozen at their seasonal (summer) high, and distillates were frozen at seasonally low prices.

The Phase II regulations allowed for price increases above August 15, 1971 levels only to the extent that they reflected cost increases. In most instances, large companies were required to give the Price Commission advance notice of price increases and to specify cost increase information.[4] Further, companies were constrained by a profit-margin limitation; the limit being defined as the highest profit rates (as a percent of sales) from two of the last three fiscal years prior to August 15, 1971.

After January 10, 1973, the Phase III program of "General Stan-

---

Phase IV: August 13, 1973 to April 30, 1974.
                    Mandatory price regulations re-imposed.

See, History, at iii for a more complete chronology. In addition, there was also a special two-week freeze (October 15-31, 1973) for petroleum products which was used for collecting and analyzing comments on proposed rulemaking to amend the Phase IV petroleum regulations. *See, History,* at 1286-1287.

3. *History,* at 1238. See also 1245, 1250, 1261, 1263, 1279, 1281, 1285, 1305, and 1308. World and U.S. oil prices have recently been quite stable in nominal terms and declining in real terms, but the general rate of inflation has accelerated due to overall monetary and fiscal phenomena.

4. Most major oil companies opted for term-limit pricing (TLP) agreements. These limited company price increases to a weighted average of 2 percent per year. The TLP agreements were subject to both cost justification provisions and profit margin limitations. TLP agreements allowed companies to allocate cost increases between product lines so long as the weighted average cost increase was below 2 percent. However, over the course of the year this did not allow petroleum companies enough flexibility to adjust the price of distillates to seasonally higher prices during the 1972-1973 heating season and still remain within the average 2 percent increase. The price controls thus tended to aggravate the heating oil shortage that winter. Independent retailers and wholesalers generally were free from controls after the adoption of the Small Business Exemption on May 6, 1972. Most small crude oil producers were also exempt, though crude prices remained stable throughout 1972.

dards" for price adjustments applied "voluntarily and on a self-administered basis" was substituted for Phase II mandatory price controls. In the face of less restrictive controls, distillate prices increased sharply after the beginning of Phase III. In February, 1973, the Cost of Living Council held public hearings on heating oil price increases. As a result, in March the Council issued Special Rule No. 1 which reimposed mandatory controls on the sale of crude and petroleum products. This rule covered the twenty-four largest petroleum firms.[5] Under the rule, price increases of more than 1 percent above January 11, 1973 prices had to be cost justified; increases of more than 1.5 percent were subject to profit margin limitations and pre-notification.

In response to the general inflationary pressures during the first half of the year, an economy-wide 60 day price freeze was declared on June 13, 1973. After this second freeze, most sectors of the economy were under general Phase IV price controls. As in Phase III, the petroleum industry was subject to more stringent consideration.

In August and September of 1973, controls were imposed on all segments of the petroleum industry, from wellhead to retail pump price. Basically, refiners and re-sellers could increase prices above base levels only to the extent that they reflected increased crude and purchased product costs on a dollar-for-dollar basis. For refiners, base prices were those of May 15, 1973. Crude oil prices were frozen at their May 15, 1973 prices plus 35 cents per barrel.[6] The distinction between "old" oil and uncontrolled "new" oil was implemented at this time.

Initially, Phase IV re-sellers and retailer margins were limited to January 10, 1973 levels. This was intended to roll back dealer margins from their higher May, 1973 levels. On September 28, 1973, the dealer margin levels were changed to those in effect on May 15, 1973. The regulations that were in effect just before the October, 1973 Arab oil embargo were designed to limit price increases to a

---

5. The premise was that since the 24 largest firms accounted for 95 percent of output, their regulation would effectively control the entire industry. This reasoning failed since these companies did not have full penetration at every level of the industry. For example, only 10 percent of retail gasoline stations were direct company operations. This anomaly created a dual market, with most supplies from refiners sold at controlled prices, while most retailers were uncontrolled. From January to June 1973, retail prices of gasoline and distillates (measured by the Consumer Price Index) increased 7.3 percent and 10.6 percent, respectively. For more on Special Rule No. 1 and the dual market, see *History*, at 1242-1250.

6. In December, 1973, in anticipation of the end of the crude oil price controls in 1974, an additional one dollar increment over the May 15, 1973 base price was added to the allowed price for old oil. This adjustment produced the $5.25 per barrel figure which is now widely regarded as the general ceiling price for old oil. See *History*, at 1308-1310.

dollar-for-dollar pass-through of increased crude and imported product costs.

There has recently been discussion of the relationship between U.S. and world product prices and the effects of decontrol of U.S. crude oil and product prices. This is a question to which we will subsequently return. There is little doubt, however, that the price controllers of the Energy Division of the Cost of Living Council perceived the regulatory apparatus as a device to encourage increased imports. As the architect of the system recounts in *History:* "What finally emerged was a system designed to keep prices in line with costs, while at the same time encouraging greater domestic production and not discouraging importation of necessary additional petroleum supplies;"[7] or "To encourage the importation of the necessary petroleum products in this country, refiners had to be permitted to recoup the higher costs of these increases by raising their prices for refined products;"[8] and "The other advantage was that the cost pass-through system allowed purchasers of incremental product to compete in the world market and yet essentially made certain that they would not reap large windfall profits as a consequence."[9] These 1973 regulations serve as the nucleus of continued petroleum price regulations. They are the basis for the multitier controls on crude oil which are now in effect.[10]

Petroleum price controls originated under the more general price control apparatus of the Economic Stabilization Act.[11] In addition, on November 27, 1973, Congress passed the Emergency Petroleum Allocation Act of 1973 (EPAA).[12] During December of 1973, petroleum price control and allocation responsibilities were transferred from the Energy Division of the Cost of Living Council to the Federal Energy Office.[13] The EPAA extended petroleum price regula-

7. See *History*, at 1264.

8. See *History*, at 1292.

9. See *History*, at 1313.

10. The various pricing categories of oil now in force or proposed include old oil (lower tier), new oil (upper tier), stripper oil, Alaskan North Slope oil, Naval Petroleum Reserve oil, enhanced recovery oil and "new new" oil. Stripper oil is oil produced from wells which for technical and economic reasons have been unable to produce more than 10 barrels per day. For a time, there was also a category of released oil which provided special incentives for increased oil production from old oil properties. In the discussion which follows, released oil is not considered. For more on released oil, *see*, ERICKSON, MILLSAPS, & SPANN, *Forecasting U.S. Crude Oil Supply under Alternative Tax and Regulatory Regimes*, (Proceedings of the Conference on the Economics of Oil and Gas Self-Sufficiency in Canada, University of Calgary, Alberta, Canada) 33-36 (1975); W. MONTGOMERY, The Transition to Uncontrolled Crude Oil Prices, Social Science Working Paper No. 186, California Institute of Technology 28-31 (1977); and *History*, at 1265 and 1306.

11. Pub. L. No. 92-210, 85 Stat. 743 (1971).

12. Pub. L. No. 93-159, 87 Stat. 627 (1973).

13. See *History*, at 1318-1320.

tion and allocation authority until August 30, 1975. After repeated efforts to fashion workable allocation procedures, the "entitlements system" was proposed in late 1974 and implemented in early 1975.[14] In December of 1975, the Energy Policy and Conservation Act (EPCA)[15] solidified the system of price and allocation regulations into their approximate present form. The provisions of EPCA provided for controls to be gradually phased out over the period from February, 1976 through May, 1979. In August of 1976, the Energy Conservation and Production Act (ECPA)[16] provided for the decontrol of stripper oil.

AN ECONOMIC RATIONALE FOR
MULTITIER CRUDE OIL PRICE CONTROLS

Crude oil price controls are a political phenomenon with a life of their own. But there is an economic rationale for multitier crude oil price controls based upon the concept of regulatory monopsonization of U.S. crude oil producers.[17] If one assumes that the elasticities of supply of crude oil from different categories of production differ, and if one assumes that an element of the objective function which guides U.S. energy policy formulation is to minimize the outlays of U.S. oil consumers (or revenues of U.S. oil producers) for any given volume of U.S. crude oil production,[18] then a stylized representation of a multitiered crude oil price control system for domestic production can be readily constructed.

In Figure 1, only three sources of crude oil are considered: lower tier domestic oil, upper tier domestic oil and imported oil. It is assumed that the elasticity of supply of lower tier (old) domestic oil is lower than that of upper tier (new) domestic oil, which in turn is lower than that of imported oil. For purposes of illustration, it is further assumed that the United States is a price taker in the world

---

14. For more detail on the history of the entitlements program, see W. Montgomery, A Case Study of the Regulatory Programs of the Federal Energy Administration, Social Science Working Paper No. 147, California Institute of Technology (1977).

15. 42 U.S.C. §6201 (1975).

16. 42 U.S.C. §6801 (1976).

17. This example follows Mark J. Frederiksen, A Theory of Multi-Tiered Price Regulations and Its Application to Domestic Crude Oil Production (mimeo presented at the Western Economic Association meetings, June, 1978).

18. See *History,* at 1303; MONTGOMERY, No. 186, *supra* note 12, at 33-40; and EXECUTIVE OFFICE OF THE PRESIDENT, ENERGY POLICY AND PLANNING, THE NATIONAL ENERGY PLAN (Washington: GPO, 1977). The most succinct statement of this rationale is that of The National Energy Plan: "Deregulation of oil and gas prices would make U.S. producers the beneficiaries of those arbitary price rises, and yield windfall profits from the increased value of oil and gas in existing fields. The producers have no equitable claim to the enhanced value because it is unrelated to their activities or economic contributions." *Id.* at 50.

FIGURE 1

A MONOPSONY PRICING RATIONALE FOR DOMESTIC CRUDE OIL PRICE CONTROLS

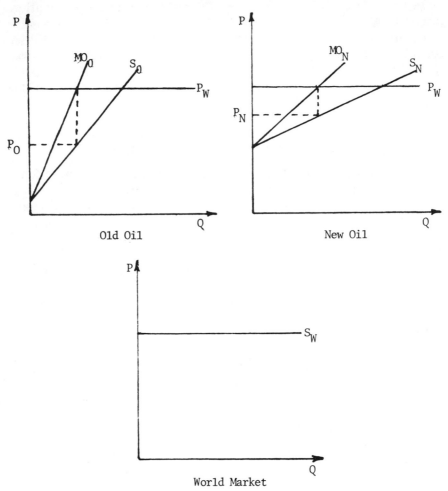

Old Oil

New Oil

World Market

oil market and faces a perfectly elastic supply of imported oil.[19] Under these conditions, the objective of minimizing consumer outlays for U.S. oil is met if the controlled prices for categories of U.S.

19. In addition, locational and quality differences among various types of crude oil are ignored. Quality differentials include such varying features of specific crude oils as specific gravity and sulphur, asphaltene, wax, heavy metal content, etc. All of these features cause crude oil to be less than fungible for a particular refinery installation. The most important heterogeneity currently may be sulphur content.

crude oil production are set such that the marginal factor cost of each source is equal to the price of imported oil. A discriminatory, multitier price control system for U.S. crude oil production thus reduces the outlay for domestic crude oil, but increases the demand for imported oil.

For such a system to be efficient in a static sense, the controllers must know the elasticities of supply of the various categories of domestic oil; the actual set of controlled prices must reflect these elasticities; there must be no interaction between the volume of U.S. imports of oil and the world oil price; the reduced outlays of consumers must be valued more highly than the foregone revenues of domestic producers; there must be no adverse strategic national security implications of increased reliance on imported oil, and the prices which consumers pay must reflect the marginal cost of imported oil.

Alternatively, if increased producer revenues are politically assigned zero social value, and if there are adverse strategic national security consequences of increased oil imports, then for static efficiency to be achieved, the cost of insuring against such implications must be less than the benefits derived by consumers due to discriminatory reduction of outlays for domestic oil. On the other hand, if national security insurance is not costless, and if no social value judgment is made concerning consumer outlays and producer revenues, then a crude oil price control system which reduces domestic output and increases imports must have negative net benefits.

The dynamic efficiency conditions are more complicated.[20] In addition to efficient consumption and national security considerations, they include short-run and long-run production effects. The long-run production considerations for conventional crude oil involve the extent of the domestic resource base and the time path of its development and use. The shorter-run production considerations involve the effects of the price control system upon the rates at which the supply curves for the various categories of established oil production drift to the left as reservoirs are depleted and secondary and enhanced recovery project opportunities are foregone.[21] The knowledge requirements for the design and administration of even a statically efficient price control system are formidable.

---

20. *See,* MONTGOMERY, *supra* note 12, at 41-60.
21. This effect, as well as the rate at which new oil prospects are acquired and drilled, may not be independent of the cash flows of producing firms if the cost of capital for internally generated funds is less than that for external funds. *See,* ENERGY ECONOMICS DIVISION, CORPORATE BANKING DEPARTMENT, CHASE MANHATTAN BANK, THE IMPACT OF CONTINUED PRICE CONTROLS AND THE CRUDE OIL EQUALIZATION TAX (COET) ON THE IMPORTED OIL REQUIREMENTS OF THE UNITED STATES (1978).

The knowledge requirements for a dynamically efficient system are even more perplexing. This is because the ultimate extent of the domestic conventional[22] crude oil resource base can only be inferred in very general terms from a priori geological information. The actual extent of the ultimate resource base can only be determined from the results of drilling and recovery investment projects. Since a price control system reduces drilling and investment incentives, it also reduces the rate at which that knowledge is acquired which is an essential input into the design of the system.[23] In the final analysis, the question is one of whether regulatory direction and the power to tax or private initiative and market incentives are the best guides for optimal oil resource development and transition to alternative sources of energy.

THE PRICE OF OLD OIL

The current average price of old oil is in the neighborhood of $5.30 per barrel.[24] There is a widespread presumption that the volume of old oil output is insensitive to the old oil price.[25] This presumption is based upon too simplistic a conception of crude oil production. Crude oil production does not simply involve drilling wells, setting casing, installing surface facilities, turning a valve, and allowing the reservoir to produce until it is depleted. Crude oil is often corrosive. The production process involves the production of fine sand grains, in addition to the oil, from the underground rock formation in which the oil occurs. Formations must be fractured or leached with acid to maintain producibility. Reservoir pressure must be maintained by injecting fluids. Pumps must be installed. Wells must be worked over as they become corroded or clogged. The density of well spacing may be increased to improve ultimate recovery or to shift production from the future to the present. Some of these expenditures are ordinary maintenance included in the lifting costs of oil production. Others are investment expenditures with payouts which stretch over the remaining life of the reservoir. Lower old oil prices increase the decline rate of established production. In this

---

22. Conventional crude oil is here used to include the output of enhanced oil recovery projects. Shale oil, tarsands oil and other sources which are based upon essentially mining rather than drilling technology are excluded.

23. In addition, the nature of reservoir engineering is such that some opportunities may be completely foregone rather than just postponed.

24. In February, 1978, the old oil price was $5.29 per barrel. *See*, U.S. ENERGY DEPARTMENT, ENERGY INFORMATION ADMINISTRATION, MONTHLY ENERGY REV. 73, DOE/EIA-0035/5 (May 1978).

25. For example, ". . . [T]he static model implies that the lower tier price will be irrelevant to production decisions." MONTGOMERY, No. 186, *supra* note 12, at 32.

connection it is worthwhile to examine how current lower tier price incentives compare to historic incentives to undertake the costs of such activities.

In Table 1, the economic incentive in the current old oil price of approximately $5.30 per barrel in current collars is converted into constant 1969-1970 dollars and compared to a reference price of $3.30 per barrel.[26] Under price controls, the real economic incentive for maintaining the production of that oil we know the most about—old oil—has declined by approximately a dollar per barrel (or about 25 to 33 percent). The long-term, cumulative effect of this erosion of incentive has negative effects upon domestic crude oil supply. First, there is a reduction in the number and type of maintenance and increased ultimate recovery investments which can be cost justified. The effect of price controls upon investment projects to increase

TABLE 1

DEFLATION OF THE ECONOMIC INCENTIVE IN THE OLD OIL PRICE

Current Old Oil Price	$5.30
Deflation Factor*	187.8
Deflated Old Oil Price	$2.82
Adjustment for Elimination of Percentage Depletion (.14 x $3.30)**	$0.46
Net Economic Incentive in The Old Oil Price	$2.36
Percentage Reduction from 1969-1970 Price	28%

*March, 1978, WPI = 203.8 (1967 = 100) Average 1969-1970 WPI = 108.6
**See E. ERICKSON, S. MILLSAPS, and R. SPANN, OIL SUPPLY AND TAX INCENTIVES, BROOKINGS PAPERS ON ECONOMIC ACTIVITY, 2:1974, at 449-478, for a discussion of the depletion component of economic incentives for crude oil supply. The adjustment used here is an approximation.

26. In 1969-1970, analysts used a representative price of $3.30 per barrel for low sulphur, high gravity crude oil at tidewater as a basis for examining U.S. oil policy. This price included the economic incentive of percentage depletion at 27.5 percent. CABINET TASK FORCE ON OIL IMPORT CONTROL, THE OIL IMPORT QUESTION 39 (Washington: GPO, 1970). The actual average price of all U.S. crude oil was $3.09 per barrel in 1969 and $3.18 in 1970. AMERICAN PETROLEUM INSTITUTE, BASIC PETROLEUM FACT BOOK, Section VI, Table 1. The wholesale price index (all items) is used as the deflator. Since oil field equipment and supplies have generally increased in cost more rapidly than the WPI, the deflated economic incentive inherent in the current old oil price is overstated. This is offset somewhat by use of the $3.30 reference price.

recovery can be quite complicated. If the project succeeds in increasing production above the Base Production Control Limit (BPCL), all the oil in excess of the BPCL qualifies for upper tier prices. However, if natural decline causes production subsequently to fall below the BPCL, the price component of the economic incentive for investments to increase ultimate recovery reverts to the old oil price. The lower tier price is less than half of the upper tier price. As a result, this potential jeopardy inhibits investment decisions.[27] Second, as the volume of old oil consequently declines more rapidly than would otherwise be the case, a larger burden of meeting the composite price stipulated by the controls is shofted to upper tier oil.[28] Since the composite price is a weighted average of lower and upper tier oil prices which is less than the upper tier price, a smaller volume of lower tier oil necessarily reduces the upper tier price. The result, under composite price controls, is to reduce the price incentive for discovering and developing new oil resources.

COST PASS-THROUGH AND PRODUCT PRICES

U.S. crude oil price controls are intended to be reflected in lower U.S. refined product prices. This intention has been embodied in price controls on refined products.[29] Refiners have thus been subject to two sets of price contraints: (1) the market constraint established by competition among refiners, and (2) the controlled price based upon cost pass-through regulation. In the event that controlled ceiling prices based upon cost pass-through exceed market prices, refiners are permitted to "bank" costs.[30]

---

27. A concrete example illustrates this effect. The SACROC unit for the Kelly-Snyder field in Texas has installed a CO_2 injection system to increase recovery. It appears to be a technical success. But production has now fallen below the BPCL and upper tier price incentives have been withdrawn. At lower tier prices, the continued operation of the project appears not to be economically feasible. SACROC is a bellwether project and its regulatory experience will condition expectations for investment in other projects. The Department of Energy is moving to allow uncontrolled prices for oil from enhanced recovery projects beginning September 1, 1978. (*Wall Street Journal*, July 27, 1978, at 6) This step could have been accomplished earlier under current law. A continuing question will be whether the administration of the program is so narrowly interpreted that U.S. oil production which would otherwise be feasible is foregone because of regulatory constraints.

28. In February, 1978, the imputed average price used for the purpose of price controls was $8.48 per barrel. *See* MONTHLY ENERGY REV., *supra* note 24, at 73. This composite price is less than the actual domestic average price ($8.84 in February, 1978) because of an adjustment for stripper oil which limits the depressing effect upon the composite price which exemption of stripper oil from price controls would otherwise have. Stripper oil has been exempt from price controls since September 1, 1976. The February, 1978, upper tier price was $11.81 per barrel.

29. Product price controls are gradually being removed. Middle distillates and residual oil are now exempt from controls. There is a pending proposal to decontrol gasoline.

30. Banked costs accumulate for specific products, and there have been various arrange-

Since the simple analytics of a price control system based upon cost pass-through are very much like that of an excise tax (see Figure 2), it is not surprising to find that all of the crude oil cost increases have not been passed through into increased refined product prices.

FIGURE 2

MARKET AND REGULATORY CONSTRAINTS FOR REFINED PRODUCTS

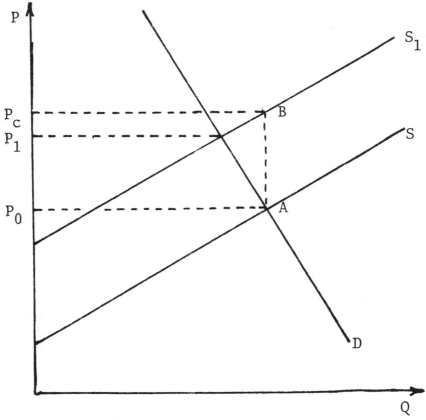

N.B.: AB = crude oil cost increase
  P_0 = initial price
  P_1 = new price
  P^2 = cost pass-through based ceiling price

ments designed to limit or permit banked costs accumulated for one product to be used to relax the regulatory price constraint for another product. These arrangements have changed from time to time. Gasoline is now the product for which there is the most flexibility in terms of using banked costs accumulated in other product sales to relax the controlled price constraint.

For refined products, the market has generally been the more binding constraint.[31]

THE U.S. AND THE WORLD MARKET

It has recently been argued that decontrol of U.S. crude oil prices would have no effect upon U.S. refined product prices.[32] In short, the argument is that world refined products are made from world crude, and the U.S. imports refined products, therefore U.S. refined product prices must reflect world crude prices. And because banked costs indicate that U.S. product markets are clearing at less than the allowable controlled ceiling prices, decontrol of U.S. crude oil prices would not cause U.S. refined product prices to increase. Unfortunately the public policy issue of crude oil price decontrol cannot be solved so simply.

The entitlements program subsidizes the importation of residual oil into the U.S. East Coast.[33] Much of the refined product imported into the United States is produced in refineries which have been built in the Caribbean or Canada particularly to serve the U.S. market. Much of this refining capacity has substantial excess capacity.[34] There is reason to believe, both analytically and empirically, that in addition to monopsonizing U.S. crude oil production, U.S. crude oil price controls have resulted in at least some temporary, modest monopsonization of suppliers of refined products to the U.S. market.[35] In 1977, the weighted average U.S. wholesale value of a component barrel of refined products did not greatly exceed the landed cost of the barrel of crude oil from which they were refined.[36] This

31. In February, 1978, unrecouped costs for refined products for the 30 largest refiners were $1.8 billion. In 1977, they averaged $1.5 billion. In E. ERICKSON, OIL, DIVESTITURE AND NATIONAL SECURITY (F. N. Trager, ed.) 61-4 (1977), it was argued that firms with market power would not bank costs. Jim Sweeney and Bob Scott have each shown in private communication that this statement is too strong. Under some combinations of price elasticity of demand and output elasticity of marginal cost, a firm with market power would bank costs. But the general conclusion holds, a firm with market power is less likely to bank costs than a firm in an effectively competitive industry.

32. See, C. PHELPS and R. SMITH, PETROLEUM REGULATION: THE FALSE DILEMMA OF DECONTROL, RAND R-1951-RC (1977).

33. See COX & WRIGHT, The Effects of Crude Oil Price Controls, Entitlements and Taxes on Refined Product Prices and Energy Independence, 54:1 Land Economics, 1-15 (February 1978).

34. John H. Lichtblau, Pricing U.S. Oil Products, Wall Street Journal, November 11, 1977, p. 16; and PIRINC, Distillate Fuel Oil in Mid-Winter: An Analysis of the Current and Near-Term Supply, Demand and Price Situation (1977).

35. See Martin J. Bailey, The Crude Oil Equalization Pass-Through Issue (mimeo, 1977), for an analytical treatment of this question.

36. See Monthly Energy Rev., supra note 19, for the landed cost of imported crude oil and the Oil and Gas J. for representative wholesale product prices. For example, in June of 1977, the refiner acquisition cost of imported crude averaged $14.63 per barrel and the wholesale value of a barrel of refined products was slightly in excess of $16 per barrel.

suggests that non-U.S. refiners' margins on product exports to the U.S. were abnormally low. In the event of decontrol of U.S. crude oil prices, U.S. crude oil prices would in general reflect world crude oil prices, with locational and quality differentials.[37] At the current level of world crude oil prices ($14 to $15 per barrel landed in the U.S.), this would mean an increase in U.S. product prices of approximately five cents per gallon for gasoline.

THE CARTER ADMINISTRATION PROPOSALS

The EPCA crude oil price controls are scheduled to phase out in May, 1979. The President, subject to veto by Congress, may extend them for two additional years. However, to replace the system of price controls and entitlements for crude oil, President Carter has proposed a Crude Oil Equalization Tax (COET) and user taxes on oil consumption.[38] This combination of policy instruments reflects the conflict in goals which has characterized U.S. energy policy formation. On the one hand, reduced reliance upon imported oil is desired.[39] On the other hand, a regulatory system intended to limit the profits of domestic oil production and subsidize oil use increases U.S. dependence upon imported oil.[40] This conflict has not been limited to the Carter Administration.

Rather than equalizing the U.S. price of crude oil and refined products with world market crude oil prices, various conservation measures such as automobile mileage standards, mandatory coal conversion, and the 55 mile per hour speed limit attempt to cause U.S. refined product users to act as if they were facing shadow prices which were at the world level (or higher), while at the same time subsidizing direct prices through the crude oil price control system.

From an analytical point of view, the proposed COET and oil user taxes represent a curious set of proposed additions to existing policy. Most analysts agree that the elasticity of supply of crude oil exceeds in absolute value the elasticity of demand for refined products. Under these conditions, proposals which rely upon demand effects

---

37. In February, 1978, U.S. upper tier prices were $41.81 per barrel and uncontrolled stripper prices were $13.90 per barrel. Old oil accounted for 40.74 percent of U.S. supply, and has been a steadily declining fraction. Monthly Energy Rev., *supra* note 19, at 73-4.

38. The National Energy Plan, *supra* note 12, at xv, xvii, 35-40, 49-52, and 60-66. As of this writing (summer of 1978) the Administration's energy proposals are making very slow progress in Congress, and consideration of COET is likely to be deferred until 1979. The user taxes on gasoline are no longer under active consideration.

39. *See,* The National Energy Plan, *supra* note 12, at 9.

40. *See* COX and WRIGHT, *supra* note 29, for an analysis which separates the effects for product and crude oil markets. U.S. crude oil imports are about three times as great as product imports. Total U.S. oil imports account for nearly half of U.S. consumption.

for most of the desired adjustment, and which restrict the price of domestic oil to less than the minimum opportunity cost of alternative supplies,[41] require substantially more tax and regulatory intervention in the economy than would a simpler policy which includes continuation of the phased decontrol of oil prices proposed under EPCA.

CONCLUSIONS

Direct crude oil and refined product price controls, allocations and entitlements have been a complicated chapter in the complicated regulatory history of the U.S. petroleum industry. The basic price control system was in place prior to the embargo and, while controls in the rest of the economy were being phased out, the embargo resulted in an elaboration and continuation of controls in the U.S. petroleum industry. The effect of U.S. crude oil price controls has been to monopsonize U.S. crude oil producers, increase U.S. dependence upon imported oil, subsidize domestic consumption and perhaps monopsonize some refiners with non-U.S. capacity targeted to the U.S. market. The Energy Policy and Conservation Act of 1975 provided for crude oil price controls to phase out in May of 1979. Such a phase-out would simplify the regulatory environment in which the U.S. petroleum industry operates, increase domestic supplies of oil and reduce reliance upon imports. The political question which now appears to be on the agenda for the U.S. energy economy is whether, and in what fashion, the crude oil price control phase-out legislated in EPCA will be allowed to occur.

---

41. Under the proposals in The National Energy Plan, *supra* note 12, at 50-2, a new tier of domestic oil production would be created. This "new new" oil would be allowed in 1980 to reach the nominal world market price which obtained in 1977, adjusted for domestic inflation. Use of the landed cost of imported oil as the minimum opportunity cost of alternative supplies does not include any national security premium.

Chapter 8

AN ECONOMIC ANALYSIS OF
GASOLINE PRICE CONTROLS

ROBERT T. DEACON*

Since August 15, 1971, the United States petroleum products industry has functioned under a complex and changing system of price regulations. Prior to March 6, 1973, these controls were part of a general system of price regulations applied to most sectors of the U.S. economy. Since 1973, a specific program of petroleum industry controls has evolved. The key to this system is a multi-tiered structure of controls on crude oil prices.[1] Regulations on subsequent stages of production, from refining to retail distribution, tie ceiling price increases to cost factors. The apparent intent is to force the industry to pass along to final consumers any savings realized from reduced crude oil prices. The question of whether or not these controls have exerted any real influence on refined product prices has been debated at length. With regard to motor gasoline, the only major refinery product that remains controlled, the debate continues.[2]

Effective November 1973, petroleum refining firms faced price ceilings set at the price charged on May 15, 1973 plus specified cost increases incurred since that date.[3] Increases in the average acquisition cost of crude oil and other petroleum product inputs were allowed to pass directly through to ceiling prices. These "product costs" were allocated across various refinery outputs on a simple volumetric basis. Price limit formulae made limited allowances for increases in such "nonproduct" cost items as labor and pollution control, but they excluded expenses for depreciation, marketing, and most taxes. Moreover, nonproduct costs could pass through to ceiling

*University of California, Santa Barbara. This research was supported, in part, by the Department of Energy (formerly Federal Energy Administration), though that agency is not responsible for the views expressed here. This paper benefited from the helpful discussions and research assistance of Vinod Agarwal and from valuable commentary provided by Walter J. Mead and David Mead (DOE).

1. Regarding crude oil price controls, *see* Erickson, et al., *The Political Economy of Crude Oil Price Controls*, Nat. Res. J. (this issue).

2. As of this writing, the Department of Energy is considering exemption of motor gasoline from price controls.

3. For a more complete description of refined product price controls, *see* Johnson, *The Impact of Price Controls on the Oil Industry: How to Worsen an Energy Crisis*, in ENERGY: THE POLICY ISSUES, (G. D. Eppen, ed., 1976) and *Federal Energy Administration Regulations*, (P. W. MacAvoy, ed., 1977).

prices only if a firm's resulting profit margin did not rise above the level experienced in a specified prior period. Refiners who chose not to apply all available cost increases to product prices were permitted to accumulate "banked costs" that could be used to justify future price increases. Although banked costs were accumulated for specific refined products, there were limited provisions for reallocating these costs across various refinery outputs.

Downstream from the refining activity, the structure of controls was similar. Individual resellers and retailers were, in effect, permitted to charge the price they paid for refined products plus their May 15, 1973 markup. With respect to retail gasoline sales, a rule of thumb was adopted which, by March 1974, permitted ceiling markups of ten cents per gallon.

During the summer of 1976 several refined products, included residual fuel oil, middle distillates, napthas, jet fuel, and gas oils were exempted from price controls. The only major refined product that remains subject to ceiling price is motor gasoline.[4]

HAVE REFINED PRODUCT PRICE CONTROLS BEEN EFFECTIVE?

The mere presence of legal price restrictions does not, of course, imply that actual market prices are effectively regulated. Indeed, several analysts have concluded that competition has imposed a more stringent discipline on petroleum product prices than has the regulatory apparatus.[5] Perhaps the most persuasive argument supporting this conclusion follows from the observation that, as a group, major refining firms and large integrated petroleum companies have not exercised all of the ceiling price increases available to them. At the industry level, banked costs for gasoline, distillates, and other products were positive in every month from 1974 through February 1978, the last month for which published data are currently available.[6] For motor gasoline, unexercised price increase allowances averaged three to six cents per gallon in 1974-75, and they increased somewhat in 1976-77. In the context of a workably competitive industry, the conclusion that price controls are superfluous follows naturally.

---

4. *See*, however, note 2.

5. The principal advocates of this view are C. E. PHELPS and R. T. SMITH, PETROLEUM REGULATION: THE FALSE DILEMMA OF DECONTROL (1976) and J. P. KALT, FEDERAL REGULATION OF PETROLEUM PRICES: REGULATORY WEALTH REDISTRIBUTION (mimeo, UCLA Law and Economics Workship, 1977).

6. *See* Kalt, *supra* note 5, at 8, and Federal Energy Administration, *Preliminary Findings and Views Concerning the Exemption of Motor Gasoline* (August 1977), and Dep't. of Energy, *Monthly Energy Review,* June 1978, 62.

The presence of refined product imports to the U.S. throughout the price control period has also been cited as evidence of the ineffectiveness of controls. If the U.S. is a price taker in the international market for refined products, then domestic prices (allowing for transportation costs, trade barriers, and so forth) are effectively set by the forces of world supply and demand. Figure 1 illustrates this point. Domestic demand and supply schedules are shown as D and S respectively. An elastic supply schedule for refined products (S^I), expressed in terms of delivered prices, has been horizontally added to domestic supply to give the total supply schedule S^T. In the absence of price controls, equilibrium occurs at the price-quantity combination P^*, Q^*; domestic production is Q^D and imports equal Q^*-Q^D. So long as imports are observed, the equilibrium domestic price is determined by the landed cost of foreign imports. A ceiling price established above P^* will have no effect on the market. To be constraining, the price limit must be set below the delivered foreign

FIGURE 1

U.S. REFINED PRODUCTS MARKET

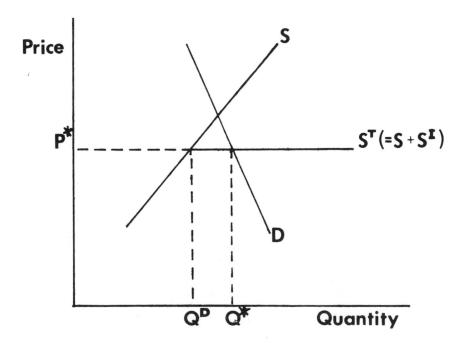

price in which case imports would be eliminated. To summarize, effective price controls and foreign imports cannot coexist.[7]

Historically, residual fuel oil has been the most important refined product (in terms of volume) imported into the U.S. Since relaxation of import quotas in 1973, motor gasoline imports have averaged only two to three percent of domestic consumption, and most of this has supplied cities on the Gulf and Atlantic Coasts. Small import volumes do not, however, contradict the proposition that foreign supplies are marginal to the U.S. market. They merely indicate that autarkic equilibrium prices in foreign and domestic markets are too close to support a larger volume of trade.

The lines of reasoning outlined above implicitly characterize petroleum product price controls as a simple ceiling price system, and consider the U.S. refining industry as a collection of homogeneous firms. As implemented since November 1973, however, the price control apparatus has contained provisions which tend to produce different ceiling prices for different firms. Prior to enactment of the entitlements program in early 1975, access to price controlled "old oil" differed among refining firms. Since average crude oil acquisition cost is a primary factor used in computing allowed price increases, such differences automatically lead to differences in ceiling prices across firms. Even after the implementation of entitlements, which tended to equalize crude oil acquisition costs among firms, details of the program (e.g., the "small refiners bias," and the preferences given to users of domestic crude oil) allowed some crude oil cost differences to remain.[8] Moreover, the base period used to compute allowed price increases was May 15, 1973. This was a time of rapidly increasing gasoline prices on world markets. Also, it roughly coincided with a switch from voluntary to mandatory price controls under Special Rule 1 of Phase III regulations, and with relaxation of U.S. quotas on imports of crude oil and refined products. In short, the base period was a time of dramatic change and possible disequilibrium in domestic petroleum markets and it may well have been characterized by temporary differences in prices listed by individual firms.

---

7. The force of this argument depends critically upon the elasticity of foreign supplies; see Phelps and Smith, *supra* note 5. Phelps and Smith extend this argument to conclude that the crude oil subsidy implicit in the entitlements program has merely altered trade flows without influencing domestic refined product prices.

8. A lucid discussion of the "small refiners bias" may be found in Roush, *Effects of Federal Price and Allocations Regulations on the Petroleum Industry,* Federal Trade Commission Staff Report (1976). The preference for domestic crude oil is analyzed in Cox and Wright, *The Effects of Crude Oil Price Controls, Entitlements, and Taxes on Refined Product Prices and Energy Independence,* LAND ECON. (February, 1978).

For all of these reasons, refined product price controls are better described as a system of firm specific ceiling prices.[9] In such a context, the banked cost argument loses much of its force, since the presence of positive banks at the industry level simply indicates that *some* firms were unconstrained. In this regard, it is noteworthy that industry banked costs for gasoline and distillates were consistently positive between November 1973 and April 1974, a period when queues at gasoline stations and alleged shortages of other products were common.[10] Further, as recently as early 1977 it was reported that three major refining firms had no banked costs for motor gasoline.[11]

In a situation where at least some firms are constrained by regulation and ceiling prices vary among firms, a degree of dispersion in the prices charged by different refined product suppliers would be expected to arise. Available evidence indicates that significant price dispersion was associated with the implementation of specific petroleum industry controls. In New York and Boston, for example, differences between daily high and low wholesale spot quotations for regular gasoline averaged seven to nine cents per gallon in 1973-1975, and 1.5 to three cents per gallon in 1976-77.[12] Some of this dispersion, particularly in 1973-74, may have arisen from the unsettling consequences of OPEC cartelization and the embargo. It is significant, however, that high-low spot price differentials in Italy and Rotterdam averaged less than 1.5 cents per gallon in 1973-75. Prior to 1973, average differences between high and low quotations never exceeded .25 cents per gallon in either foreign or domestic markets.[13]

The characterization of controls as firm specific price constraints also has interesting implications for the refined products imports argument. In the presence of domestic price dispersion, foreign supplies need only be competitive with high priced domestic gasoline

9. Other sources of dispersion in individual firm's ceiling price schedules existed. *See* W. J. Mead and R. Deacon, PRICE CONTROLS AND INTERNATIONAL PETROLEUM PRODUCT PRICES, Department of Energy, June 1978.

10. *See* Phelps and Smith, *supra* note 5, at 25.

11. *Preliminary Findings and Views . . .; supra* note 6, at 113.

12. The gasoline price data cited are from Platt's Oilprice Handbook (New York: McGraw-Hill, various years). For more detailed evidence on this phenomenon, see Mead and Deacon, *supra* note 8, Ch. 3.

13. Clearly, such dispersion implies excess demand for the supplies of price constrained firms. However, the rationing problem is not necessarily as severe as would be the case under a simple industry wide price ceiling. If some firms are not controlled, their marginal supplies could effectively clear the market. In other words, buyers who are unable to obtain products at a low controlled price could still satisfy their demands at a higher marginal price. It should also be noted that the FEA operated a mandatory refined product allocation program throughout this period. *See* Roush, *supra* note 7, for further details.

produced by uncontrolled firms. The presence of imports does not refute the proposition that price ceilings are binding for some domestic producers and that the average domestic price is effectively constrained. A second and more damaging conclusion follows from regulatory provisions which allow the cost of imported crude oil and finished products to pass through to domestic ceiling prices. Under this policy, price controlled firms may well opt to import gasoline and other products even at prices that exceed levels they are allowed to charge domestic customers. Such imports offer one way for constrained firm to increase its price ceiling. Although the firm's average cost would be increased by such action, dollar-for-dollar pass-throughs for imports raise its ceiling price by the same amount; in terms of profits, such changes are a matter of indifference. The effect of this is to essentially eliminate any necessary relationship between domestic and delivered foreign prices.

THE DELIVERED PRICE OF FOREIGN GASOLINE

Actual comparisons of foreign and domestic wholesale gasoline prices can shed light on the effectiveness of gasoline price controls. Substantial equality between domestic and imported gasoline prices, though not conclusive (due to pass-throughs), would provide prima facie evidence that U.S. price regulations have not been effective. On the other hand, if import prices consistently exceed prices from domestic suppliers, it would indicate that controls have been binding and that observed imports are directly attributable to cost pass-through provisions exercised by constrained firms.

Price comparisons were conducted for three foreign supply sources and three domestic consumption points; thus a total of nine comparisons were examined. The three foreign export centers are Italy, Rotterdam, and the Caribbean; during 1975-77 these three regions accounted for 66 to 74 percent of all gasoline imports into the U.S.[14] During this same period, most imported gasoline entered U.S. customs districts I, II and V-VI (combined). The three domestic consumption points studied, i.e., Boston, New York, and New Orleans, are major population centers in these three respective districts.

The domestic price series employed[15] are daily wholesale (ex-refinery) quotations, recorded at mid-month, for regular gasoline. Given the preceeding discussion of price dispersion, comparisons

---

14. The only major excluded supply source is Canada, which was dropped from analysis for lack of consistent price data. *See* Mead and Deacon, *supra* note 8, Chapter 5.

15. Gasoline prices were taken from Platt's, *supra* note 12.

were conducted for both "average" (simple mean of high and low quotations) and "high" domestic prices.

The delivered foreign price for a particular origin-destination combination is computed as the sum of foreign FOB price, tanker transport charges (including insurance, port fees, etc.), and U.S. import tariff. Since foreign price dispersion was relatively insignificant during this period, the simple mean of high and low daily foreign quotations (at mid-month) was used. Price quotations for European gasoline are described as actual transaction prices. However, the minimum lot size for Rotterdam quotation is smaller than that appropriate for tanker shipments and, as a consequence, Rotterdam prices are slightly overstated (one to two cents per gallon). The only Carribean prices available are postings by major petroleum firms. That posted prices may differ from true transactions prices is, of course, well known and this caveat should not be ignored when interpreting the results.[16] Tanker transport charges for foreign imports are consecutive voyage rates for clean cargoes shipped aboard vessels in the 22,000 to 45,000 (Dead Weight Cargo Tons) class. The effective import tariff on crude oil and refined products varied over time and among individual importers. In all computations, the import duty applicable to those not holding duty free licenses under the old Mandatory Oil Import Program was used; this is appropriate since such licenses merely confer a rent to the holder. The most important change in import fees occurred in 1975 with the imposition of a $1.00 per barrel supplemental tariff in February which was raised to $2.00 per barrel in June, and discontinued in December 1975.[17]

Price comparisons are presented in terms of the following two hypotheses: (i) the landed foreign price of gasoline was equal to the *average* domestic price, and (ii) the landed foreign price equalled the *high* domestic price. The overall period studied, 1975-1977, was split into two subperiods, 1975-76 and 1977. This was done primarily because certain changes in price control policy (e.g., exemption of several products, an alteration in the formula for computed banked costs, and increased allowances for nonproduct costs) were instituted in the last half of 1976.

Table 1 shows domestic wholesale prices and differences from landed foreign prices. All figures are in cents per gallon and are

16. *See* M. A. Adelman, THE WORLD PETROLEUM MARKET, 38. The pattern of monthly data revealed that posted Caribbean prices followed the general trend of European prices, but that Caribbean price changes tended to follow changes in other world markets only after delay of several months.
17. *See* Mead and Deacon, *supra* note 8, Ch. 4 for further discussion of data sources.

TABLE 1

FOREIGN–DOMESTIC GASOLINE PRICE COMPARISONS
(all figures in cents/gallon; t statistics in parentheses)

	Boston		New York		New Orleans	
	1975-76	1977	1975-76	1977	1975-76	1977
1. Average Domestic Price:	35.99	38.83	34.48	38.43	33.13	37.13
Differences from Landed Foreign Prices:						
2. Rotterdam	4.47*	.19	5.96*	.60	7.78*	2.26*
	(8.00)	(.25)	(13.80)	(.99)	(19.10)	(3.91)
3. Italy	2.51*	−1.17	4.03*	−.76	5.77*	.91
	(4.52)	(1.49)	(9.02)	(1.20)	(13.73)	(1.54)
4. Caribbean	2.05*	2.94*	3.48*	3.24*	4.77*	4.43*
	(3.89)	(3.95)	(12.16)	(8.00)	(14.91)	(9.80)
5. High Domestic Price:	37.90	39.84	35.65	39.09	34.89	38.04
Differences from Landed Foreign Prices:						
6. Rotterdam	2.56*	−.82	4.79*	−.06	6.02*	1.27
	(4.59)	(1.04)	(11.10)	(.10)	(15.34)	(2.29)
7. Italy	.59	−2.18*	2.86*	−1.42	4.01*	−.07
	(1.09)	(2.83)	(6.52)	(2.30)	(9.96)	(.13)
8. Caribbean	.13	1.92	2.31*	2.57*	3.01*	3.45*
	(.25)	(2.52)	(8.33)	(6.56)	(9.61)	(7.79)

Sources: see text.
* significant at 1%

means of monthly data for the periods indicated. The delivered foreign price may be obtained by *adding* the reported difference to the domestic price. Thus a positive difference indicates that the delivered foreign price exceeds the domestic price. The statistics in parentheses are appropriate for the null hypothesis that mean price differences equal zero.

For the period 1975-76, all landed foreign prices significantly exceed *average* domestic prices (see rows 1-4 in Table 1). Similarly, delivered foreign prices exceeded *high* domestic prices in 1975-76 for all comparisons and, with two exceptions, these differences are statistically significant. Estimated price differences for this period are not only generally significant, they are large in an absolute sense. For *average* domestic price comparisons, foreign supplies were priced two to eight cents per gallon above domestic gasoline. *High* price comparisons involving New York and New Orleans reveal a differential of approximately two to six cents per gallon. These results are, therefore, inconsistent with the proposition that foreign gasoline supplies effectively determined either the average or marginal U.S. wholesale price of gasoline during 1975-1976.[18]

18. When comparing price differences from Italy versus Rotterdam, recall the earlier comment on the basis for price quotations.

The monthly price data reveal that foreign-domestic price differentials were consistently observed during 1975-1976. The delivered price of foreign gasoline (from all three sources) exceeded the average New York price in every month of this period, and exceeded the high New York Price in all months except one. Similar monthly patterns are evident for Boston and New Orleans. Moreover, imports from Europe and the Caribbean were observed in almost all months of 1975-76. The only obvious explanation for this phenomenon is the availability of cost pass-throughs for constrained firms. Ironically, the presence of imports during this period strongly indicates the effectiveness of price controls on gasoline.

Comparing price differences in 1975-76 to those in 1977, a marked trend toward equality is evident. From the monthly data, this trend began in late 1976. In 1977, landed European (non-Caribbean) prices did not significantly exceed *high* domestic prices in any of the U.S. cities examined; thus imports from Europe during 1977 can be rationalized without appeal to the pass-through argument. Moreover, European imports were significantly more expensive than *average* domestic supplies only in New Orleans, and here the difference could easily be attributed to the rather small lot sizes upon which Rotterdam prices are quoted.[19]

In contrast to European differentials, the price spread between domestic and Caribbean gasoline did not decline in 1977 (and imports from the Caribbean were observed, though at substantially reduced volumes). In all likelihood, the lack of similarity in European and Caribbean price changes is due to the fact that the latter are company postings and may well be biased. Although the degree of bias is not known with any precision, the estimated price differentials appear sufficiently small to be considered inconclusive.

On balance, observed price relationships and import activity provide strong support for the proposition that gasoline price controls were effective, at least for some U.S. refiners, in 1975 and 1976. By 1977, however, foreign and domestic prices had reached virtual parity. Though the evidence is not conclusive, it is consistent with the contention that U.S. price ceilings had become ineffective by 1977.

THE SOURCES OF FOREIGN AND DOMESTIC PRICE INCREASES

Between 1970, prior to the imposition of U.S. price controls, and 1977, wholesale gasoline prices in domestic markets rose about twenty-five cents per gallon. This fact alone demonstrates consider-

---

19. Monthly price comparisons indicate that even this difference was eliminated by mid-1977.

able flexibility in the U.S. system of price regulation. Over the same period, however, prices in European markets increased by thirty cents per gallon. Although the analysis of gasoline import prices suggests that U.S. controls were ineffective in 1977, these differences in foreign and domestic market price increases are sufficiently large to merit further scrutiny.

Significant differences between foreign and domestic prices naturally might be attributable to influences other than U.S. price regulations. Factors such as U.S. import quotas on crude oil and refined products (prior to 1973), differences in foreign and domestic tax policies, current U.S. controls on crude oil prices, etc. would all affect the pattern of gasoline price increases in foreign and domestic markets since 1970. To address the question of whether such factors can fully account for differences in realized gasoline prices, wholesale price increases in four major U.S. cities—Boston, New York, New Orleans and Los Angeles—were compared to price changes in the Netherlands.[20] The methodology employed implicitly assumes that refined product price differences in the two countries can be traced to differences in marginal costs, and that marginal cost differentials can be attributed entirely to differences in factor prices and taxes. The first assumption is essentially one of competitive supply in both countries. The latter assumption is accurate if both nations have access to the same refining technology and if, at the industry level, refining takes place at constant returns to scale.[21]

Comparisons of this sort are complicated by the joint production nature of refining, since the marginal cost of a particular item depends upon the mix of final products produced. Any change in the

---

20. The choice of a comparison country was largely dictated by available data and by the requirement that the foreign price series be free of government controls. Retail petroleum product prices are subject to government control in the Netherlands, as is the case in virtually all industrialized nations. However, these regulations do not apply to products produced for export. Nevertheless, retail controls may affect production decisions and thus influence wholesale prices indirectly, and this fact should be recognized in the interpretation of results. For further discussion, see Mead and Deacon, supra note 8, Ch. 5.

21. With constant returns to scale, the marginal cost of refined products, C, can be expressed as function of factor prices. In the two factor case, where r_1 and r_2 are input prices,

$$C = f(r_1, r_2).$$

Changes or differentials in marginal cost are specified by taking a total differential

$$dC = (\partial f/\partial r_1)dr_1 + (\partial f/\partial r_2)dr_2.$$

From cost minimization, it follows that

$$dc = (x_1/q)dr_1 + (x_2/q)dr_2$$

where q is the output of refined products and x_1 and x_2 are levels of inputs used. Thus, changes in factor prices are simply weighted by input-output ratios. Adjustments for specific or ad valorem taxes on refined products are straightforward.

mix of outputs will alter the marginal cost of each product, even if
factor prices remain constant. Refinery yields in the U.S. and the
Netherlands differ markedly; between 1970 and 1977, motor gasoline accounted for 43 percent to 45 percent of U.S. refinery production as compared to 8 percent to 11 percent in the Netherlands.
Although widely different, gasoline yields in the two countries were
quite stable during the 1970's. For this reason it was assumed that
marginal cost changes induced by output mix changes were insignificant.[22]

In summary, wholesale gasoline price changes (net of cost changes)
between a precontrol period (1970-71) and 1977 were compared for
the two countries. The specific cost factors taken into account were
crude oil prices, including tanker transport costs and import duties
where applicable, and taxes levied directly on refined products. Each
cost factor was expressed in cents per gallon for use in computing net
price changes.

The cost of crude oil to domestic refiners was directly influenced
by mandatory import quotas prior to 1973, and by crude oil prices
controls after mid-1971 since both policies created differences between U.S. and international crude oil prices. During 1970-71, the
marginal supply of petroleum to U.S. refiners was from domestic
sources, and crude oil input cost was computed as the domestic
wellhead price, plus gathering and pipelining charges, plus tanker
transport costs where relevant. In 1977, on the other hand, the price
of domestically produced petroleum, and hence its supply, was controlled. For this period foreign petroleum was the marginal supply
and the landed price of foreign crude is the relevant input cost item.
Further, the entitlements feature of domestic crude oil price controls
resulted in an effective subsidy to U.S. refiners who imported petroleum in 1977. Throughout the 1970's, most of the crude oil refined
in the Netherlands was imported from the Persian Gulf and delivered
crude oil costs from this supply source were used to adjust foreign
prices.[23]

The foreign and domestic price series reported in Table 2 are net
of excise taxes and represent the price received by the seller. The

---

22. Assuming constant returns to scale, the marginal cost of a given refinery output can
be expressed as function of factor prices and percentage yields of various final products. If
yields remain constant, the formula in note 21 can be used to compute changes in the
marginal cost of a particular refined product.

23. Regarding crude oil import tariffs, the fee applicable for U.S. importers not posses-
sing duty free licenses was used. Petroleum imports to the Netherlands were not subject to
tariffs during the 1970's. All petroleum input cost estimates (for both foreign and domestic
refiners) were based upon crude oil of 34° (API) gravity and 1.7% sulfur content. A detailed
discussion of data sources may be found in Mead and Deacon, *supra* note 8, Ch. 4, 5.

only other tax taken into account in adjusting prices is the value-added tax (i.e., a noncumulative sales tax) levied in the Netherlands. Although the rate remained constant between 1970 and 1977, it is levied on an *ad valorem* basis so the actual levy depends upon the price of the product.

Table 2 displays the results of adjusted price comparisons. All items in this Table (except those in row 7) are expressed in U.S. cents per gallon and are means of monthly data for the periods indicated. The first three rows report changes in mean prices between the precontrol period and 1977. Changes in delivered crude oil costs (wellhead price plus transportation and tariff charges) and taxes on refined products appear in Row 4. Although the entitlements program is actually a part of the structure of price controls on crude oil rather than refined products, the effect of entitlements upon U.S. crude oil costs and refining margins is reported separately in Row 5 to highlight its influence.

From Row 6 it can be seen that increases in refining margins

TABLE 2

CHANGES IN WHOLESALE PRICES, REFINING COSTS
AND REFINING MARGINS
1970-71[a] versus 1977

	New York	Boston	New Orleans	Los Angeles	Rotterdam
1. 1977 Wholesale Price	38.43	38.83	37.13	38.04	36.57
2. 1970-71[a] Wholesale Price	13.48	13.12	12.65	11.63	6.46
3. Price Change (1-2)	24.95	25.71	24.48	26.41	30.11
4. Total Cost Change Excluding Entitlement	22.40	22.34	23.24	23.03	23.01
5. Entitlement Benefit	5.44	5.44	5.44	5.44	---
6. Margin Change Including Entitlement (3-4+5)	7.99 (.90)	8.81 (.90)	6.68 (.98)	8.82 (1.07)	7.10 (2.33)
7. t statistics[b]	1.50	3.09	−.59	2.73	

Note: All figures are in cents per gallon and are means of monthly data for the periods noted. U.S. wholesale prices are derived from averages of high and low daily quotations. Figures in parentheses are standard errors.

[a] January 1970 through July 1971.

[b] t statistics are constructed under the null hypothesis that the *mean* change in a particular U.S. refining margin is equal to that in the Netherlands. The critical level for rejection at 1 percent is 2.47.

between precontrol and control periods were actually larger in three of the four U.S. cities examined than in the Netherlands. Only in New Orleans is the increase lower than that experienced in the comparison country, and here the difference is less than 0.5 cents per gallon. On average, adjusted price increases in the U.S. exceeded those in the Netherlands by slightly less than one cent per gallon.

Figures in Row 7 are *t* statistics constructed under the null hypothesis that price increases (net of cost increases) in the uncontrolled foreign market have been identical to those experienced in the U.S. The only items in this row that are statistically significant involve comparisons of Boston and Los Angeles where margin increases exceed those in the Netherlands. In a statistical sense, therefore, these results are inconsistent with the proposition that U.S. gasoline price increases (as of 1977) have been abnormally low when judged against an uncontrolled foreign situation. Thus, a measure of corroboration for the analysis of refined product import prices is obtained. Moreover, a comparison between cost adjusted prices in the U.S. and the Netherlands as of 1976 indicates that foreign price increases exceeded domestic increases by 2.0 to 2.5 cents per gallon between 1970 and 1976. This is consistent with the earlier indication from import price comparisons that U.S. controls on wholesale gasoline prices were binding as recently as 1976.

The overall difference between foreign and domestic price increases as of 1977 (about one cent per gallon, on average) appears to lie within the bounds of confidence one can place upon the underlying data and methodology. The difference could be due to variations in environmental regulations such as U.S. restrictions on the use of lead as an octane enhancer, to unmeasured differences in product quality, or to other factors. Although regulations on gasoline prices are apparently ineffective, price controls imposed upstream on crude petroleum (and implemented with entitlements) are evidently holding refined product prices down. The magnitude of the effect on the wholesale price of gasoline is shown in Row 5 of Table 2. If crude oil controls and the entitlements program are phased out as planned, the cost of marginal barrels of crude oil to U.S. refiners will increase, and corresponding refined product price increases, perhaps mitigated by product imports, can be expected. It is possible that offsetting gains through reduced government involvement and complying company administration costs will also occur.

CONCLUSIONS

The central conclusion that emerges from this analysis is that competition, not regulation, is enforcing the current structure of gasoline prices in the U.S. Thus it is difficult to see why controls should continue; they appear to do little more than to impose an administrative burden on government and industry. It is possible that a few petroleum product suppliers remain effectively constrained. However, in the context of a firm specific price control system, decontrol of such firms need not result in unamibiguous product price increases. Prices charged by constrained firms would presumably rise with decontrol, and this would be reflected in increases in low market price quotations. But these price increases would induce greater supplies from previously constrained firms, placing downward pressure on unconstrained prices. Spreads between high and low price quotations would be reduced, but average prices could either rise or fall.[24]

Although the ineffectiveness of current price regulations is a sufficient basis to argue for decontrol, it is not necessarily the only basis upon which the argument can be made. The inefficiencies in production and exchange induced by general price ceilings are familiar. Price increases for refined products are merely symptomatic of a more fundamental change—in this case, reduced world supplies of crude petroleum. It makes little difference whether this scarcity stems primarily from international political events or from purely physical or market phenomena. Suppressing the symptoms of the change hinders market responses that would alleviate its effect. In addition, the U.S. system of refined product price controls contains its own peculiarities that are difficult to rationalize. For example, firms that are able to demonstrate high production costs are rewarded with ceiling price increases, and refiners who limit production are granted preferential treatment.[25] Moreover, the general attempt to reduce gasoline prices paid by final consumers coexists with regulations to improve gasoline mileage in new automobiles and thereby reduce consumption.

The present system of gasoline price controls reflects an attempt to redistribute the windfall gains accompanying world crude oil price increases from domestic oil producers to consumers of final products. The complexity of this multi-tiered regulatory structure attests to the difficulty of the task. If nothing else, the U.S. experiment with petroleum product price controls has demonstrated the inefficiency of the gasoline pump as a tool for redistribution.

---

24. Of course, the current situation may change; a reduction in the entitlement subsidy or a rise in foreign oil prices could set off future gasoline price increases. However, given the cost pass through allowances in the present control policy, refined product price increases would result regardless of whether or not price controls are in effect.

25. Preferences exist in the "small refiners bias" feature of the entitlements program and in an attractive pass through formula available to those refiners who limit production to within 10% of 1973 levels. *See* Mead and Deacon, *supra* note 8, Ch. 1.

Chapter 9

ENERGY CONSERVATION POLICIES*

ALLEN V. KNEESE**

INTRODUCTION

In a classic article "What is Conservation," written many years ago by Orris Herfindahl, but still well worth reading, numerous definitions of conservation are reviewed. The well known early conservationist Gifford Pinchot appears to have been the most prolific creator of such definitions. On close examination they all prove to be high-sounding bits of nonsense. The following are a few examples. "Conservation is the use of natural resources for the greatest good of the greatest number for the longest time." Clearly this definition requires the impossible by demanding the achievement of simultaneous conflicting objectives. Another Pinchot thought on the matter is: "Conservation implies both the development and the protection of resources, the one as much as the other." This statement naturally neglects the fact that the two stated objectives are normally in conflict with each other. A final example with a ringingly conclusive sound: "Conservation is simple, obvious, and right." H. L. Mencken is said to have paraphrased this statement into: "For every problem economists have an answer, simple, obvious, and wrong."

While I would not deny that there is considerable truth in the last statement, economic theory does provide a conceptual framework for consideration of conservation policies. In this paper the economic conceptual framework is used to consider a number of questions surrounding the matter of the proper rate of use of energy resources.

But what is conservation? History has shown the bootlessness of trying to formulate a general definition which will be both understandable and satisfying to everyone. Therefore I will not attempt to define it. The issue I will examine, however, concerns the economic justification for slowing down the depletion of a natural resource below the rate which would otherwise occur, by means of deliberate public policies and the instruments for implementation of these policies. In general the pertinent public policy instruments fall into two

---

*Parts of this paper draw heavily on portions of a report *Natural Resources Policy 1975-1985* prepared by the author for the Joint Economic Committee of the United States Congress.

**Professor of Economics, University of New Mexico.

categories: (a) altered economic incentives, such as taxes on certain activities or release of controlled prices, and (b) administratively enforced standards, e.g., prohibitions on certain acts such as driving above a prescribed speed.

The present paper concludes that when measured against "ideal" market behavior, the actual functioning of the economic system in the United States contains multiple biases in the direction of excessively rapid use of natural resources, including energy resources. These biases result both from systematic failure of markets to function in an ideal manner and because public policies developed in the past, many of which are still in place, have tended to encourage rapid resource development.

Before proceeding to develop these points, it is appropriate to inquire whether we are in fact addressing an issue of import. Is it in fact technically possible to substantially reduce the rate of growth of energy usage without drastic reduction in the quality or quantity of production and consumption services which would otherwise occur? A number of recent studies on the subject conclude that it is possible. The greatest possibilities appear to exist in three areas, at least in the relatively near future:

(a) More economically efficient energy usage in transportation, especially improved automobile gasoline mileage.
(b) Construction and operation of buildings in a manner which would reduce the energy needed for space conditioning.
(c) Improved energy efficiency in industry, including cogeneration of electric power (e.g., the simultaneous production of electricity and process heat).

In general the energy savings would occur by some substitution of capital for energy and from design changes aimed at achieving greater energy efficiency. It is not my purpose here to evaluate the details of any of the particular studies of possibilities for reduced energy usage, but simply to point out that in general they suggest considerable elasticity in energy demand, especially after a few years.[1] Thus, it seems likely that conservation policies aimed at lower rates of energy usage per unit of economic output could in principle be effective in influencing the rate of energy demand growth without necessarily causing widespread economic disruption.

The question then becomes what, if any, rationale would there be for undertaking such policies and what would be the most suitable

---

1. This is already reflected in the fact that with the increased level of energy prices which has already occurred most public and private projections of energy usage are below historical trends.

instruments for implementing them. This question will be approached by first providing a review of how economic theory envisages an ideal market in operation.

THE IDEAL MARKET

Economic theorists have found that the results of market exchange may be regarded as desirable or normative if a certain basic value judgment is accepted and if the market exchange economy displays certain consistent structural characteristics. The value judgment is that the personal wants and preferences of the individuals who constitute the present members of a society should guide the use of that society's resources. This is also the premise which is at the root of Anglo-American political theory.

The three structural characteristics in a desirable market exchange are:

(1) All markets are *competitive*. This means that no specific firm or individual can influence any market price significantly by decreasing or increasing the supply of goods and services offered by that specific economic unit. Competition must extend to all markets, including those for money.

(2) All participants in the market are *fully informed* as to the quantitative and qualitative characteristics of goods and services and the terms of exchange among them.

(3) All valuable assets in the economic system can be *individually owned* and managed without violating the first assumption of perfect competition. Individual ownership of all assets, plus competition implies that all costs of production and consumption are borne by the producers and consumers directly involved in economic exchanges. A closely related requirement is that there must be markets for all possible claims. This is particularly pertinent to the consideration of questions of conservation and the role of futures markets.

If all of these conditions are met, it can be concluded that the best social solution to the problem of allocating the society's scarce resources is to limit the role of government to merely deciding questions of equity in income distribution, providing rules of property and exchange, enforcing competition, and allowing the exchange of privately owned assets in markets to proceed freely. The connection between this market exchange model and the real working economy has always been tenuous at best. But the idealized model has served as a standard against which an actual economy could be judged as a resource allocation mechanism for meeting consumer preferences.

Ways in which the real world functioning of markets departs from the theoretical ideal will now be reviewed, and then some implications for rates of resource use will be covered.

I will start with a consideration of the assumption that all valuable assets can be privately owned in view of the reality of common property resources. The latter idea has largely been used to help explain the economic origins of environmental problems but its additional pertinence to conservation questions can be explained by introducing into the picture a simple concept from physics: mass balance, the first law of thermodynamics. While I will discuss the concepts of common property resources and mass balance in the general context of natural resources development and use, they have a special pertinence to energy because, in our economy, the mass of energy resources used is so large and the use of common property resources by that sector so heavy.

MASS BALANCE AND COMMON PROPERTY[2]

When materials such as minerals, fuels, gases, and organic materials are obtained from nature and used by producers and consumers, their mass is essentially unaltered. Material residuals generated in production and consumption activities are therefore about equal in mass to that initially extracted from nature. Similarly, all energy converted in human activities is discharged into the environment.

Conservation, in the physical sense of mass-energy, taken together with the peculiar characteristics of environmental resources, has important implications for the allocation of resources in a real market system as contrasted with the ideal market system. While most extractive, harvesting, processing, and distributional activities can be conducted relatively efficiently through the medium of exchange of private ownership rights just as the idealized market model envisages, the process of returning into the environment the inevitable residuals generated by production and consumption activities makes heavy use of common property resources.

The term "common property resources" refers to those valuable natural assets which cannot, or can only imperfectly, be held in private ownership and which therefore cannot be exchanged in markets as can ordinary commodities. Important examples are the air mantle, watercourses, large ecological systems, landscapes, and the audial and electromagnetic spectrums. When open and unpriced access to such resources is permitted, it is apparent what must hap-

---

2. For a fuller discussion of these concepts and their relationship to economic theory see A. KNEESE, R. AYRES & R. D'ARGE, ECONOMICS AND THE ENVIRONMENT: A MATERIALS BALANCE APPROACH (1970).

pen. From careful study of particular common property or common pool problems like oil pools and ocean fisheries, it is well known that unhindered access to such resources leads to overuse, misuse, and quality degradation. With respect to environmental degradation, this takes the form of large masses of materials and energy being discharged into watercourses and the atmosphere, thus degrading their quality. Furthermore, resource extraction processes themselves can cause visual degradation and other forms of pollution such as clear-cut forests, mine tailings, unreclaimed strip mine land, and acid mine drainage.

Costs associated with the destructive effects of these situations are of no consequence to the enterprises involved, inasmuch as they are imposed on or transmitted through common property resources. The impacts of these effects, referred to as "external costs," are imposed on society as a whole. Pareto optimality is not gained through exchange because private ownership of natural assets must be incomplete. Without ownership, the market by itself can generate no incentive to protect environmental resources.

Conservation of mass-energy dictates that as economic development proceeds and as the mass of material and energy flowing through the economy increases, and if environmental resources remain in their common property status, environmental conditions must display a tendency to get systematically worse as the economy grows. The systematic degradation of air quality in many parts of the country over the past few decades is an illustration of this problem. Efforts at controlling this phenomenon have been made, as will be discussed later. First, however, it will be useful to consider the relationship between common property, mass balance, and the rate of use of natural resources commodities.

COMMON PROPERTY—THE PRICE STRUCTURE AND RESOURCE ALLOCATION

The combination of the two simple but revealing concepts introduced in the previous section—conservation of mass and common property resources—provides considerable insight into the basic nature of environmental problems involving pollution in a market system. But the implications are not limited to environmental matters. When the use of certain environmental resources is not priced, the entire price structure is then distorted. Thus the price of extractive resource commodities, which are exchanged in markets, will deviate substantially from the actual social costs of their use. This comes about in two major ways.

First, the extraction and processing of extractive resource commodities involves particularly heavy use of environmental resources. Strip mining, copper processing, coal conversion, the making of steel, and oil refining are obvious examples. In the ordinary course of market exchange the social costs associated with any damage to these environmental resources are not reflected in the private costs incurred by the producers of resource commodities and by the ultimate users of the products produced from them.

Second, when such commodities are devoted to their end uses they further generate social costs which the market does not reflect. Junkyards, litter in the countryside, and the combustion of fuel in automobile engines are random but obvious examples.

Thus the market generates a *systematic bias,* the result of which is to essentially publicly subsidize the production of extractive resource commodities. The larger the impact on environmental resources in the extraction, processing and use of resource commodities, the larger the subsidy. Furthermore, as environmental resources become increasingly scarce and thus more valuable, and as the production of environmentally destructive resource commodities increases, the societal subsidy of such production correspondingly increases.

The natural tendency of markets to work in this unfortunate manner is bad enough. But policies formed to stimulate the production of resource commodities during the euphoria of extreme abundance, and made in the interest of rapid economic growth, aggravate the situation. For example, special tax treatment of extractive industries, prominently including the energy industries vis-a-vis ordinary industries, abounds.

The ultimate result of market malfunctioning and of the biases of policy is excessive use of materials and energy in general, excessive use of virgin materials in particular, too little recovery and reuse of materials and energy, and excessive environmental deterioration. With this set of ideas in mind I will turn to a consideration of natural resources policies which affect rates of energy use, turning first to environmental policies.

ENVIRONMENTAL POLICY ISSUES BEARING ON
REDUCED RATES OF USAGE

I will not linger over the matter of environmental policy in the United States, as it is an area I have discussed extensively elsewhere.[3] The essential point to be made is that the development of environ-

---

3. *See, e.g.,* A. KNEESE & C. SCHULTZE, POLLUTION, PRICES AND PUBLIC POLICY (1975).

mental policy in the United States has been built around a combination of subsidies and direct regulation and has not recognized the economic sources or the possible remedies for the problem. Many studies, in addition to my own, have concluded that a system of economic incentives in the form of fees for the use of common property resources (effluent and related fees), has a sounder basis in economic theory than the presently used approach and can be defended on the basis of improved efficiency, effectiveness, and equity. In any case environmental concerns provide one basis, albeit an indirect one, for energy conservation as defined in this paper. Changes in economic incentives to take account of costs imposed on common property resources would recognize the distortions in the price structure which otherwise occur. One response among others is that energy use would tend to be restrained because energy users then bear a greater percentage of the social cost.

The direct regulation policy presently pursued to restrict the use of common property resources can also have the effect of raising costs as emissions and other environmental controls are required. But, as mentioned, many questions have been raised by economists and other scholars about the effectiveness, equity, and efficiency of this policy and its implementation.

To summarize thus far: the energy industries have been unusually heavy users of common property resources, as have the final consumers of energy. Historically, the whole energy conversion process has fallen far short of meeting the full social costs of production. This tendency to undershoot social costs has been aided significantly by a number of different types of special tax treatment. In general, it is common knowledge that the extractive sector of the economy is one of the most lightly taxed ones. In part this limited taxation is a result of special provisions for extractive industries, such as depletion allowances and capital gains for timber, coal, and iron, and expensing of exploration and development expenditures. But it is also partly due to the special ability of the extractive industries to take advantage of uniform provisions in the tax code; for example, the foreign tax credit and capital gains treatment. It is now generally agreed upon by students in the area that investment in extractive industries has been at least 50 percent greater (and possibly much greater than that) than it would have been if taxation of these industries had been on the same basis as other industries.[4]

A combination of unpriced use of common property resources and

---

4. S. Agria, in THE TAXATION OF INCOME FROM CAPITAL (A. Harberger & M. Bailey eds., 1969).

a light tax burden has made energy artificially cheap and has stimulated the development and use of energy-hungry technologies throughout our economy. As already indicated, this has led to excessive rates of natural resource materials use, excessively rapid rates of resource depletion, and as was emphasized in the previous section, environmental pollution on an enormous scale. Approximately 60 percent of the total weight of materials flow in the United States consists of mineral fuel materials.[5]

A DYNAMIC CONSIDERATION IN REGARD TO RATES OF ENERGY USAGE

In considering the environmental dimension of the energy usage question I have emphasized market failures resulting from the presence of common property resources. Other types of market failures such as monopoly elements in the energy industry and national security problems could also be considered in this context.[6] However, in this concluding section I will address only one other aspect of the question—the absence of markets for future claims.

As has been stressed several times, one of the characteristics of the "ideal" market model is that markets for all goods and services in fact exist. So far, we have considered this requirement in a static context and have found that the condition is not met in reality. But in a dynamic context there is the further implication that a full set of futures markets must exist if the market system is to have the desired normative property of optimal allocation of resources use over time, as well as at a given time. This means that it should be possible today to make contracts about deliveries of goods and services in the future. For example, an owner of a nonrenewable resource should be able to sell a claim today on one unit of the resource to be delivered fifteen years from now. This is a requirement of profound importance for ideal markets with respect to extractive resources because they are depleting resources, and such a full set of futures markets does not exist.

The absence of futures markets causes a systematic incentive to produce too much of a nonrenewable resource in the present at the expense of production in the future. This is perhaps the most fundamental rationale for levying severance taxes and undertaking other non-environmentally based conservation measures with respect to extractive industries.

---

5. This calculation excludes construction materials.
6. *See,* the joint Economic Committee paper.

CONCLUDING COMMENTS

Perhaps the most profound aspect of the conservation question, the one that is intergenerational, has not been addressed in this paper. This is an exceedingly difficult problem and one on which research is just beginning to yield some interesting results. But this paper has argued that there are multiple biases in the system which, in the past, have led to excessively rapid exploitation of natural resources including energy resources, even when only the preferences of the current generation are considered. In the broadest general sense these biases are institutional—partly results of a policy structure conducive to rapid resources use, and partly results of the inability of the market to function effectively with respect to some important values.

To the extent that a policy response to this situation has been made, a piecemeal approach has been taken relying on an increasingly detailed, cumbersome, and inefficient direct regulation approach that has been chosen by Congress. This paper suggests that there is indeed a case to be made for conservation, in the sense used here, but that the proper approach to incorrect economic incentives is to replace them with better ones. Elements of a coherent economic program would be price deregulation, the cessation of special tax treatment for certain industries, and use of the tax system to counter any insufficiency of attention by the market to the future.

Chapter 10

TAXATION AND THE POLITICAL ECONOMY OF THE ENERGY "CRISIS"

GERARD M. BRANNON*

The issues of tax policy in the energy "crisis" make up a political problem of some subtlety. The battle of who shares the gains and losses (on domestic oil and natural gas) generated by the international market has continued for four and one half years, and still seems far from solution.[1] This article examines these issues as a problem of public choice, a matter of both politics and economics.

SOME PRELIMINARIES

As an economic problem of allocation of resources, the so-called energy crisis presents no overwhelming mystery, even though there are uncertain elements. Given the fact of a high price for imported oil, which is out of the United States' control, it follows that the efficient policy for the United States is to increase the output of domestic energy resources until their marginal cost is equal to the cost of equivalent oil imports, and to reduce oil consumption until its marginal utility rises to the cost of imports.[2] Since both the demand and supply of oil and oil substitutes is price inelastic in the short run, a period of continued high, but falling, imports is the economic solution.

A great deal, but not all, of an efficient solution for allocating energy resources could be achieved by simply letting markets work, which means that the market prices for energy resources would rise sharply in the U.S. The nub of the political "crisis" of energy policy is that most Americans would see this price rise as imposing "excessive" burdens on consumers and generating "excessive" windfalls for many energy producers and resource owners.

The public choice problem we focus on is how much to use

---

*Dr. Brannon is a Professor of Economics at Georgetown University.

1. As of this writing, May 1978, the House-Senate Conferees have not agreed on an energy bill. I do not expect their compromise to be the ultimate solution.

2. "Marginal Utility" is a convenient way to refer to consumer satisfaction from using oil. We could substitute "until consumers are indifferent at the margin between using more oil, using an oil substitute or not using so much energy." The only economic assumption involved is that as consumers use less oil, the marginal amount consumed becomes more valuable relative to the alternatives and at some point it will be efficient to import high cost foreign oil.

market mechanisms to bring about basic adjustment to the current world oil market. Posing the problem this way does not present a claim that the market for energy resources is efficient in all respects, but only that very specific market defects call for specific remedies. The following are market defects and their corresponding specific remedies:

(1) The market price of imports does not make provisions for the special security costs involved in dependence on imports subject to boycott. This problem calls for a reserve inventory financed by an import tax and a still higher market price.

(2) The market price of imports does not reflect that heavy imports affect our exchange rate and impose a further burden on Americans. Consequently, a still higher import price is necessary.

(3) Most energy alternatives to oil involve environmental and health hazards that are not internalized in costs. Internalizing the externalities would require some pollution taxes and/or regulations which further increase the cost of alternative fuels.

(4) An optimum amount of research and development is not likely to be undertaken in private markets because much of the benefits of successful research and development (R&D) is captured by others than the investor. Subsidized research is necessary.

These uncertain elements are serious, and much work needs to be done to quantify and solve the problems of imports, pollution, safety and research.

However important, these externality problems are separable from the central energy policy problem that this paper addresses—the extent to which we use the market system, by means of transferring real income, to deal with the basic tasks of (1) reducing U.S. consumption of oil and energy, and (2) increasing U.S. production of oil and oil substitutes. The problems of specific market defects can be handled whether we rely on market prices or government controls to deal with these basic tasks. Thus, we will largely put these specialized problems to the side and concentrate on the politics and economics of using a market solution to the problem of the increased price of oil imports.

THE POLICY RANGE

Since the increase in world oil prices of 1973-1974 the U.S. has been engaged in public and legislative debates about oil price control and various taxes on the production and use of oil. Since the 1950's, we have had a national debate on the regulation of the field price of natural gas. During the last few years there has been a flurry of activity in some states over the imposition of increased severance taxes on coal and uranium. These issues have a common core: they are concerned with the transfer of income away from producers and owners of energy resources.

Three consecutive Presidents have proposed changing the price-control tax on oil to a more specific windfall tax. The difference is hardly crucial to producers. A specific tax deprives producers of actual revenue; price control deprives producers of potential revenue.[3]

The unique difference between price control and windfall taxes is that the effective "tax" under price control is immediately "spent" by the government as a consumer subsidy. Each consumer benefits from maximum price control in proportion to his or her consumption. Cadillac drivers benefit far more from gasoline price control than do bus riders. Windfall tax revenues, on the other hand, can be distributed to the public to compensate for the price increase on some average consumption basis. Alternatively, the proceeds could be spent by the government on the public's behalf. The obvious third alternative policy is to do nothing; let consumers face market prices, and make this income available to producers.[4]

Both the windfall tax and the price control form of tax will necessarily change producer incentives. Any output and reinvestment incentives that would have come from market prices are lost, and there may be new incentives inadvertently created to do things that reduce or avoid taxes. In addition, the price control, through its consumer subsidy feature, will change consumer incentives.

These incentive distortions must be regarded as bad. Typically, governments try to supplement policies of capturing producer surplus with a variety of regulations or other tax incentives to reinduce the behavior that is discouraged by taxing income away from producers and subsidizing consumption.[5]

Briefly, the policy alternatives are as follows:

(1) free market prices (externality corrected), or
(2) free market prices plus special producer taxes ("windfall" taxes)
   (a) with specific distribution of the proceeds to the public, and/or

---

3. On the claim that the economic regulation issue is really about allocation of income, see Stigler, *The Theory of Economic Regulation*, BELL J. ECON. MANAGEMENT SCI. 2:3 (1971) and Pelzman, *Toward a More General Theory of Regulation*, J. L. ECON. 19:211 (1976).

4. Recall that externality problems are being left aside.

5. For a discussion of these problems of incentives in relation to energy policy, see articles by Wright, Mead, Brannon, Penmer, Bryer and Drapkin, GROWTH AND CHANGE (Jan. 1979).

126

      (b) with other incentives or regulations to induce desired pro-
           ducer behavior, or,
    (3) price control with or without other incentives and regulations to
    induce desired producer and consumer behavior.

These policies of transferring producer surplus are not novel.

In the 1950's and 1960's, the present issue of basic energy policy existed in exactly the opposite form to that of 1973-1974. Two decades ago the world price of oil was low and national policy, which consisted of an import quota, a lower income tax on crude oil production via percentage depletion and the deduction of intangibles, and national support for state prorationing, was concerned with diverting a potential consumer surplus into higher income for producers. This policy could also be described as shifting a negative producer surplus to consumers.

The same income redistribution issues underline the argument of a military draft vs. an all volunteer armed force. It is irrelevant to pose the question, "Is a drafted army better than an all volunteer army?" The answer to that question is that if we pay enough for a volunteer army, it can attract the same soldiers that we would have drafted. To achieve this parity, of course, we would have to set the pay levels and the acceptance qualifications high, especially for new entrants.

The present political talk about going back to a draft is largely a response to earlier claims that a volunteer army would save money. The evidence is now clear that for an equal quality army, the short run cost of volunteers is much higher than the cost of draftees. Economically, the draft is a way of enforcing price control on military service.

The military draft issue is like the issue of oil price control. In one case we don't want the oil companies to exploit energy customers. In the other case we flabby, middle-aged Americans do not want young people to exploit the market for defense.

The assumption of this paper is that the issue of taxes in the energy program is not merely a matter of populist pique at rich oil companies but a manifestation of a very general social problem of a change in income distribution which is perceived as non-functional (i.e., undeserved). Some deeper understanding of the tax issues in energy policy can be achieved by looking at them in relation to this social (i.e., political) problem of income transfer.

THE SIMPLE OPPOSITION OF PRODUCERS AND CONSUMERS

At root, the energy policy options involve a political contest between producers and consumers. The outcome of such a contest is simply indeterminate. Consumers far outnumber producers; therefore consumer interests have an initial edge in any democratic policy. On a per-capita basis, however, producers would have high gains from a market price policy without windfall taxes. Consequently, it is possible that the producer interest can prevail by means of logrolling.

Legislators representing producer interests will trade their votes on other issues that are not of much concern to their constituency. Legislators whose districts cover only energy consumers will observe that the gain to any consumer from price control will be small. Therefore, an anti-consumer vote on this issue might not be remembered when these legislators go back to their districts for re-election. Legislators who represent consumers might profit from trading away proconsumer votes on energy issues in order to get support on other topics that are of greater concern to their constituency.[6]

The foregoing argument does not predict that energy producers will prevail by means of logrolling, only that this development might overcome the numerical advantage of consumers. In energy policy the record is mixed. In the 1950's and 1960's the producer interests succeeded in obtaining import quotas and low taxes for oil and gas companies, but they were unable to prevent natural gas price regulation.

A commentary on the close balance between the legislative power of producer and consumer interests was offered by the income tax changes with regard to percentage depletion that was debated in the Congress in 1974 and 1975.[7] The facts were that the drastic reduction in percentage depletion was not enacted until 1975, and favorable depletion was preserved for medium-sized oil and gas producers as well as for producers of other minerals. The inference is that it was only the massive size of the oil price increase that tipped the balance against the producer interests.

The device that brought about a change in the law in 1975 was a compromise that protected the interests of medium-sized independent drillers by limiting percentage depletion to about $4,000,000 to $6,000,000 of receipts.[8] This provision has very little to do with

---

6. Another discussion of this producer-consumer conflict which suggests a number of circumstances in which consumers should win, see Buchanan and Tideman, Gasoline Rationing and Market Pricing: Public Choice in Political Democracy, Center to Study Public Choice, VPI Blacksburg, Virginia, (research paper, Jan. 1974).

7. Morrison, *Energy Tax Legislation; the Failure of the 93d Congress,* 12 HARV. J. LEGIS. 369 (1975).

8. Bennett and Heath, *Tax Reduction Act Severely Cuts Depletion Allowance, Tax Credit on Foreign Operations,* 42 J. TAX. 337. Also McDonald, *The Taxation System and Market Distortion* in R. KALTER & W. VOGLEY, ENERGY SUPPLY AND GOVERNMENT POLICY (1976).

output incentives since a nonintegrated producer whose receipts are already at this level would get no tax benefit on marginal output. In price terms, assuming a 48% tax rate and a net value of the percentage depletion deduction of 15%, this gross allowance is equivalent to a $0.75 price increase for lower tier oil and an increase of $1.70 for upper tier oil. For a taxpayer in the 70 percent bracket who might be regarded as an influential constituent in an oil district, the real price equivalent of this percentage depletion allowance is about $1.85 for lower tier and $4.00 for upper tier.[9]

A similar pattern can be seen in the provision in the price control system for crude oil to treat stripper wells as producing upper tier (high priced) oil.[10] From an efficiency standpoint, this must be overall counter-productive (compared to other ways of dealing with pumping costs). Under the price control arrangement a producer can substantially increase income from a low yield well by *reducing* output to bring it within the definition of stripper (10 bbls a day).[11] One reason price control on oil has survived is that a very numerous body of potential opponents have been bought off.

The benefits in both of these provisions go to groups that would make up part of the producer lobby. Those benefits serve to reduce the willingness of producers to provide the intense political support necessary to logroll their position over the far more numerous consumer interests.

A further complication in the producer-consumer politics of oil is that independent refiners and distributors have an interest in preserving price control. From the standpoint of the independents, increased crude oil prices would mean increased profits for integrated companies with the prospect that profits on crude would be available to improve their competitive position in refining and distribution.[12]

By 1978 it has been widely reported that the mechanics of price control, especially the complex arrangements for rolling-in prices of

---

9. We assume that the net benefit of 22% percentage depletion is 15% for lower tier oil, the reduction accounted for by the net income limitation, the cost depletion foregone and the minimum tax. *See* Brannon, *The Present Tax and Subsidy Provisions Relating to the Energy Industries* in STUDIES IN ENERGY TAX POLICY (G. Brannon, ed., 1974). *See also* McDonald *supra,* note 7. For upper tier oil, the net income limitation will be less restrictive so we put the value of percentage depletion at 18%.

10. Mead, *Oil, an Unregulated Industry,* in ENERGY SUPPLY AND PUBLIC POLICY 155 (1976).

11. Renshaw, *The Taxation of Crude Oil, Gasoline, Related Fuels and Commodities such as Motor Vehicles,* GROWTH AND CHANGE (Jan. 1979) (forthcoming).

12. *See* M. WOOLRICH, ADMINISTRATION OF ENERGY SHORTAGE: NATURAL GAS AND PETROLEUM (1976). There is a discussion of industry structure at 111-119 and a number of references to measures to protect independents in Chapter 6.

high and low cost resources for refiners and distributors, including imported gasoline, have produced a pump price of gasoline which is more nearly consistent with the world crude price than the U.S. crude price. These circumstances provide a further group of producers who are willing to support the consumer side of price control politics.

On the face of things, producers and consumers have different kinds of strength in the political conflict over income redistribution—intensity of interest versus sheer numbers. Because of the ability of redistribution schemes to isolate subgroups of producers, the outcome of this conflict must be regarded as indeterminate.

THE OUTPUT PENALTY

Our public choice approach to the treatment of energy incomes makes the basic assumption that decision makers respond to the self interested views expressed to them by their constituents. This assumption appears to leave little room for government policy to be directly affected by considerations of economic efficiency, a topic so prominent in economic analyses of the energy crisis.

A useful way to integrate economic efficiency questions within the political context of the present discussion is to refer to the output penalty. In any situation in which an industry enjoying a windfall price increase exhibits a high level of price elasticity of supply, an attempt to capture the windfall profits, either by price control or by special taxes, will reduce output substantially. This reduction is an output penalty. In this way, the tax creates an excess burden over and above the burden of income transferred from producers to consumers.

A significant excess burden is likely to fall on labor as increased unemployment. Where the labor group involved is organized, there will be opposition to the price control from a constituent of the federated labor union organization. This opposition will make it difficult for the central labor organization to support the consumer interest. In U.S. politics, support of organized labor is an important condition for success of consumer-oriented causes.

So far as the energy price issue is concerned, there is debate about the size of the output penalty. Ostensibly, the two tier price control system leaves a strong inducement to new well drilling, but impairs incentives with regard to old wells. Where there are multiple owners of property interests in one nonunified oil pool, existing owners would not likely risk loss of ultimate recovery by deferring output. In the aggregate, however, we can only say that there has been some loss in ouptut of old oil.[13] The loss, however, is less than would appear from lowered production figures because oil left in the ground can be extracted later.[14] A relevant observation is that the output penalty does not diminish existing jobs, and it would be unlikely to trigger much labor opposition to a tax on producer incomes.

Consumers can influence the political decision regarding output penalty. A shortage that was obviously induced by regulation would generate considerable demand for decontrol. There is no shortage of oil involved since an indefinite supply of foreign oil is available at some price. Consumers generally do not give as much notice to oil prices as they do to oil shortages since the energy resource component of energy service prices is quite small.

A detailed look at how the output penalty has entered the political debate in natural gas is revealing as to the oil situation. On some obvious grounds, 1978 is a most unusual year for repeal of natural gas price regulation. On the political side, the consumer-oriented interests were stronger than they had been in most Congresses since field price regulation began, and the Administration was in favor of continued price control. At the same time, massive increases in field prices had already occurred under price control; the Carter energy program was providing a controlled price for natural gas almost six times higher than the field price that prevailed in the U.S. in the 1960's! Why, under these circumstances, has it been so difficult politically for the Administration to get a continuation of price control on natural gas?

With only slight facetiousness, I suggest the explanation of the cold winter of 1977. Consumers have been made increasingly aware of the output penalty through a cumulation of effects from unsatisfied demand, restriction on new installations of gas home-heat, unemployment from interruptions of industrial service, and finally, the restriction on the availability of heating gas during an exceptionally cold winter.

It has taken almost 15 years for the output penalty involved in natural gas price regulation to assume sufficient importance to change the balance of forces in the politics of the producer-consumer

13. Rostow, Fisher and Woodson, *National Energy Policy, Sept. 1977: An Interim Overview,* in COUNCIL ON ENERGY RESOURCES, NATIONAL ENERGY POLICY: A CONTINUING ASSESSMENT (1978).

14. Renshaw, *supra.* A qualitative assessment which seems to express a greater concern with the output penalty is provided by Russell, ENERGY IN THE 1978 BUDGET SETTING NATIONAL PRIORITIES (J. Pechman, ed., 1978). *See also* the comment on Renshaw's paper by Geo. VonFurstenburg, GROWTH AND CHANGE (Jan. 1979) (forthcoming).

opposition. Understandably, the far more subtle penalty associated with price control on oil (which is merely excessive imports) is unlikely to have a significant impact on consumers.

POLITICAL AWARENESS

The next ingredient of a public choice analysis of the treatment of windfall profits on energy resources can be identified as the general public awareness of the issue, which really means the state of consumer awareness. It is useful to distinguish windfall profits from the output penalty that we just discussed. The separation of these two topics facilitates concentration on states of mind and general expectations as distinct from actual observed consequences. It has been recognized in the literature that one source of strength on the producer side of the conflict is the large per capita benefits to producers from policies of decontrol with no windfall taxes; producers can spend money to change the public awareness of the issue.[15]

What has happened in the matter of the profits underlying the energy crisis illustrates the extreme complexity of this issue awareness. While producer outlays on advertising will have significant effects at the margin, there appears to be a broad variety of almost accidental circumstances that change the state of awareness.

In the matter of natural gas price regulation, the succession of historical accidents is amazing. The regulation of field prices grew out of a Supreme Court interpretation of highly ambiguous statutory language.[16] What was certain to be a Congressional override of the decision was frustrated by a fortuitous scandal involving allegations of an improper offer to one Senator.[17] Since the public enjoys reading about scandals more than about economics, this raising of awareness led directly to the long reign of natural gas price control, in the face of powerful economic arguments against this price control (i.e., that the control reduced the royalty income, not a monopoly profit and created a shortage).

The significant publicity factor in the energy crisis of 1974 was the fortuitous oil embargo that directed public attention to the energy problem in a unique way due to long waiting lines at gasoline stations. Also of some importance was the fact that a price control mechanism left over from President Nixon's New Economic Policy of 1971 already existed. Of the two circumstances, the preexisting price

15. Peltzman, *supra.*
16. Phillips Petroleum Co. v. Wisconsin, 347 U.S. 672 (1954).
17. Breyer & MacAvoy, *The Natural Gas Shortage and the Regulation of Natural Gas Producers,* 86 HARV. L. REV. 941 (1973).

control was undoubtedly the less important. The announcement of a major international political event, an embargo against the U.S. at the beginning of the winter heating season, immediately set the media to talking about how the suddenly limited supplies would be allocated. The serious health implications of heating oil shortages, even on a local basis, would seem to make inevitable a public demand for a nonprice allocation system.

If further consciousness raising were necessary, it was provided by the identification of large U.S. oil companies with the governments in several key OPEC countries and the resulting persistence of conspiracy theories about the whole oil crisis. There is undoubtedly some general good will in the American public for a market-price argument. The relevance of adopting a domestically free price as a response to a foreign cartel beyond our control is a somewhat subtle point, however. With a widespread suspicion that our oil companies were somehow involved in the foreign cartel, the chances of dislodging a price control system already in place were very slight.

The awareness issue was very clear in 1975. President Ford's administration, whose sympathies might be presumed to rest on the side of market prices and production incentives, proposed merely the substitution of an explicit windfall tax with distribution of the proceeds in lieu of a price-control tax. The proposal was defeated by a populist demand for crude price control.[18]

THE ADMINISTRATIVE COSTS OF REGULATION

In assessing the potential gains to consumers from either a price control or a tax approach to dealing with a producer surplus, the cost of enforcing a redistribution system is potentially an offset to those consumer gains. This argument is similar to the point about economic efficiency in that we would not expect to find a strong constituency for efficiency in government expenditures as such. The public choice significance of this feature will depend on its absolute size, as well as precisely how the administrative costs are reflected in the policy decision.

In the present case, for a number of reasons, there were in existence a number of oil and oil products reporting systems plus a reasonably small number of refineries. The entire regulatory system has been handled at an administrative cost of under $0.5 billion on the government side.[19] Even if these costs were subtracted from the

---

18. For review of this legislative battle, *see* Brannon, *Prices and Incomes: The Dilemma of Energy Policy*, 13 HARV. J. LEGIS. 445 (1976).
19. Russell, *supra* at 330, referring to the results of an inter-agency study.

proceeds of a producer tax, this would make a very small dent in the size of excess profits.

A POLITICAL ANALYSIS OF THE CARTER ENERGY-TAX PROGRAM FOR OIL

The central feature of the Carter energy tax program as it relates to oil is the crude oil equalization tax (COET). In political terms a proposal more or less like this one should be regarded as inevitable. Oil price control was extended by the 94th Congress (1975) with its principal support from President Carter's party, and that party was in stronger control of the 95th Congress than it was of the 94th.

Impressively, the opposition to COET in the Ways and Means Committee was a combination of the 12 Republicans voting plus the Democrats from the oil producing states of Texas (2), Louisiana, and Oklahoma. The measure carried by 21-16.[20] Clearly the opposition was not a vote for price control but for ultimate decontrol with gain accruing to energy producers and owners of energy resources. This inference is strengthened by the appearance of exactly the same line-up (with yeas and nays reversed) on an amendment to allow oil companies to keep 20 percent of the COET revenues for investment in finding more oil.[21]

The President had brought around the non-oil-state Committee Democrats (many of whom had been price control supporters in 1975) to the position of allowing consumers to face the import price of oil with regard to their marginal decisions.[22] The President had certainly moved his constituency to a more economically defensible position. It would have been quite unrealistic to have expected a Democratic President to completely abandon his own constituency to advocate no price control and no windfall tax.

The COET was keyed to the import price of oil which meant that it involved two important economic problems. The import externality problems noted in our introduction remained, and there was some output penalty.

Although we have argued that the output penalty was not potent politically, it will be useful to look a bit more closely at COET to see how it deals with output issues. The tax would move the U.S. crude oil price to the world price level by 1980 with the reservation that the U.S. price might not be permitted to rise fully to the world price

---

20. TAX NOTES, June 20, 1977, at 3.
21. *Id.*
22. An exception to this proposition is noted *infra* at note 24.

if that price after 1977 rises by much more than the rate of U.S. price inflation, now an unlikely possibility.

COET would recapture "windfalls" by applying different tax rates to different oil types. Different types of oil are defined as follows:

    (1) old oil, as defined by the pre-1977 price regulations, broadly oil produced from a field not in excess of the production in 1973;

    (2) new oil, which does not fall in any of the other categories;

    (3) new-new oil—oil discovered from wells drilled after April 20, 1977 (at a minimum distance from old wells on shore or from old leases off-shore) plus oil obtained from existing wells by tertiary recovery methods;

    (4) stripper oil—from wells with output below 10 bbl/day;

    (5) Alaskan oil and oil from the Naval Petroleum Reserves.

COET would be defined as the market price less an allowed factor price. The factor prices for old oil and new oil are the 1977 regulated prices, $5.28/bbl and $11.56/bbl respectively, increased annually for general inflation. The factor price for new-new and stripper oil would be the 1977 world market price, $14.25, also increased for inflation. Table 1 provides some calculations of the COET for 1980 assuming that the world market price for oil rises at 5 percent or 7 percent a year while the U.S. prices increase about 5 percent a year.

Table 1 illustrates the division between producers and consumers of the increased market cost of raising the crude oil prices. We have simply assumed a plausible level of U.S. outputs for 1980; our intention is not to predict a particular output response, but to look at the financial implications of a plausible output.

An OPEC price, rising at the U.S. inflation rate, should be about $16.50 in 1980, delivered East Coast, U.S. (1980 case #1). If U.S. production is 3.56 billion bbls, this will create a market cost of $58.8 billion in 1980. Under price controls in 1977, Americans paid $25.7 billion for crude produced in the U.S. To get a fair picture of the cost to U.S. consumers of the higher prices, we include in the 1977 cost the value of an amount of oil that was imported in 1977 but will be produced in the U.S. in 1980, the quantity X in Table 1. (U.S. consumers will pay for other imports in 1977 and 1980 but these are irrelevant to the immediate focus of U.S. product.)

For an amount of crude oil for which Americans are now paying $34.5 billion (the $25.7 billion noted *supra* plus $8.8 billion of imports) the cost in 1980 at the market price will be about $60 billion, a few billion more or less depending on the OPEC price. If we assume 5 percent inflation, the U.S. consumers should expect the current cost to rise to $40 billion by 1980 with no increase in real

TABLE 1

U.S. PRODUCTION OF CRUDE OIL, PRICES, MARKET COST AND PROPOSED CRUDE OIL EQUALIZATION TAX, 1977 AND 1980

Oil Type	1977			1980 (1)				COET		1980 (2)		COET	
	Output bbl/y	Market Price $	Cost $bil	Output bbl/y	Market Price $	Cost $bil	Factor Price $	Per bbl $	Total Rev. $ bil	Market Price $	Cost $	Per bbl $	Total Rev. $ bil
Old oil	1.34	5.20	7.0	0.91	16.50	15.0	6.40	10.10	9.2	17.50	15.9	11.10	10.1
New oil	1.10	11.00	12.1	1.20	16.50	19.8	14.20	2.30	2.8	17.50	21.0	3.30	4.0
New-new oil	0.07	11.20	0.8	0.40	16.50	6.6	16.20	0.30	0.1	17.50	7.0	1.30	0.5
Stripper	0.36	13.50	4.9	0.40	16.50	6.6	16.20	0.30	0.1	17.50	7.0	1.30	0.5
Alaskan	0.07	13.50	0.9	0.58	16.50	9.6	16.50	–	–	17.50	10.2	–	–
NPR	–	–	–	0.07	16.50	1.2	16.50	–	–	–	1.2	–	–
X	0.62	14.25	8.8	–	–	–	–	–	–	–	–	–	–
	3.56		34.5	3.56		58.8			12.2		62.3		15.1

burden. The net increase in burden on U.S. consumers is then $19-22 billion. Under the proposed windfall tax, the federal government captures $12-15 billion, leaving $7 billion to producers, along with approximately $9 billion that U.S. producers set for displacing some imports. This is a gross increase in U.S. producer real income of $16 billion. One obvious qualification to the producer income is that the 1980 production includes an increase of 0.51 bbl of Alaskan production, which entails special costs of almost $4 billion (transportation at $6/bbl and Alaskan Tax of about $1.25/bbl). These special costs reduce the net increase in producer income to $11 billion.

To relate this to output changes we must consider the normal decline rate in old wells. Putting aside the new-new and Alaskan oil in 1977, the remaining production is 2.7 billion bbls.; in three years this should decline normally by about 0.6 billion bbls. To produce a net output gain of 0.6 billion bbls, the total new production must be around 1.2 billion bbls. As proposed, the COET drives a hard bargain with producers. Even if producers achieve an appreciable output increase, the gain to the companies per barrel of increased output is only about $10.

This much windfall tax would appear to be "buying" considerable output penalty. Some recognition of this situation was shown by newspaper reports of proposed regulation changes wherein oil producers would be offered substantial increased revenues.[23] The techniques of driving the Congress to a strong anti-producer position that is to be modified later by administrative action seems to create an inept political operation. Basically, it seems clear that the details of COET can be modified to achieve more producer income.

However these output aspects of COET might be handled, the externality problems related to high imports remain. It is not inconceivable that the Carter administration could have advanced a price solution—an import tax plus correspondingly higher taxes on U.S. producers and higher distributions to consumers. Considering the price control forces to be dealt with, it is not surprising that this avenue was not pursued.

Since the externality problems remained, the questions were how non-price adjustments would be allocated between classes of consumers, and whether the adjustments would be brought about by regulation, tax penalties, or tax incentives. (Although there was no constituency for further restrictions on oil consumption, we think an administration must anticipate that continuation of economically

---

23. Washington Post, April 15, 1978, at 1.

unsound positions in this case, increasing oil imports, will generate a future political liability.)

With regard to the first part of this remaining problem of allocating more energy reductions, we can infer from the administration proposals and from Congressional reaction, a priority scale which was approximately as follows, starting with the most favored group:

(1) users of home heating (non-electric)
(2) users of petro-chemicals
(3) users of residential and commercial heating (non-electric)
(4) auto drivers and agricultural users
(5) public utilities
(6) industrial users (of oil) not convertible to coal
(7) industrial users, convertible to coal.

The Ways and Means Committee has consistently worried about imposing high oil costs on home heating bills. This reluctance was reflected in the amendment to COET to provide that certain home heaters could obtain COET refunds in proportion to their purchases, which is an expensive way of retaining price control. The root of this amendment was the concern that coal heating of homes is no longer feasible, which with a natural gas shortage leaves home heaters with few alternatives (lower temperatures or more insulation). This problem was seen as peculiar to northern states. The regional nature of the problem adds to the voter recognition of the issue. The vote alignment supporting this rebate was substantially the same as that supporting COET, except two Republicans, from Northern New York and Pennsylvania, shifted to vote for rebate and one southern Democrat shifted to vote against it.[24]

After a decision to leave home heating systems facing too low a price of oil (and gas) it was predictable that consumers would do too little insulation, and too little investment in alternatives. It was, therefore, obvious to induce economic behavior by introducing subsidies for home insulation and solar heat. Arguably solar heating would be advanced more readily by more research outlays rather than by consumer subsidies for buying the present high-priced systems. The subsidy for insulation is limited in amount per taxpayer and in the form of a credit; it is probably not appreciably worse than any other subsidy that could have been proposed.

Users of petro-chemicals and operators of multi-residential and commercial heating systems were left alone with the price decontrol.

---

24. TAX NOTES, July 4, 1977, at 3.

Automobile drivers were handled gingerly. The political wisdom was that a straight-out increase in the automobile tax was anathematic after the crushing defeat of the Ways and Means Committee's gasoline tax proposal in 1975.[25]

The Administration opened up an ingenious approach toward using price mechanisms to reduce gasoline consumption. Studies of price elasticity of demand for gasoline reveal a low short term elasticity, about 0.2, and a long term elasticity that is considerably higher.[26] The obvious meaning of these figures is that higher gasoline prices have little effect on driving habits, assuming consumers drive the autos they already own. Given time, the rational response to higher gasoline prices is to put more weight on gasoline economy in choosing a new car. (The obvious reason why European cars are so much smaller than American cars is the historically high levels of gasoline taxes in Europe.)[27]

This situation points to an obvious political strategy—taxation of new car owners. Such discrimination would be impossible to administer at the gasoline pump, but it could be accomplished by collecting in advance a gasoline tax on new car purchases (at a discount for pre-payment) on the expected gasoline consumption over the life of the car. A car driven 100,000 miles in ten years with a average of 20 miles per gallon will consume 5,000 gallons. At a 9 percent discount rate, the value of a 1 cent/gallon tax will be, at the time of purchase, $33. Similar calculations for a car of 15 miles per gallon yields a purchase tax of $50 and for 30 miles per gallon, $22.

The roughly 20 gallons of gasoline refined out of a barrel of crude accounts for about 55 percent of the value of product. Consequently, gasoline buyers could be faced with the equivalent of a $1/bbl higher price for crude by a tax of about 3 cents/gal. Assuming we wanted to induce behavior consistent with a real cost of imports $3 above the nominal import price, the appropriate scale of the new car tax would be as follows:

Gasoline consumption	Tax
12 miles/gal	$500
15 miles/gal	400
20 miles/gal	300
30 miles/gal	200
35 miles/gal	173

25. *See* Brannon, Price and Incomes, *supra* note 18.
26. U.S. INTERNATIONAL TRADE COMMISSION, THE FUEL EFFICIENCY INCENTIVE TAX PROPOSAL: ITS IMPACT UPON THE FUTURE OF U.S. PASSENGER AUTOMOBILE INDUSTRY, U.S. SENATE, COMMITTEE ON FINANCE (July 1977).
27. N. GUYOL, ENERGY IN THE PERSPECTIVE OF GEOGRAPHY 99 (1971).

This scale represents the current value of an extra 9 cents/gal gasoline tax.

This strategy is inherently attractive in that it avoids a relatively pointless burden on drivers of existing cars. In this way, existing car owners are like those who heat homes; they face no viable options, and see the income transfer associated with high prices as both useless and burdensome. The observation that such a tax burden is not politic as well reflects a fundamental rationality in the political process.

Unfortunately, the apparent "way around" the bad politics of a gasoline tax carries its own problems; a significant penalty on new car sales. Assuming an average price of a new car at $5,000, an average tax of $300, and a price elasticity of demand around 1.2, car purchases would decline about 7 percent.

Pursuing the will-of-the-wisp of a weightless burden, the administration came up with a means to impose a differential burden on gasoline consumption of new cars by making the tax high on low gasoline mileage cars, zero on average cars and negative (i.e., a tax credit) on gasoline economy cars. This is a way of refunding the car tax to customers, while continuing a price differential for gasoline economy and not significantly reducing car purchases. (From an energy policy standpoint, reducing new car purchases would have been sensible but impolitic.)

Fascinated with its discovery of weightless burdens, the Administration sought to push the technique very hard. The significance of these proposals can be seen by comparing a zero revenue variant of the 9 cent gasoline tax proposal with the President's proposal:

Gasoline Consumption	9 cent gasoline tax prepaid adj to zero revenue	Carter Proposal 1980
12 mil/gal	200	666
15 mil/gal	100	333
20 mil/gal	0	0
30 mil/gal	(100)	(333)
35 mil/gal	(133)	(428)

This severe economic burden on varying gasoline mileage makes little economic sense. It was in fact presented by the President in terms of a lot of moralistic talk about "gas guzzlers." A station wagon carrying 5 people may be much more fuel efficient than a small car carrying one person. A straight out "real cost of gasoline" basis for the auto tax could have avoided the anti-family aspect of a punitive tax on station wagons. Another political defect of the Administration's plan was that foreign cars would be over-represented in the refund category. A study called for by the Senate Finance Committee produced the estimate that the plan would reduce 1985 sales of U.S. and Canadian produced cars by 330,000 and increase imports by 300,000.[28]

Ultimately, the fate of the fuel economy incentive tax was to be reduced to a fairly trivial device to enforce some crude mileage regulation imposed on car producers. When the problem was seen by the public as amenable to a regulatory solution, price burdens appeared unproductive.

The remaining three classes of fuel users, all in large industry, elicited only modest sympathy. Presumably the industries involved would pass most of higher fuel prices on to customers. These industries would be left with the market price of crude, and progressively between 1978 and 1983 there would be imposed an extra excise tax from $1.50 to $3.00/bbl on crude oil (and a similar tax on natural gas). The details are unimportant so we comment only on some broad features of industrial user treatment.

Public utilities were subjected to the lowest tax, presumably because of the continuing protest about electric rates. These are sensitive because rates are set by politically appointed public utility commissions. In industrial situations in which conversion to coal is not feasible, the extra tax is also low, in line with the limited option principle. Finally, large classes of industrial users, small and medium sized firms, and the inevitable farmers were spared the industrial user tax.

The other features of the industrial user tax were two tax rebates. Firms paying the tax were to be allowed a full rebate for installation of oil substitute equipment while all firms were to be allowed an extra investment credit for installation of any of a broad range of equipment to utilize new energy sources or to produce more economical use of energy.

Neither rebate feature was brilliantly designed. The refund of excise tax involves a 100 percent offset of cost and would induce much outright waste of useful capital. The investment credit fails on the ground that the amount of the credit is a function of the amount of capital cost, not of the relative energy efficiency. The problem is basically one of disorganized political decision-making. The Administration could have designed a more efficient subsidy for energy efficient new investment, but the constraint was that it had to be worked into the same tax package as the industrial user excise tax,

---

28. U.S. INTERNATIONAL TRADE COMMISSION, *supra* note 26.

and the subsidy had to be designed not on energy policy grounds but on grounds of workability within the tax system.

CONCLUSION

The energy "crisis" is a political one. It mostly arises from the combination of historical accidents that led to a national response of price control. In some political circumstances, political leadership or industry influence may have led to a more market oriented response. In the politics of the 1970's in the U.S. a market solution was not possible; price control was demanded. The problem for successive administrations has been to find popular ways to modify the price/profit control system so as to come closer to market results.

Chapter 11

PROTECTING ENERGY TURF: THE DEPARTMENT OF ENERGY ORGANIZATION ACT

DANIEL M. OGDEN, JR.*

On August 4, 1977 President Jimmy Carter signed the first of a series of key new laws which were designed to lay the foundations for his new Administration's energy policy: the Department of Energy Organization Act.[1] Although conflict over the National Energy Plan gained far greater national attention because of the protracted policy conflict in Congress in the late fall and winter of 1977-1978, the earlier act is equally notable for what it did not achieve.

The Department of Energy Organization Act is a particularly compelling demonstration of two basic principles of national policy making:

First, national policy is made through a system of power clusters[2] which operate quite independently in each of the major substantive fields of policy. Except for atomic energy, most of energy supply long has been a sub-cluster within the broader Natural Resources power cluster and has, in fact, operated in several other sub-clusters within Natural Resources, primarily in water and in minerals. On its face, it would appear that the establishment of a Department of Energy would do no violence to the power cluster system and thus should have been an attainable proposition.

Second, administrative agencies jealously guard their subject matter "turf." They yield jurisdiction only after a major struggle and only in the face of overwhelming political force. They can and will muster counter political forces to protect their turf.[3] Reorganization which involves realignment of established jurisdictional relationships and the sharing of duties formerly lodged in one agency are especially difficult to achieve, because the original agencies continue with their established functions and can successfully resist the new arrangements. Thus, for example, attempting to give the Fish and Wildlife Service responsibility for managing wildlife in the National

*Dr. Ogden is a Professor of Political Science at Colorado State University, and is currently on leave to serve as Director, Office of Power Marketing Coordination, Department of Energy.

1. 42 U.S.C. § 7101 (1977) (hereinafter The Act).
2. D. OGDEN, HOW NATIONAL POLICY IS MADE, INCREASING UNDERSTANDING OF PUBLIC PROBLEMS AND POLICIES–1971 5-10 (1971).
3. H. SEIDMAN, POLITICS, POSITION, AND POWER (2d ed. 1975).

Parks would be an organizational disaster. Neat as it may look on paper and logical though it may sound to have one federal agency responsible for the management of fish and wildlife on all federal property, the overriding management responsibilities of the principal agency would simply make life impossible for the secondary one. The Department of Energy Organization Act clearly reflects the impact of both of these principles.

First, the Act assembles several energy agencies from various places in the government and establishes a few new ones. Two previously independent agencies, the Federal Energy Administration and the Energy Research and Development Administration, a lineal descendent of the post-war Atomic Energy Commission, are abolished and their functions transferred to Energy. The Nuclear Regulatory Commission, the other part of the old Atomic Energy Commission, remains independent. All of the electric power marketing bureaus of the Department of the Interior are moved to Energy: the Bonneville Power Administration, the Southwestern Power Administration, the Southeastern Power Administration, the Alaska Power Administration, and the power marketing functions of the Bureau of Reclamation converted to the Western Area Power Administration. The Federal Power Commission is abolished and all its powers transferred to the new Department. A new, five-member Federal Energy Regulatory Commission is "established within the Department (as) an independent regulatory commission." It has all of the regulatory functions of the old Federal Power Commission over hydroelectric licenses, power rates, natural gas rates, and service. The Secretary of Energy receives all other authority from the Federal Power Commission, especially the information functions.

The Act also creates several new bureaus. An Energy Information Administration will be "responsible for carrying out a central, comprehensive, and unified energy data and information program."[4] An Office of Energy Research is to advise the Secretary on the many research functions assembled in the Department. To direct internal auditing and insure honest administration, an Office of Inspector General is also established.

Second, the Act transfers to the Secretary several energy-related functions from other agencies. From Interior comes the power to promulgate leasing regulations for coal, oil, and natural gas on the Outer Continental Shelf and on public and private lands that are subject to the Mineral Lands Leasing Act, the Mineral Leasing Act for Acquired Lands, the Geothermal Steam Act of 1970 and the

---

4. *See,* The Act, *supra* note 1, § 205.

Energy Policy and Conservation Act. This includes setting diligence requirements and rates of production, fostering competition in bidding, and specifying the procedures, terms, and conditions of federal royalty interests. But the Secretary of the Interior remains "solely responsible for the issuance and supervision of Federal leases and the enforcement of all regulations . . . including . . . lease terms and conditions and production rates,"[5] and the Secretary of Energy is expressly denied authority to "restrict or limit" that authority. Moreover, Indian lands remain exclusively under Interior's jurisdiction. This awkward arrangement is institutionalized with a Leasing Liaison Committee composed of equal representatives from Energy and Interior.[6]

From Housing and Urban Development comes the power "to develop and promulgate energy conservation standards for new buildings."[7] Yet "all other responsibilities, pursuant to Title III of the Energy Conservation and Production Act, shall remain with the Secretary of Housing and Urban Development."[8]

From Transportation no powers are transferred. The Secretary of Transportation is merely directed to "consult with the Secretary of Energy" in carrying out his duty to promote fuel economy.[9] The carpooling provisions of the Energy Policy and Conservation Act go the other way; from the Federal Energy Administration to Transportation.[10]

From Agriculture nothing is transferred. The Administrator of the Rural Electrification Administration, in making loans to build generation, transmission, or distribution facilities, is merely directed to "consider such general criteria consistent with the provisions of this Act as may be published by the Secretary of Energy."[11]

From the Interstate Commerce Commission the Act transfers responsibility for the regulation of transportation of oil by pipeline, and from the Navy jurisdiction over several naval oil reserves is transferred. From the Department of Commerce comes the small Industrial Energy Conservation Program, which had been delegated there by the Federal Energy Agency.[12]

Third, the Act assigns to the new Department broad planning and

5. The Act, *supra* note 1, §303(a).
6. The Act, *supra* note 1, §210.
7. The Act, *supra* note 1, §304.
8. The Act, *supra* note 1, §304.
9. The Act, *supra* note 1, §305.
10. The Act, *supra* note 1, §310.
11. The Act, *supra* note 1, §709(f).
12. Department of Energy Organization Act: *Hearings before the Comm. on Governmental Affairs*, 95th Cong., 1st sess. 723 (1977).

coordinating functions to encourage energy conservation. Title VIII directs the President to propose a "National Energy Policy Plan" and makes elaborate provision for both state and local government and private input as well as Congressional review.

Recognizing that each power cluster would have to do its bit to win the energy war, the Act directed the Secretaries of Defense, Commerce, Housing and Urban Development, Transportation, Agriculture, and Interior, the Postmaster General, and the Administrator of the General Services Administration to designate one person at the level of Assistant Secretary to be "the principal conservation officer of such Department" who "shall be principally responsible for planning and implementation of energy conservation programs . . . and for coordination with the Department of Energy."[13]

A recitation of these provisions readily reveals that more energy management is left out of the new Department than is included. Two distinct conclusions emerge. First, the Department of Energy is responsible primarily for energy *supply*. Its duties in conservation are limited to planning, encouraging others, and data gathering and publication. The real decisions which could bring about energy conservation have been left as an integral function of those power clusters that consume rather than produce energy. Thus the Department of Transportation will continue to worry about improving the energy efficiency of automobiles, trucks, trains, airplanes, and other means of conveyance. The Department of Agriculture will continue its concern for conservation of energy on the nation's farms. The Department of Housing and Urban Development will continue its responsibilities to improve energy savings in existing homes and other buildings, where the real savings have to be made.

Second, in the energy supply area, the new Department is responsible primarily for research, regulation and part of electric power marketing. It has virtually no responsibility for managing the basic water and fossil fuel sources of energy, and it does not regulate nuclear power.

Such a limited assignment is especially remarkable because the United States Government owns the bulk of the basic energy resources of the nation. It owns all of the hydroelectric power and has developed many of the major hydro sites itself. The other sites have been licensed to private entrepreneurs on a 50-year recapture basis. The United States Government also owns all of the offshore oil and gas reserves beyond the 3-mile limit. It owns a major part of the oil and gas reserves in Alaska and much of the remaining reserves in the

---

13. The Act, *supra* note 1, §656.

continental United States, including in particular most of the oil shale reserve. It leases these to private companies for development and extracts bonus bids and royalties. Of the nation's huge coal reserve, fully half is under federal lands or has been retained in federal ownership under the Mineral Leasing Act of 1920.[14] The government itself pioneered the development of nuclear energy and has retained a permanent government monopoly over it, primarily for defense reasons. It has licensed private development of electric energy using nuclear reactors with extensive subsidies, but the source of the energy remains as federal property and under tight federal controls.

The lack of jurisdiction of the new Department of Energy is therefore very significant. In the hydroelectric field, where the federal government has been an active generator and transmitter of power for generations, the Department has responsibility for no power generation at all and for only part of the federal power marketing. The Tennessee Valley Authority, the largest federal electric power system, remains independent and intact. The generation of power at federal dams continues in the hands of the dam-building agencies, specifically the Corps of Engineers in the Department of Army and the Bureau of Reclamation in the Department of the Interior. The Rural Electrification Administration remains essentially untouched in Agriculture.

In coal, oil, and gas, the Bureau of Land Management in the Department of the Interior continues to issue all leases on public lands, including the Outer Continental Shelf, and the Geological Survey in the Department of the Interior continues to oversee the operations of lessors. The regulation of the surface mining of coal and the restoration of damages caused by both surface and subsurface mining of coal have been assigned to the newly established Office of Surface Mining Reclamation and Enforcement in the Department of the Interior. In nuclear power, the licensing and regulation of nuclear reactors for domestic power production are left outside the Department in the independent Nuclear Regulatory Commission.

When confronted with a crisis the President has labeled "the moral equivalent of war,"[15] how could the Congress have left so much of the control of energy in other hands? The stark truth is that the President did not ask for a Department of Energy which would

---

14. *See,* ENERGY POLICY PROJECT, A TIME TO CHOOSE 270-S (1974).

15. *The President's Energy Program: A compilation of documents printed by the Committee on Energy and Natural Resources,* 95th Cong., 1st sess. (1977). It appears in the President's address to the nation of April 18, 1977.

assemble all federal energy responsibilities under one roof. He really asked for very little more than he got.

Carter apparently called on a task force of experienced natural resources administrators to write the strongest bill they thought could be passed. Being well aware of the strength of the power clusters and of the propensity of all agencies to protect their turf, they wrote a bill which would avoid antagonizing the most effective of these clusters and attacking the turf of the energy agencies.

Charles F. Luce, Chairman of the Board of the Consolidated Edison Company of New York, and formerly Bonneville Power Administrator and later Under Secretary of the Interior under Presidents Kennedy and Johnson, accurately characterized the Administration's bill to the New York delegation:

> By no means does the bill create a strong Energy Department. I assume that it creates as strong an Energy Department as the President believes the Congress would approve. But the fact is that the head of the Energy Department will be powerless to assure that domestic energy resources are tapped, or new energy facilities built, unless the Interior Department, the Environmental Protection Agency, and, in the case of nuclear facilities, the Nuclear Regulatory Commission concur in his decisions.[16]

The application of a strategy of avoiding confrontation with other power clusters and avoiding confrontation over turf with well-established intra-cluster agencies is particularly clear in the electric power field. There were two explicit lines of attack.

First, the Administration's bill, S. 856, avoiding attacking agencies which were capable of arousing vigorous defense of their turf in Congress. The Tennessee Valley Authority was completely ignored, as though it did not exist. It is mentioned nowhere in the bill. Moreover, it is mentioned in neither the testimony of the Administration's key spokesmen, James R. Schlesinger or John F. O'Leary, before the Senate Committee on Governmental Affairs,[17] nor in the President's April 18, 1977 address to the Nation.[18] In his address to the joint session of Congress on April 20, President Carter mentioned the TVA only in passing and then only as implementing its own programs to conserve energy.[19] The power generating functions of the Corps of Engineers and the Bureau of Reclamation were similarly ignored.

Second, Title III of the bill attempted to transfer to the Secretary

---

16. Dept. of Energy Organization Act *supra* note 9, at 719. Luce's elaboration of this point is very clear and well done.

17. *Id.* at 4-53.

18. *The President's Energy Program, supra* note 12, at 1-5.

19. *Id.* at 10.

of Energy the powers and functions of agencies which the bill drafters apparently thought would be unable to resist such a transfer. Rather than proposing to transfer these agencies intact, however, the bill very precisely and explicitly proposed to transfer to the Secretary of Energy "all the functions vested by law" in the Federal Power Commission and the four separate power marketing administrations in the Department of the Interior, plus the electric transmission and marketing functions of the Bureau of Reclamation.[20]

This language very skillfully preserved the famous "Bone red line formula" established in the Bonneville Act of 1937.[21] Senator Homer T. Bone of Washington had struck a compromise between the Corps of Engineers and the Secretary of the Interior, Harold Ickes, which preserved the "integrity" of managing all functions of the dam itself for the Corps but handed the power to Interior at the bus bar for transmission and sale. That pattern had subsequently been followed throughout the nation except in the Tennessee Valley.

The bill drafters guessed right about the Federal Power Commission. As an agency, it proved to have few champions. They guessed wrong, however, about the support for continued independence and collegial decision making in the Federal Power Commission's regulatory functions and about the power marketing agencies.

The proposal to transfer the power marketing functions only avoided attacking the turf of the Corps of Engineers, and they accordingly stayed out of the fray. But it did attack the turf of the Bureau of Reclamation, which had marketed all federal power in the West except in the Pacific Northwest and Alaska. It also threatened every one of the power marketing agencies, for it opened the possibility of a single, centralized power marketing administration headquartered in Washington. All of the power marketing administrations and the Bureau of Reclamation have strong local support from their preference customers, the publicly and cooperatively owned utilities. These groups in turn are heavily supported by key members of the Congress, and especially by the leadership of the Senate Committee on Energy and Natural Resources. Moreover, two key Senators on the Energy committee are also ranking members of the Committee on Governmental Affairs which handled the Department of Energy bill.

The drafters of these proposals also apparently did not perceive the double trouble they would create by burying an amendment to

20. *Dept. of Energy Organization Act, supra,* note 9, at 7-9. *See* sections 301 and 302 of the proposed act.

21. Daniel M. Ogden, Jr., The Development of Federal Power Policy in the Pacific Northwest, ch. 7 (unpublished doctoral dissertation, The University of Chicago, 1949).

the Rural Electrification Act of 1936 in section 712(h) of Title VII of the Department of Energy Organization Act. That section, entitled, "Transitional, Savings, and Conforming Sections" sounded routine and unimportant. It was not. Section 712(h) proposed to add a new section to Title I of the Rural Electrification Act:

> Sec. 16. In order to insure coordination of electric generation and transmission financing under this Act with national energy policy, no loan for the construction, operation, or enlargement of any generating plant or electric transmission line or system shall be made or guaranteed under this Act except after consent by the Secretary of Energy or a determination by the Secretary of Energy that such consent is not necessary.

Section 712(h) was a major political intrusion into the Agriculture power cluster and it invited Agriculture alliance with the public power people to protect both the Rural Electrificiation Administration and Interior's power marketing agencies.

At the hearings, on March 24, 1977 Robert D. Partridge, Executive Vice President and General Manager of the National Rural Electric Cooperatives Association went right to the point:

> First and foremost, we are opposed to section 712(h) . . . We do not feel that adding another layer of government bureaucracy through which the REA loan documents would have to pass for generation and transmission financing for electric cooperatives is a proper approach to . . . coordination.[22]

He was seconded by Alex Radin, Executive Director of the American Public Power Association.[23] Both men also supported the transfer of the power marketing *agencies.* As Partridge put it, "We would strongly recommend that the integrity of the power marketing agencies be maintained, that they not be abolished."[24]

Neither proposal really had a chance. The bills reported from both houses responded to the wishes of the publicly owned and cooperatively owned utilities. The Act transfers the *functions,* as the Carter administration wanted, but then adds two explicit paragraphs directing that each of the power marketing administrations "shall be preserved as separate and distinct organizational entities within the Department," that each shall keep its principal office within its region, that a separate administration shall be established to operate the power transmission and marketing functions of the Bureau of

---

22. *Dept. of Energy Organization Act, supra* note 12, at 504.
23. *Id.* at 513.
24. *Dept. of Energy Organization Act, supra* note 9, at 505.

Reclamation, and that the new agency shall maintain regional offices in its huge service territory.[25]

The amendment to the REA Act mildly directs the administrator to "consider such general criteria consistent with the provisions of this Act as may be published by the Secretary of Energy."[26] Thus did the power marketing agencies and their constituencies on the Hill and in the interest groups unite to protect their turf.

The opposite fate of the Federal Power Commission is equally instructive. Since 1930, when a five-person independent regulatory commission was established to replace the interagency commission composed of the Secretaries of the Interior, War, and Agriculture, the Federal Power Commission had had a rather stormy career. Under the vigorous leadership of Leland Olds from 1939 to 1949, it had effectively implemented the Natural Gas Act and backed up the intent of the Public Utility Holding Company Act. Not only had the regulated electric utilities sought to avoid regulation by refraining from building inter-state interconnections, but also the oil and gas industry had led the charge to prevent Mr. Olds' reappointment to a third term.[27] In 1954 in the Phillips Petroleum Company case, the United States Supreme Court ruled that the Commission had authority to regulate the wellhead price of natural gas moving in interstate commerce.[28] This touched off a major effort to deregulate natural gas production which has had a stormy 24 year history. During the 1950's the Commission, dominated by Republican appointees, became much more industry-oriented,[29] and in particular generously issued or extended hydroelectric licenses to the outrage of public power groups.[30] Its subsequent record had not built a confident relationship with any of its clientele groups.

The Commission was therefore without friends to defend it from abolition and the transfer of its functions to Energy. But it did have long-time defenders who wanted to preserve the functions the Commission had performed, the commission system for decision-making, and the independence of the process.

If the Commission wished to resist a change which would end its independence, it needed the support of leading liberals to be convincing to a Democratic Congress. The people it needed most, however, defended its functions but were willing to see the Commission

25. The Act, *supra* note 1, §302(2)(3).
26. The Act, *supra* note 1, §709(f).
27. *See,* ROBERT ENGLER, THE POLITICS OF OIL, 319-322 (1961).
28. Phillips Petroleum Co. v. Wisconsin, 347 U.S. 672 (1954).
29. Engler, *supra* note 27, at 322.
30. U.S. Congress, Senate Committee on Interstate and Foreign Commerce, *Nomination of Jerome K. Kuykendall* (G.P.O. 1957).

abolished as an Independent entity in favor of a new agency within the Department of Energy.

"Two former Democratic Chairmen of the Commission, Joseph C. Swidler and Lee C. White, endorsed transfer of the functions of the Commission to the new Department, but urged careful preservation of its powers and duties. They both characterized the Administration's proposal as "not carefully thought through."[31]

Alex Radin and Robert Partridge for the public and cooperative electric power systems took the same position. Mr. Radin, for example, started off his testimony, "The Federal Power Commission has justifiably been criticized in recent years, and our organization has joined in such criticism," but he similarly was dissatisfied with the Administration's alternative.[32] Stewart L. Udall, Secretary of the Interior for Presidents Kennedy and Johnson, simply said, "I think it has served its main purpose, I think its functions can be folded into the proposed Cabinet department."[33]

Throughout the hearings, markup, and debate on the floor of both houses, the fate of the Federal Power Commission as an agency was treated as decided: the agency was to be abolished. Attention focused on how the new Department would be organized and empowered to carry out the Commission's essential functions.

The Administration's proposals contained two administrative features which created suspicion and distrust across the political spectrum. An Economic Regulatory Administration would be established in the Department with a single administrator appointed by the President with Senate confirmation. The Secretary would delegate to it any function under the Emergency Petroleum Allocation Act of 1973 and any function of the Federal Power Commission "which relates to establishment of rates and charges." A separate Board of Hearings and Appeals was also proposed to hear any matter which required an agency hearing on the record or any other matter the Secretary might decide.[35]

This arrangement was much too loose and vague to suit the affected parties, liberal and conservative alike. George H. Lawrence, President of the American Gas Association, supported abolition of the Federal Power Commission, transfer of its functions to the Department of Energy, and, of course, deregulation of production of new natural gas. Yet, he pointedly wished to keep utility regulation

---

31. *Dept. of Energy Organization Act, supra* note 12, at 203-213.
32. *Id.* at 513.
33. *Id.* at 369.
34. *Id.* at 7.
35. *Id.* at 12.

of interstate gas pipelines "in accordance with longstanding, workable utility type regulatory procedures for which the Natural Gas Act of 1938 was designed."[36] His views were echoed by Willis A. Strauss, Chairman of the Interstate Natural Gas Association,[37] and Frank N. Ikard, President of the American Petroleum Institute, who labeled "counterproductive" the lumping of several regulatory functions which "are fundamentally different in what they seek to accomplish."[38] They were joined by Charles F. Wheatley, Jr., General Counsel of the American Public Gas Association, normally an opponent of the private gas companies, who said the administration bill "would deprive consumers of long-established safeguards under the Natural Gas Act and the Federal Power Act." "The net result, I fear, is the establishement of a new procedural system which could facilitate future de facto administrative deregulation of gas and electric rates to the detriment of the American consumer."[39] Charles F. Luce was almost alone in saying, "I do not see the advantages of merging the FPC into the new Energy Department."[40]

The Congress responded by transferring the functions but establishing a new "independent" Federal Energy Regulatory Commission in the Department to which it specifically assigned the regulatory functions of the Federal Power Commission. Like its predecessor, the new Commission has five members, but they serve four-year overlapping terms.[41]

Major debate took place on the floor of both houses over the manner of handling the Federal Power Commission's functions. The Senate Committee had leaned toward the Administration's proposal by accepting a three-person Energy Regulatory Board to which it had assigned pricing authority.[42] The House, adopting an amendment from the floor by Congressman John E. Moss of California, empowered a five-member Federal Energy Regulatory Commission to set the wellhead price of natural gas and to exercise the regulatory functions of the Federal Power Commission.[43] Fear was expressed in both Houses that too much power was being assigned to the Secretary of Energy.

Thus the Federal Power Commission, as such, was abolished as an independent regulatory commission. But it was, for all practical pur-

---

36. *Id.* at 320.
37. *Id.* at 330-338.
38. *Id.* at 315-318.
39. *Id.* at 388.
40. *Id.* at 720.
41. *See,* The Act, *supra* note 1, §401 and 402.
42. CONGRESSIONAL QUARTERLY WEEKLY REPT., 952-3 (May 21, 1977).
43. CONGRESSIONAL QUARTERLY WEEKLY REPT., 1009 (June 4, 1977).

poses, recreated under a new name as an "independent" regulatory commission within the Department of Energy.

The leasing of federal fossil fuel resources reflected still another form of agency ability to resist change. While the administration was drafting the bill, elaborate negotiations were undertaken between Mr. Schlesinger, whom everyone expected would become Secretary of Energy, and Secretary of the Interior Cecil D. Andrus. Schlesinger had attempted to acquire control over leasing of fossil fuels on public lands. Andrus had insisted that management of the public lands could not be divided. One agency had to be in charge. The upshot was the division of responsibility which was finally proposed and enacted. Energy would set down policy guidelines for the leasing of fossil fuel resources, but Interior would continue to do the leasing and supervise execution. A special Leasing Liaison Committee would insure coordination. In the struggle, Interior found strong allies in the environmentalist groups, which trusted Andrus and his strongly pro-environmental staff, but distrusted Schlesinger. Marc Messing, a director of the Environmental Policy Institute, was quoted as saying, "If Interior is going to have any integrity at all, it's got to have control over public lands."[44]

Thus the Department of Energy emerges as a paper tiger to wrestle with the foremost problem besetting the United States today. It has virtually no authority to conserve energy, but instead must depend on the work of other departments, state and local governments, and private industry, and voluntary efforts by consumers. Moreover, the Department is also virtually powerless to expand the nation's production of domestic energy to meet rising demand by digging more coal, producing more oil and natural gas, or building more nuclear fueled steam-electric plants. The Department of Energy can only encourage these efforts by others.

To compound its weakness, several other agencies have the authority to check or stall energy development. The Environmental Protection Agency can impose reviews and delays from its point of view. The Nuclear Regulatory Commission can refuse to grant licenses. The Department of the Interior can view other uses of the public lands as more important, and can lock up large areas for wilderness or other special uses. These agencies march to different drums and seek different goals than the Department of Energy.

Reconciliation of these differences unavoidably will fall on the White House and probably on the President himself. But even if such reconciliation can be achieved, any dissatisfied party can still take a

---

44. CONGRESSIONAL QUARTERLY WEEKLY REPT., 403 (March 5, 1977).

particular case through the federal courts. An effective and coherent energy policy can emerge from this system of divided authority and conflicting purposes only through the most effective and diligent presidential leadership.

Thus the energy act demonstrates one of the principal corollary conclusions from observation of the nation's power cluster system. Power clusters often try to resolve major inter-cluster problems by themselves by using organizational structures and procedures appropriate for simple, intra-cluster problems. Energy, clearly, is chief among the nation's current major inter-cluster problems which cannot be left to single-cluster decision making. The President, therefore, must himself provide dynamic leadership in the energy field to develop new sources of energy, to expand the supplies of traditional sources, to reduce dependence upon the Arabian oil cartel, and to promote efficient use of energy among our people by using all of the instruments of government which he commands.

Chapter 12

FREE ENTRY INTO CRUDE OIL AND GAS PRODUCTION AND COMPETITION IN THE U.S. OIL INDUSTRY*

RUSSELL O. JONES,* WALTER J. MEAD** and PHILIP E. SORENSEN***

INTRODUCTION

The thesis of this paper is that a condition of free entry into crude oil and gas production in the United States prevails and that this condition, in conjunction with the existing structure of the petroleum industry, effectively guarantees that all phases of the industry's operations—production, refining and marketing—will be competitive in the long run.[1] There is an unfortunate predilection in human nature to seek scapegoats for unhappy historical events such as the recent rise in the price of oil. U.S. oil companies are very large, their early history was characterized by monopolistic behavior, and they are still the beneficiaries of some discriminatory tax laws. But appropriate public policy toward the oil industry should be based, not on a recitation of the sins of the past, but on objective analysis of the present structure, conduct, and performance of the industry.

We believe analysis shows that workable competition currently exists in all phases of the U.S. oil industry. Because the industry is effectively competitive, we believe proposals to amend the O.C.S. Lands Act to change the method of bidding for oil and gas leases on the Outer Continental Shelf (H.R. 1614, 95th Cong., 1st sess. (1977)) or to force vertical or horizontal divestiture of the major, integrated oil companies (S. 2387, 94th Cong., 2d Sess. (1976)) are unnecessary and ill-advised.

I. MARKET POWER

Monopoly is not presently a relevant issue in relation to the U.S. oil industry. The only realistic hypothesis concerning non-competitive behavior within the industry would be that of "shared monopoly" carried out through some form of explicit collusion or through a strategy of "conscious parallelism." Following this hypoth-

*This research was supported by U.S. Geological Survey Contract No. 14-08-0001-16552. The views and conclusions are those of the authors.
**University of California, Santa Barbara.
***Florida State University, Tallahassee.
1. We exclude pipeline transportation because of federal and state regulatory control over this phase of the industry.

esis, the leading firms in the industry would operate as an informal cartel and, by means of limitations on either inputs or outputs, raise prices above the levels which would be observed under competitive conditions.

To appraise the shared monopoly hypothesis, consider the problems an informal cartel of the kind suggested above would be likely to face (ignoring, for now, the threat of antitrust prosecution and attendant civil suits for triple damages).

> A cartel faces one external and four internal problems. The external problem . . . is to predict (and if possible, discourage) production by nonmembers. The internal problems are, first, to locate the contract surface; second, to choose a point on that surface (the sharing problem); third, to detect; and fourth, to deter cheating.[2]

Management of these internal and external problems is extremely difficult in the short run and perhaps impossible in the long run, even in the case of a formally-recognized cartel such as OPEC, which is shielded from legal and political reprisals.

The central economic threat facing a hypothetical oil industry cartel is entry by new firms. If new firms enter the industry but not the cartel, the cartel market share will decline. Entry into the cartel leads to increased problems of coordinating cartel behavior. In mathematical terms, a two-firm industry may be represented by a two-dimensional contract surface. As the number of firms in the industry rises to n, the number of dimensions required to solve for the cartel profit-maximizing output solution also rises to n. Concentration ratios (as cited below) are a shorthand method of expressing this relationship between the number of firms operating at each level of an industry's activities and the potential for collusive behavior through shared market power.

A successful cartel must control the use of at least one essential input in the production process and it must prevent potential entrant firms from gaining access to this input. The most effective barriers to entry are:

(1) Government imposed barriers;
(2) Ownership of sources of raw materials;
(3) Patents;
(4) Large capital requirements;
(5) Economies of scale which create a limit-pricing situation;
(6) Product differentation; or
(7) The threat of predatory behavior by the cartel.

---

2. Osborne, *Cartel Problems*, 66 AM. ECON. REV. 835, 835 (Dec. 1976).

We shall examine these potential barriers to entry, first in relation to the refining sector of the U.S. oil industry.

A. Refining

Access to crude oil is the *sine qua non* for a refinery operator. Such access has been relatively free in the U.S., as is shown in later sections of this paper.

There are no existing patent restrictions or technical-engineering barriers facing potential entrants to refining. U.S. refineries have traditionally been built by engineering-contracting firms, not by the major oil companies. New entrants are able to contract for refinery construction on the same terms as existing firms. The technology involved is widely known and easily duplicated.

Large capital requirements cannot serve as a barrier to entry into refining, given an efficient U.S. capital market. If an oil industry cartel sought to earn monopoly profits at the refinery level, it would restrict refinery outputs (and inputs) until marginal revenue for the cartel firms was equal to marginal cost assuming the sharing problem was perfectly solved. Since the price of refinery outputs at this point would exceed marginal cost, a potential entrant to refining could expect to earn greater profits than any member firm having the same cost structure. This is true because the entering firm would expand its output to the point where its marginal cost was equal to market price determined by the cartel's activity. As long as excess profits were earned in refining, additional entry would occur, ultimately undermining the cartel's strategy.

Economies of scale do not prevent entry into refining either. It is possible for a limit-pricing situation to arise in an industry having very large economies of scale. In this case, a new entrant is forced to achieve a high level of output in order to operate at an efficient scale. Its entry at this scale of output will lower market prices below the break-even level of costs, assuming existing firms in the industry maintain their levels of output. But this kind of limit-pricing situation typically requires that the optimum scale of plant for any firm must constitute at least 25-30 percent of industry output. Oil refining in the U.S. does not fit this model.

The largest operating oil refinery in the U.S. (as of January 1, 1978) was the Exxon Baytown, Texas refinery which has a daily capacity of 640,000 barrels, or only 3.8 percent of U.S. capacity.[3]

3. *Oil and Gas Journal,* March 20, 1978, at 113-134. Environmental constraints on new refinery construction implicitly favor expansion of existing plants. The Baytown refinery is unique, furthermore, in being located at the heart of the U.S. oil transportation system. Purely engineering considerations, therefore, have little to do with the large size of the refinery.

Data concerning new refinery construction in the U.S. contradict the limit-pricing hypothesis. The most recent survey of industry construction plans indicates that seven new grassroots refineries are currently either planned or under construction in the U.S. Four of the new refineries will have capacities of 30,000 barrels per day or less; the other three are in the range of 183,000 to 250,000 barrels per day.[4] Under the survivor principle, uneconomic plant sizes would not be chosen.[5] It must be concluded that economies of scale are not a factor inhibiting entry into U.S. refining.

Product differentiation arises at the marketing level of the oil industry, not in refining. This issue will be considered below.

Potential predatory behavior by existing firms is not a valid entry barrier in oil refining. Such behavior is illegal under the Robinson-Patman amendments to the Clayton Act.[6] The legal and civil penalties which can be meted out for predatory price cutting are substantial. An industry whose behavior is as closely monitored as the oil industry could hardly escape notice if it undertook to drive new entrants from the field through the use of predatory pricing tactics. In fact, significant new entry into U.S. refining has occurred, as is shown in the data relating to new refinery construction cited above and in the more general evidence that thirteen major new independent refiners have entered the industry since 1950 (each of which has constructed 50,000 barrels per day or more of new capacity).[7] The capacity of these thirteen independent refiners totaled about 2 million barrels per day in 1975, approximately 15 percent of U.S. capacity.

Data relating to trends in industrial concentration in U.S. refining are presented in Table 1. These data indicate that refining is not a concentrated industry, by any of the visual standards. They further indicate that concentration levels in refining have declined since 1960 and have continued to decline since the Arab embargo, as measured by market shares of both the Big-4 and Big-8 firms. The fact that concentration levels in refinery *runs* are consistently higher than same year concentration levels for refinery *capacity* throws further doubt on the cartel hypothesis, because it indicates that large refiners on the average have higher output-capacity ratios than do

---

4. *Oil and Gas Journal,* April 25, 1977, at 124-131. None of these refineries is being built for a company among the top twenty in U.S. refining capacity.

5. It should be noted that small refineries receive a subsidy in the form of additional crude oil entitlements, at the expense of larger refiners, assuming the parent company's total refining capacity is less than 175,000 barrels per day. F.E.A. Regulations, Par. 13,650, Nov. 1974.

6. Section 2(a).

7. W. JOHNSON, COMPETITION IN THE OIL INDUSTRY, 94 (1976).

smaller refiners. This outcome would not have occurred if large refiners had attempted to restrain outputs to obtain monopoly rents.

TABLE 1

CONCENTRATION RATIOS—SEGMENTS OF THE
U.S. ENERGY INDUSTRY

	1954	1955	1960	1965	1970	1975	1976
Proven Crude Oil Reserves[A and C]							
Big-4					37.2	36.2	38.7
Big-8					63.9	55.5	57.3
Proven Natural Gas Reserves[A]							
Big-4						26.9	26.2
Big-8						39.7	38.6
U.S. Crude Oil Production[A]							
Big-4		18.1	20.8	23.9	26.3	26.0	25.5
Big-8		30.3	33.5	38.5	41.7	41.2	40.5
U.S. Natural Gas Production[A]							
Big-4		21.7	16.8	20.8	25.2	24.2	23.5
Big-8		33.1	28.4	33.6	39.1	36.8	35.6
U.S. Oil Refinery Capacity[B]							
Big-4			32.0	30.4	32.5	29.9	29.7
Big-8			55.0	54.3	57.5	53.5	51.8
U.S. Oil Refinery Runs[B]							
Big-4		33.1	33.2	31.0	34.2	32.9	32.7
Big-8		57.7	56.8	55.3	61.0	57.7	56.9
U.S. Gasoline Sales[B]							
Big-4	31.2				30.7	29.5	29.3
Big-8	54.0				54.6	50.3	49.9

Sources:

[A] American Petroleum Institute, "Concentration Levels in the Production and Reserve Holdings of Crude Oil, Natural Gas, Coal and Uranium in the U.S.," 1955-1976, Discussion Paper No. 4R, September 1977.

[B] American Petroleum Institute, "U.S. Petroleum Market Shares: 1950-1976 Individual Company Data," Discussion Paper No. 3R, September 1977.

[C] Thomas D. Duchesneau, *Competition in the U.S. Energy Industry* (Cambridge, Mass.: Ballinger Press, 1975), p. 39.

B. Marketing

Barriers to entry arising from product differentiation have been recognized as a significant potential source of monopoly power since the classic work of Bain.[8] It has been argued that·the source of cartel power for the large oil companies in the U.S. has been their domina-

8. J. BAIN, BARRIERS TO NEW COMPETITION (1965).

tion of major brand gasoline retailing.[9] But the validity of this argument in respect to the U.S. oil industry is seriously undermined by the combined facts of relatively low absolute levels of concentration in gasoline marketing over the period 1954-1976 and declining market shares for the Big-4 and Big-8 gasoline retailers over this same period (as shown in Table 1). Because this argument has been urged with particular vigor since the Arab embargo of 1973—the assertion being that major refiners have denied independent marketers their usual access to gasoline supplies—it is significant to note that concentration ratios in marketing continued to decline in 1975 and 1976.

Major oil companies may have succeeded in creating the image of a superior product as a result of many years of advertising and developing networks of branded retail stations. But this perceived product differentiation has not shut out independent marketers. The quality image of the branded stations has been achieved at a cost. Through economies in marketing, independent retailers have been able to sell their lesser-known products at a discount of two to five cents per gallon. Consumers have therefore been given a choice between a higher priced "quality" product and a lower priced "no frills" product. The rise in the market share of independent retailers since 1954 shows that any efforts by major oil companies to preempt gasoline marketing through product differentiation have not succeeded.

There are presently no technical or financial barriers to entry into gasoline marketing in the U.S. Paradoxically, the only real barrier to entry has been created by government regulations. Gasoline allocation regulations, initially promulgated by the Federal Energy Office, still survive in the new Department of Energy (DOE). These rules require potential new gasoline marketers to obtain DOE approval before opening a new service station in any area. The approval will not be given unless the government believes the market area involved is not adequately served by existing retailers.[10] By this rule, the federal government has conferred on existing marketers some of the cartel power they could not have obtained by means of a strategy of product differentiation.

C. Access to Crude Oil

We have argued that monopoly power in the U.S. oil industry has not been obtained through restrictions on refinery construction (or outputs) nor through control over gasoline retailing. We have not yet

---

9. F. ALLVINE & J. PATTERSON, COMPETITION, LTD. (1973).

10. Furthermore, the D.O.E. must notify "potentially aggrieved parties" (i.e. other service stations in the market area) before deciding on the approval. See 10 C.F.R. § 211.12 (e)(2) (1977), and 10 C.F.R. § 205.39 (1977), and Appendix thereto.

dealt with the most important potential source of cartel power for the industry: control over crude oil supplies. It is apparent that new entrants to refining must have a secure and competitive source of raw material inputs in order to risk entry to the oil industry. In the absence of new entry to refining, constraints on the supply of gasoline could eventually result in the creation of monopoly power at the marketing level. Thus access to crude oil supplies is the crucial factor affecting present and future competition in the oil industry.

It might be argued that the ending of oil import quotas in 1973 has, by itself, created the conditions necessary for competitive access to crude oil supplies, when combined with the entitlements program of the U.S. government (which was introduced to equalize the cost of imported and domestic crude oil for all U.S. refiners). This supposition is incorrect, for reasons involving both external and internal political policies.

First, total dependence on foreign crude oil would expose a new refinery to the vagaries of international politics, and especially to the risk of another Arab-Israeli war. While future embargoes on the export of foreign oil to the U.S. are believed to be unlikely, it must be remembered that the 1973 embargo was also said to be unlikely or even impossible.

Second, total dependence on foreign oil would put a new refinery under the threat of changes in U.S. policy toward imports. For various reasons—balance of payments, strategic non-dependence, etc.—the federal government might in the future invoke restrictions in imports of crude oil by means of quotas, high tariffs or other limitations. Such restrictions would severely damage the operations of a new refinery wholly dependent on imported crude oil.

Since potential new entrants to refining quite likely would not perceive access to foreign crude oil as being either secure or competitive, some form of access to domestic crude oil would have to be available in order for entry to occur. Domestic crude oil supplies could be obtained in two ways: first, by means of purchases from domestic producers through either short or long-term contracts; and second, by developing future production within the firm through participation in the domestic oil and gas lease market. Short-term oil supply contracts offer no security to an entering refiner. Because of the uncertain regulatory environment, suppliers may be unwilling to enter into long-term crude supply contracts. Further, crude producers tend to be tied into pipeline systems and buyers, and they may not be willing or able to shift supplies to new entrants. Thus, new refiners could obtain neither secure nor competitive supplies of crude oil in the direct contract market. Access to the domestic oil and gas lease market is the only alternative which offers a new refiner both security of supply and competitive cost of raw materials.

II. THE DOMESTIC CRUDE OIL LEASE MARKET

The market for crude oil leases may be divided into two general categories: developed and undeveloped properties. Purchasers of an undeveloped property engage in exploration, and if oil is discovered in commercial quantities, they make decisions about the rate of development and production. Buyers of developed properties gain immediate access to crude oil production. Prices of the two kinds of properties (assuming they have the same expected production potential) are approximately equal after adjustment for cost and risk.

Existing firms might attempt to discourage entry into refining by buying up developed and undeveloped crude oil properties.[11] Both kinds of properties would have to be controlled since exploration and development, like refinery construction, are usually carried out by contractors and not by the major oil companies. Potential entrants to refining would have access to these contractors on the same terms as the major oil companies. Therefore, in order to maintain output restrictions, existing refiners would be forced to absorb newly offered crude oil properties into their reserve inventories. Their ability to maintain this policy would be undercut by two factors. First, the federal government has set an initial term of five years on all its crude oil leases (the major source of new oil properties in the U.S. at present) and has further imposed "due diligence" requirements on all leaseholders.[12] Second, oil properties which are not presently in production often encounter "common property" problems when contiguous properties are under production. Since crude oil will migrate to the lands under production in these cases, the holder of lease inventories will suffer unacceptable losses if he refuses to produce from his lands.[13] In addition to these factors, an important economic consideration would affect the ability of lease buyers to profitably follow the strategy of adding all newly offered oil properties to their land inventories: if the in situ price of oil was expected to rise at a slower rate than the existing rate of interest, the cost of carrying this oil would be an offset against the monopoly rents which

---

11. Restrictions on output could not profitably be effected through large-scale storage of crude oil or products since such storage is prohibitively expensive.

12. O.C.S. Regulations, 30 C.F.R. § 250.33 (1977).

13. This factor forced the federal government to produce from its lands in Wyoming (Teapot Dome) and California (Elk Hills) earlier than was desired; it also convinced the government to conduct the O.C.S. lease sale offshore from Santa Barbara, California in 1968.

could be earned through output restrictions. On the other hand, if the in situ price was expected to rise faster than the rate of interest, these gains from conservation would be augmented by any monopoly gains.

The limited data relating to crude oil reserves holdings by the Big 4 and Big 8 oil companies (Table 1) do not support the hypothesis of preemptive lease buying. Additional evidence on this question is provided by an analysis of the conditions of competition in the domestic lease market.

Suppliers in the domestic crude oil lease market fall into four principal categories:

1. The federal government controls the supply of potential producing properties on the Outer Continental Shelf (OCS), an area beginning at the three mile limit for all states except Texas and Florida, and extending seaward to the limit of operability. It also controls onshore lands in the public domain and influences the leasing of Indian lands onshore.

2. States control the supply of offshore lands within their jurisdiction as well as some onshore lands, particularly in Alaska and Texas.

3. Other legal entities within some states (i.e., the City of Long Beach, the University of Texas, American Indians, native associations in Alaska) control potential oil properties.

4. Privately owned lands continue to be a major source of onshore leases.[14] The Federal Energy Administration (FEA) has estimated that a continuing decline in the rate of oil production from existing (1976) wells will mean that only one third of current production will continue into 1985. This drop in production will be replaced, according to the FEA, as follows: 40 percent from new fields, 40 percent from expansion of known fields, and 20 percent from tertiary recovery. The new fields are expected to be developed almost entirely in two areas: OCS and state lands offshore and Alaska onshore.[15] Since all offshore and Alaska lands will be leased under competitive leasing procedures, entry of new producers over the next decade will be extremely difficult to forestall.

III. THE STRUCTURE OF THE LEASE MARKET

A. Buyer Concentration

Concentration data are reported in Table 2 for acreage, bonus

14. Oil producing firms are rarely owners of oil lands. They are lessees and pay royalties to the land owners (lessors) listed above. As lessees, they have less discretion concerning the rate of development and production, and a smaller economic incentive to attempt to restrict output.

15. FEA NATIONAL ENERGY OUTLOOK, 63-65 (1976).

bids, and production for OCS leases. Acreage and bonus bids are both proxies for ownership of the resources in question: oil and gas. Both proxies are reported because, while larger acreage may correspond with larger ultimate production, larger bonus payments may correspond with greater likelihood of finding oil or gas in producible quantities. Concentration ratios are reported on a year-by-year basis, 1954 to 1976, for each year in which more than 100 leases were bid on. Big-4 and Big-8 firms were chosen on the basis of rankings in crude oil production, U.S. and worldwide, for 1969-1970.[16]

Concentration data reveal considerable variation in C_4 and C_8 ratios for bonus payments on a yearly basis, but the trend has been generally downward (Table 2). Concentration ratios in acreage show a definite downward trend except for a large rise in C_8 in 1964.

Concentration ratios for production show increases from the initial values of 1960 (the first year calculated) to maximum values in 1965 ($C_4 = .64$ and $C_8 = .86$), with declines occurring thereafter. One probable explanation of the 1965 "hump" is that, due to the high risk of entry into offshore oil and gas production, Big-8 firms may have had an initial comparative advantage in locating reserves or in developing leases to maximum productivity.

Summarizing the concentration data, all ratios for the 1970's are below the four-firm and eight-firm levels of 50 percent and 70 percent frequently used to demarcate non-competitive market structures. Though individual ratios rose above these levels in certain years (particularly 1964 and 1968), the weighted average ratios over the entire period for bonus payments, acreage, and production are all below these critical levels. Most importantly, the ratios are much lower in recent years than in the 1964-69 period.

These OCS lease concentration ratios may be compared to averages computed for 292 U.S. manufacturing industries by Mueller and Hamm, who reported Big-4 concentration to be 41.5 percent and Big-8 concentration to be 54.3 percent in 1970.[17] Relative to the Mueller-Hamm averages, we find concentration ratios in all our applications to be low on a weighted average basis, except for the C_8 ratios for liquid production and for acreage leased (which are still below the Bain critical level of 70 percent).

---

16. These eight firms correspond exactly with those currently cited in antitrust action by the Federal Trade Commission (F.T.C. Docket #8934). If firms had been selected on the basis of total acreage acquired over the 1954-76 period (rather than by production), the only change would have been the replacement of Shell by Sun Oil Company.

17. Mueller & Hamm, *Trends in Industrial Market Concentration, 1947 to 1970*, 65 REV. ECON. STATISTICS 512, (1974).

TABLE 2

CONCENTRATION IN THE OCS OIL AND GAS LEASE MARKET,
1954-1976

Year	Number of Leases Issued	Bonus C_4 Yearly	Bonus C_8 Yearly	Acreage C_4 Yearly	Acreage C_8 Yearly	Liquid Production C_4	Liquid Production C_8	Gas Production C_4	Gas Production C_8
1954	109	.418	.653	.506	.710				
55	121	.244	.508	.274	.664				
56	**	**	**	**	**	see note		see note	
57	**	**	**	**	**	***		***	
58	**	**	**	**	**				
59	42	*	*	*	*				
60	147	.142	.440	.163	.568	.430	.732	.073	.458
61	**	**	**	**	**	.395	.849	.138	.471
62	420	.436	.652	.354	.612	.441	.785	.118	.445
63	57	*	*	*	*	.473	.803	.136	.513
64	124	.418	.750	.212	.817	.554	.827	.200	.534
65	**	**	**	**	**	.642	.866	.320	.622
66	42	*	*	*	*	.621	.855	.436	.758
67	158	.278	.582	.301	.551	.573	.819	.385	.668
68	197	.563	.672	.472	.585	.545	.790	.356	.671
69	36	*	*	*	*	.500	.726	.284	.585
70	138	.149	.264	.141	.299	.431	.684	.232	.510
71	11	*	*	*	*	.362	.633	.233	.504
72	178	.196	.387	.194	.428	.340	.633	.236	.490
73	187	.231	.412	.151	.425	.289	.623	.218	.461
74	348	.305	.580	.258	.491	.268	.577	.192	.393
75	321	.301	.542	.280	.588	.267	.575	.208	.397
76	246	.274	.503	.315	.558	.288	.572	.206	.392
Weighted Average		.287	.508	.294	.570	.376	.657	.232	.474

*fewer than 100 tracts bid on
**no lease sales
***not calculated prior to 1960 due to small
  levels of production

Derived from: a) U.S. Bureau of Land
  Management, *OCS Statistical
  Summaries.*
  b) U.S. Geological Survey,
  LPR 11.8.1 (process date
  9/22/77).

Note: All concentration ratios are calculated
using firm shares of jointly
owned leases.

C_4: includes Exxon, Texaco, Gulf
and Chevron.
C_8: includes C_4, Shell, Mobil,
Standard Oil of Indiana and
Atlantic Richfield.

B. Conditions of Entry into the Lease Market

The potentially significant barriers to entry into the OCS lease
market are (1) the capital cost of the bonus payment which must be
tendered prior to development or production; and (2) the high risk

of a dry hole or an uneconomic discovery leading to a total loss of both bonus payments and exploration-drilling costs. The device of joint bidding is a means of reducing these barriers to entry.

The record of entry into the OCS lease market is reported in Table 3. Twenty firms participated in winning bids in the first OCS lease sale (1954). The number of firms participating in winning bids had doubled by 1966 and doubled again by 1972. Through 1976, 137 separate firms had participated in winning bids for OCS leases.

The practice of joint bidding has greatly increased over time. From 1954 through the February 6, 1968 lease sale, 33 percent of all winning bids were joint bids. In subsequent sales (through 1977), the share of joint winining bids increased to 54 percent. This increase in successful joint bidding occurred at the same time that the share of leases won by the Big-8 firms showed a modest decline from 66 percent in the 1954-1968 period to 59 percent in the 1968-1977 period.[18] This suggests that joint bidding has produced pro-competitive results by lowering barriers to entry.

TABLE 3

RECORD OF ENTRY INTO THE OCS OIL AND GAS LEASE MARKET, 1954-1976

Year of Lease Sale	Number of Tracts Bid On	Number of Firms Winning Bids (Solo or Joint)	Number of Firms Entering Market For First Time	Cumulative Number of Firms In Market
1954	116	20	20	20
1955	121	21	5	25
1959	*	*	3	28
1960	173	24	2	30
1962	436	31	9	39
1963	*	*	1	40
1964	101	15	0	40
1966	*	*	0	40
1967	172	34	9	49
1968	237	46	18	67
1969	*	*	1	68
1970	148	41	4	72
1971	*	*	0	72
1972	192	55	11	83
1973	193	59	8	91
1974	435	74	11	102
1975	395	91	25	127
1976	271	71	10	137

*Fewer than 100 tracts bid on
Derived from: U.S. Department of Interior, Geological Survey, Conservation Division, *LPR 11.8.1* (process date 9/22/77).

18. BUREAU OF LAND MANAGEMENT, SUMMARY OCS STATISTICS (1954-1976).

Our interpretation is supported by an analysis conducted by Wilcox which found a significant negative relationship between firm size (asset value) and the percentage of tracts won through joint bidding, indicating that "smaller firms more frequently utilize the joint bidding structure than larger firms."[19]

An analysis by Dougherty and Lohrenz concluded that joint bids tend to occur on leases with a higher average number of bids per lease and a higher average bid per acre. They further found that "joint bidding is a method whereby bidders with limited financial resources moderate their risk while competing for the more expensive and sought-after leases," and on these leases they "tend to bid higher on the average than their solo-bidding competitors."[20] Markham's analysis of the history of bidding for OCS oil and gas leases in 1968 reached a similar conclusion: ". . . the evidence does not support the hypothesis that joint bids are at the expense of solo bids; indeed, if one were forced to guess, the better guess is that joint bids increase rather than reduce the total number of bidders."[21]

The theoretical expectation that joint bidding should increase participation by small firms in OCS leasing by lowering front-end capital requirements and spreading risk over more tracts is born out in the empirical analyses cited above. Furthermore, any potential anti-competitive consequences of joint bidding by large firms, which are fully able to bid separately on a large number of tracts, have been obviated by a 1975 regulation issued by the Interior Department banning joint bids among firms that individually produce more than 1.6 million barrels of crude oil equivalent per day.[22] The net impact of joint bidding, therefore, is to increase the number and size of bids (on average) and to increase the share of bids won by smaller firms.

Although there is no evidence in the record implying dominance of the OCS lease market by major oil companies, a suspicion still remains that such companies may have attempted to withhold production in order to capture monopoly gains. This possibility is greatly reduced by a stipulation in all federal and most state leases which permits cancellation of the lease if no production has been

---

19. S. Wilcox, Joint Venture Bidding and Entry into the Market for Offshore Petroleum Leases, 106-107 (unpublished Ph.D. dissertation, University of California, Santa Barbara, March 1975).

20. E. Dougherty & J. Lohrenz, *Statistical Analysis of Bids for Federal Offshore Leases,* 1976 J. PETROLEUM TECH., 1137, 1781.

21. Markham, *The Competitive Effects of Joint Bidding by Oil Companies for Offshore Leases,* in INDUSTRIAL ORGANIZATION AND ECONOMIC DEVELOPMENT 124 (Markham & Papanek, eds., 1970).

22. Promulgation by the Secretary of Interior, Oct. 1, 1975. 43 C.F.R. §11.3300 (1977).

developed within five years.[23] The lessee could attempt to produce from a lease at less than the maximum efficient rate, but even this possibility is constrained by the right of the government to insist upon "prompt and diligent" development of production.

The only proven instance of monopoly restraint over domestic crude oil production which created artificially high prices occurred under state controls through market demand prorationing. This exercise of market power was authorized by federal government legislation. Moreover, the federal government directly supported the program by cutting allowable production from its OCS leases. This program was not a reflection of private monopoly, but one of government monopoly exercised on behalf of the crude oil production industry in the U.S.[24]

The evidence reported here indicates that entry into the OCS lease sale market is relatively free and that the joint bidding device facilitates additional entry, primarily by small firms. With the exception of federal onshore lands not on a "known geological structure," federal and state oil leases are sold under competitive auction bidding conditions similar to those governing the OCS, generating similar free entry and competitive pricing results. We have discovered no evidence that lease buyers are constrained from entering these lease markets.

C. Constraints on the Supply of Leases

The supply of new crude oil leases is not subject to direct control by the private oil industry. Private oil companies might conceivably influence the rate of leasing through lobbying activities within federal or state governments, but there is no evidence in the record to indicate that such power was ever sought or exercised. Indeed, the record indicates the opposite—that the oil industry has consistently urged an accelerated leasing program. Leasing restraint, particularly since 1969, has come about primarily because of the objections of environmental groups.

The record of leases supplied offers little evidence of intentional supplier restraint by the federal government. OCS lease offers are initiated by the Bureau of Land Management (BLM) which publishes a Call for Nominations in the *Federal Register,* indicating an interest

---

23. The five-year rule may also constrain the optimum allocation of resources over time. Under competitive conditions, if producers of oil expect its in situ value to increase at a rate greater than its opportunity cost (the interest rate on investments of similar risk), they should reduce current production in favor of future production. By forcing earlier production, the five-year rule contradicts the goal of conservation.

24. The market demand prorationing system was effectively ended in 1972.

in leasing lands in a specified area. Interested parties are invited to nominate tracts for lease within this area. These nominations are reviewed by BLM which may add additional tracts to the sale list as well as delete any tracts which are deemed to pose environmental or other risks. The sale is then scheduled.[25] Over the 1954-75 period of OCS leasing, 49.1 percent of all tracts offered for lease received no bids.[26] This large percentage indicates an absence of government restraints on the supply of potential producing properties. Recent delays in federal lease sales have been created by Congressionally-mandated requirements for environmental studies and by the actions of federal judges in granting injunctions against development, not by a desire on the part of sellers of leases to withhold properties from the market.

VI. BEHAVIOR AND PERFORMANCE OF THE LEASE MARKET

The observed condition of relatively free entry into the lease sale market is of critical importance in evaluating competition in all phases of the petroleum industry. With free entry into the lease market, and consequent free entry into crude oil production, any attempt by private firms to reduce output in order to raise prices would produce only short-term monopoly profits.

If refiners attempt to reduce output and raise prices, they must either (1) accumulate inventories of crude oil or products, or (2) reduce the flow of crude oil by controlling its production. Storage of large quantities of crude oil or products is prohibitively expensive; even the federal government has rejected conventional storage methods for its strategic crude oil reserves. Long-run control of crude oil output by private firms is impossible given entry into the lease market.

Concentration ratios in petroleum refining are below the Mueller-Hamm average for all U.S. manufacturing. Big-4 and Big-8 concentration ratios in refining capacity were 29.7 and 51.8 percent, respectively, in 1976.[27] In that same year, 55 separate refining companies in the U.S. had refining capacity exceeding 30,000 barrels per day.[28] With existing concentration ratios and a large number of operating firms, successful collusion among firms to restrict output is probably impossible since colluding firms would be forced to yield market share to non-colluding rivals. Collusive behavior among refiners is

---

25. O.C.S. Regulations, 30 C.F.R. § 250 (1977).
26. Calculated from Bureau of Land Management, O.C.S. Statistical Summaries.
27. See Table 1.
28. NATIONAL PETROLEUM REFINERS ASSOCIATION, U.S. REFINING CAPACITY ON JANUARY 1, 1971-77 (1977).

constrained in the long run by free access to crude oil supplies through the lease market.

Performance in the lease sale market is predictable from structural data cited above. Modest concentration and free entry conditions lead to an expectation of normal profits (an absence of monopoly profits) in oil and gas production from such leases.

To test the hypothesis that the OCS lease market has produced competitive results, we have analyzed the private profitability of all OCS oil and gas leases sold in the first twelve lease sales conducted by the federal government over the period 1954-1962. Eight hundred thirty-nine individual leases were included in our analysis. Bonus, rental and royalty payments as well as oil and gas production and revenue on each lease through 1976 are known precisely from U.S. Geological Survey (USGS) records. Exploration, development, and production costs were estimated on the basis of engineering data, plus knowledge of the precise number and depth of wells drilled on each lease through 1976 (again from USGS data). Future production from leases still in production in 1976 was estimated using a constant percentage decline forecast for production.

Future oil prices were assumed to be the 1976 price plus 5 percent per year through 1985 with a maximum price of $18.29 per barrel. In 1986, all leases were assumed to receive a price of $18.29 per barrel, with this price increasing 5 percent per year thereafter. The future natural gas price assumed for each lease was the 1976 price plus 20 percent per year through 1985, with a maximum price of $3.00 per thousand cubic feet (MCF). The price in 1986 was assumed to reach $3.83 per MCF on all leases, increasing at 5 percent per year thereafter.

Leases were assumed to shut down in the first year in which marginal costs exceeded marginal revenues from the lease. All leases were assumed to shut down in the year 2010.

The preliminary results of our analysis are found in Table 4. In the aggregate (all 839 leases), lessees earned a 9.49 percent *before-tax* rate of return on their investments. Non-Big-8 firms earned higher rates of return than Big-8 firms. Joint bidding firms earned higher rates of return than solo bidding firms. Reflecting their greater risk, wildcat leases earned higher rates of return than drainage leases.

For all categories of leases shown in Table 4, rates of return are low relative to other business earnings. For example, all manufacturing firms in the U.S. earned an average 19.2 percent rate of return before taxes over the period 1954-1975.[29] The low rates of return

29. Calculated from FEDERAL TRADE COMMISSION, QUARTERLY FINANCIAL REPORTS OF MANUFACTURING CORPORATIONS (1954-76).

reported in Table 4 are convincing evidence that the OCS lease market is highly competitive; indeed, it could be argued that oil producers paid too much for these leases, in comparison with opportunity costs. Monopsony profits clearly were not earned.

TABLE 4

INTERNAL RATE OF RETURN (BEFORE TAXES) ON OCS
OIL AND GAS LEASES IN THE GULF OF MEXICO, 1954-62

All leases (839)	9.49%
Big-8 leases (500)	8.76%
Non-Big-8 leases (339)	10.29%
Solo bid leases (616)	8.38%
Joint bid leases (223)	11.51%
Wildcat leases (811)	9.63%
Drainage leases (28)	6.77%

Note: These results are preliminary and are subject to revision due to subsequent corrections in the USGS data base, or to different assumptions in our analysis.

V. CONCLUSIONS

The structure of the crude oil lease market is competitive. Concentration ratios in OCS lease acquisition are low for the Big-4 and about average for the Big-8 oil companies. Entry into the lease sale market is relatively free.

Free entry into all lease markets where federal or state governments are the suppliers, plus relatively low concentration ratios in oil refining and marketing, mean that collusive behavior to restrain outputs and increase prices is unworkable in the long run. Successful collusion would require either (1) storage of crude oil or products, or (2) control over access to crude oil supplies. The former is prohibitively expensive; the latter does not exist.

Performance in the OCS lease sale market shows no evidence of monopsony profits. To the contrary, the rate of return earned on 1954-1962 OCS leases is below normal. The competitive bonus bidding system has returned more than normal economic rents to the public owners of OCS oil and gas resources. Free entry into domestic crude oil production has led to a competitive structure in oil refining and marketing in the U.S., producing workably competitive performance at all levels of the U.S. oil industry.

Chapter 13

ENERGY PRICES AND
THE U.S. ECONOMY, 1972-1976

EDWARD A. HUDSON and DALE W. JORGENSON*

INTRODUCTION

The purpose of this paper is to analyze the impact on the United States economy of higher energy prices resulting from the establishment of the OPEC oil cartel in late 1973 and early 1974. The year 1972 is the last year of the "old" regime of energy prices and provides the starting point for our study. The year 1976 is the most recent year for which detailed data on energy prices are available and it provides the termination point for our study. These years correspond to periods of vigorous expansion following the recessions of 1970 and 1974. However, they differ drastically with regard to the level of energy prices.

The main conclusions of our analysis of the impact of higher energy prices on the U.S. economy are the following:

1. GNP: Real GNP in 1976 was reduced by 3.2 percent because of the increase in energy prices from 1972 to 1976.

2. Energy: Total energy consumption in 1976 was reduced by 8.8 percent because of the increase in energy prices, resulting in a sizeable fall in the energy-GNP ratio.

3. Capital: The level of capital stock in 1976 was reduced by $103 billion in constant dollars of 1972 because of the increase in energy prices. This can be compared with 1976 gross investment of $165 billion in constant dollars.

4. Labor: Despite the reduction in GNP growth, employment in 1976 declined by only 0.5 million jobs as a result of higher energy prices. As a consequence, productivity growth fell substantially over the period 1972-1976.

Our overall conclusion is that higher energy prices have had a dramatic impact on the U.S. economy over the period 1972-1976. This impact is not limited to a reduction in the growth of energy consumption, but it has also resulted in a slowdown in economic growth, a weak recovery of capital spending, a substantial increase in employment and a decline in the growth of productivity. We now turn to a detailed examination of the mechanisms through which energy prices have affected the U.S. economy. We examine the shift

*Data Resources, Inc.

in the composition of total spending away from energy and energy-intensive goods and services. We will next consider the impact of a reduction of energy and energy-intensive inputs into the production sectors of the economy. Finally, we will analyze the impacts of these changes on investment and capacity and on employment and labor productivity.

ANALYTICAL FRAMEWORK

Our analysis of the effects of higher energy prices is based upon a dynamic general equilibrium model of the U.S. economy. The original form of the model was developed for the Energy Policy Project of the Ford Foundation.[1] Subsequent development of the model is outlined by Hudson and Jorgenson.[2] Production activity in this model is divided among ten sectors: agriculture and construction, manufacturing, transportation, services, and six energy sectors. There are thirteen inputs into each sector—intermediate inputs consisting of output from the ten producing sectors, together with three primary factors of production, including capital services, labor services and imports. Each producing sector supplies output to each of the ten intermediate sectors and to the four categories of final demand: personal consumption, investment, government purchases and exports.

The technology of each producing sector is represented by an econometric model giving the supply price of output as a function of the prices of primary and intermediate inputs and the level of technology.[3] Also, technical coefficients giving the use of each type of primary and intermediate input per unit of output for each producing sector are derived as functions of prices and productivity from these models of technology. Consumer preferences are represented

1. The original form of the model was presented in E. HUDSON & D. JORGENSON, ENERGY RESOURCES AND ECONOMIC GROWTH, FINAL REPORT TO THE ENERGY POLICY PROJECT Ch. 5 (1973).

2. A comprehensive description of the current version of the model is given in E. HUDSON & D. JORGENSON, THE LONG TERM INTERINDUSTRY TRANSACTIONS MODEL: A SIMULATION MODEL FOR ENERGY AND ECONOMIC ANALYSIS, FINAL REPORT TO THE APPLIED ECONOMIC DIVISION, FEDERAL PREPAREDNESS AGENCY (1977). A related discussion of the model in the policy analysis context is given in D. BEHLING, E. DULLIEN & E. HUDSON, THE RELATIONSHIP OF ENERGY GROWTH TO ECONOMIC GROWTH UNDER ALTERNATIVE ENERGY POLICIES (1976).

3. The econometric model of production also is described in E. BERNDT & D. JORGENSON, ENERGY RESOURCES AND ECONOMIC GROWTH, FINAL REPORT TO THE ENERGY POLICY PROJECT Ch. 3 (1973) and in Christenson, Jorgenson & Lau, *Transcendental Logarithmic Utility Functions*, vol. 55, no. 2, 65 Rev. Econ. Statistics 3 (Feb. 1973). A related application of the production model is given in Berndt & Wood, *Technology, Prices, and the Derived Demand for Energy*, 57 Rev. Econ. Statistics 259-68 (Aug. 1975).

by an econometric model giving the allocation of personal consumption expenditures among goods and services as a function of prices and income.[4] Given the final demands and the technical coefficients, the level of output from each sector can be determined. Then, using the levels of output and the technical coefficients, each sector's demand for intermediate and primary inputs, including energy, can be calculated.

In each period, the relative prices of all commodities are determined by the balance between demand and supply. Technical input coefficients are determined simultaneously with the prices. Final demands are also functions of these prices. Final demands and input coefficients together determine sectoral output levels and input purchases from the condition that there is balance between total demand and supply for each type of output. The condition that demands for capital and labor equal their supplies yields the prices of these primary inputs.

The supply of capital in each period is fixed by past investment. Variations in demand for capital services affect the price but not the quantity of these services. Similarly, the supply of labor time in each period is fixed by past demographic developments. Variations in demand for labor time by the producing sectors and by the household sector for consumption in the form of leisure affect the price of labor and the allocation of labor time between these market and nonmarket activities. Finally, the supply of saving by the household sector must be balanced by final demand for investment by the producing sectors. Dynamic adjustment to higher energy prices is modeled by tracing through the impact of investment on capacity expansion.[5]

Our dynamic general equilibrium model was used to simulate two economic growth paths over the 1972-1976 period. In the first simulation, actual values of the exogenous variables, including world oil prices, were employed as the basis for model solution. This simulation provides an estimate of the actual development of the U.S. economy between 1972 and 1976. In the second simulation, 1972

---

4. The econometric model of consumption is described in D. Jorgenson, *Consumer Demand For Energy*, INTERNATIONAL STUDIES OF THE DEMAND FOR ENERGY 309-28 (W. Nordhaus ed. 1977). The theory of this model also is developed in Christensen & Jorgenson, *The Structure of Consumer Preferences* vol. 4, no. 1 ANNALS SOCIAL ECON. MEASUREMENT 49-101 (1975) and Christensen, Jorgenson & Lau, *Transcendental Logarithmic Utility Functions*, vol. 65, no. 3 Am. Econ. Rev. 367-83 (June 1975).

5. A theoretical analysis of the dynamic adjustment process, in a macroeconomic growth model context, is presented by HOGAN, *Capital Energy Complementarity in Aggregate Energy-Economic Analysis*, ENERGY MODELING FORUM, INSTITUTE FOR ENERGY STUDIES, STANFORD UNIVERSITY (Sept. 1977).

energy prices were employed over the whole 1972-1976 period; i.e., world oil prices were held at their 1972 real values. As world oil prices are the only set of exogenous variables to change between the two simulations, the differences in simulated economic activity can be attributed solely to the impact of the oil price increase. (Other energy prices are affected by the oil price change so all energy prices change between the simulations.) Therefore, comparison between the two simulations provides the basis for analyzing the impacts of the energy changes on energy use and on the level and structure of economic activity.

OVERALL ECONOMIC IMPACT

The energy price increases, and the associated changes in energy use, have significant impacts on both the quantity and the price aspects of overall economic activity. The level of real GNP is reduced, or the rate of economic growth is slowed as a result of the energy changes, while the structure of spending and production is also changed. The overall price level is increased, or the rate of inflation is raised from the energy changes, at the same time as the structure of relative prices is altered.

The rise in energy prices leads to a reduction in real GNP. The simulated level of real GNP for 1976 under actual energy price conditions was 3.2 percent lower than its simulated level under 1972 energy prices. There are two broad sets of reasons for this decline, one centering on input productivity and one centering on capital. Producers can economize on energy by substituting other inputs for energy. This substitution is not perfect, so that productivity is adversely affected. In addition, any additional input used as a substitute for energy must be taken from some other use, further detracting from overall productive potential. The result is that a given set of primary inputs can sustain a lower real GNP than would be possible without the restructuring of production patterns caused by the energy price increases.

A second result of the energy-induced changes is a reduction in the demand for capital services. The rise in energy prices leads to a decline in the rate of return on capital. This reduces the incentive for saving and investment, slowing the rate of capital formation. In addition, the energy price increase and the reduced level of real GNP lead to less saving and to a change in the allocation of income between consumption, on the one hand, and saving and investment on the other. This further slows the rate of capital formation. There is, then, a slowing of the rate of growth of productive capacity with the result that the level of potential GNP is lower than would have been the case at lower energy prices. The combination of substitution and capacity expansion effects results in an estimated reduction in 1976 real GNP of 3.2 percent.

The rate of economic growth, as well as the level of real GNP at any time, is affected by higher energy prices. The substitution or productivity changes affect the level of GNP; after the adjustment to the new spending and production patterns has been made there is no further pressure from this source tending to reduce GNP. This results in a shift to lower economic growth path but it does not depress the underlying growth rate. The capacity expansion effect, however, can have a longer lasting impact. At reduced GNP levels, under higher energy prices and with the reduced rate of return, savings and investment account for a smaller fraction of income. The resulting slowdown in the rate of capacity expansion works to reduce the rate of economic growth. Only in the long run will the rate of growth return to the underlying trend. Since this new economic growth path is, at every point, below the previous path, the loss of income or production resulting from higher energy prices is permanent.

Inflation will be accelerated by the higher energy prices, since the direct impact of higher energy prices is to raise the level of output prices as the energy prices are passed through the whole cost structure. In addition, the shift from energy towards other inputs results in some loss of productivity and some further increases in unit costs, adding to inflationary pressures. The inflationary effects can be complicated by the labor productivity changes. If wage and salary demands are based on past trends, and if they are granted, then the slowdown in labor productivity growth means that unit labor costs will rise more rapidly than previously, giving further impetus to inflation. All of these effects, however, correspond to a transition to a higher price level, not to a higher rate of price increase. They give inflation only a temporary increase. It is only if some additional feedback mechanism such as a price-wage-price spiral comes into operation that these short-run inflationary impacts can be translated into a permanent rise in the rate of inflation.

EFFECT ON ECONOMIC STRUCTURE

The structure of economic activity, as well as the level of output, changes as a result of the energy price increases. Higher energy prices raise the whole price structure. In addition, the pattern of relative prices is changed with the more energy intensive goods experiencing the largest price increases. These price changes induce a shift in the pattern of final demand spending away from the now more expensive energy intensive products. Similarly, the pattern of inputs into production is altered with the role of energy being reduced. Since both the mix of final demand and the way in which output is made are adjusted away from energy, the composition of total output shifts away from energy and energy-intensive sectors. Thus, the energy content of each dollar of GNP is reduced.

Final demand patterns alter as a result of the energy price rises, partly in response to the price increases themselves and partly as a result of the associated reduction in income levels. The essence of the final demand changes is a movement away from energy intensive, and now more expensive, products. Table 1 shows the change in the pattern of final demand between the high and low energy price simulations. This gives the allocation of real final demand—personal consumption expenditure, investment, government purchases and exports—over the four non-energy products and delivered energy. The principal change is the reduction in the relative importance of energy purchases.

TABLE 1

COMPOSITION OF REAL FINAL DEMAND IN 1976
(PERCENT OF TOTAL REAL FINAL SPENDING)

	Simulated with 1972 energy prices	Simulated with actual energy prices
Agriculture, Construction	12.3	12.0
Manufacturing	32.4	32.2
Transportation	2.6	2.5
Services, Trade, Communications	48.8	49.9
Energy	3.9	3.4
Total	100.0	100.0

The share of energy in total real final demand declines from 3.9 percent under low energy price conditions to 3.4 percent with higher energy prices. Purchases of transportation and of agriculture and construction show the next largest declines while the share of manufacturing is reduced slightly. Purchases of services are increased, absorbing the expenditure directed away from each other type of output. The services' share of total real final demand rises from 48.8 percent at the lower energy prices to 49.9 percent under the higher price conditions. In sum, final demand is redirected from energy to non-energy products and, within the non-energy group, it is redirected to the purchase of services.

Producers respond to higher energy prices in a way analogous to final demand. The motivation is to minimize unit costs in the face of the new price structure. The direction of adjustment is to economize on energy input and, given time to adjust, significant reductions in energy use are cost-effective under a regime of high energy prices. This reduction in energy use is not costless; it is achieved by increases in the use of labor services, capital services and other intermediate inputs. What is involved, therefore, is a redirection of input patterns away from energy, not a net reduction in input levels. The changes in input patterns can be represented by changes in input-output coefficients. These coefficients are given in Table 2 for four input categories—capital services, labor services, energy, and materials (all other intermediate inputs)—into each non-energy producing sector. Two sets of coefficients are given for each sector, one the simulated 1976 coefficients, the other the coefficients simulated for 1976 on the basis of the 1972 energy prices.

The result of the adjustment from lower to higher energy prices is that for every sector the energy input coefficient is reduced. Thus, considerable energy savings are achieved in production activities. The greatest proportionate energy reductions are estimated to occur in services and in manufacturing, where the energy input coefficient is reduced by about 15 percent. Agriculture, construction and transportation obtain energy savings of half this amount. There are also considerable differences among the sectors as to how the other inputs are adjusted to compensate for reduced energy use. Labor input is increased in all sectors and capital input is decreased in all sectors other than services. Manufacturing shows particularly noticeable adjustments: the 16 percent reduction in the energy coefficient is accompanied by a 4 percent reduction in the capital coefficient, with both of these reductions being offset by the 3 percent increase in labor intensity of production.

Patterns of input into production in each sector move toward less energy use. Final demand patterns are adjusted away from energy-intensive goods and services. These two changes in combination mean that the pattern of gross sectoral outputs is altered and that the nature of this change is a shift away from energy and energy-intensive products. Table 3 summarizes these changes. The relative importance of the energy sector is reduced substantially, from 5.9 percent to 5.0 percent of total output. Transportation shows the next largest relative decline while agriculture, construction and manufacturing show smaller reductions. The role of services increases significantly. There is, then, a redirection of production in the economy away from energy, and to a lesser extent away from goods and towards service activities.

TABLE 2

INPUT-OUTPUT COEFFICIENTS FOR INPUTS INTO PRODUCTION
(SIMULATED COEFFICIENTS FOR 1976)

	Coefficient Corresponding to Energy Price For:		Difference[1] (Percent)
	1972	1976	
Agriculture:			
Capital	.2242	.2222	−0.9
Labor	.2532	.2591	2.3
Energy	.0219	.0204	−7.0
Materials	.5007	.4983	−0.5
Manufacturing:			
Capital	.1059	.1015	−4.1
Labor	.2822	.2909	3.1
Energy	.0215	.0181	−15.8
Materials	.5904	.5895	−0.2
Transportation:			
Capital	.1777	.1743	−1.9
Labor	.4102	.4135	0.8
Energy	.0415	.0380	−8.4
Materials	.3706	.3742	1.0
Services, Trade, Communications:			
Capital	.2962	.2995	1.1
Labor	.4262	.4347	2.0
Energy	.0176	.0143	−18.8
Materials	.2599	.2515	−3.2

1. Percentage difference of the coefficients corresponding to 1976 energy prices relative to those based on 1972 energy prices.

These changes in the structure of economic activity are significant. First, they imply that all aspects of the economy are affected by the energy price changes, despite the relatively small fraction that energy represents in total economic output. Thus the relative sizes of the different sectors of the economy are affected as well as spending patterns and production patterns. In addition, the use of capital and labor inputs will be affected throughout the economy. Second, these structural changes have the effect of reducing the energy content of spending and of production. This means that, under the higher energy prices, each dollar of GNP requires less energy input.

REDUCTIONS IN ENERGY USE

In 1972 the U.S. used 72.0 quadrillion Btu's of primary energy input to sustain a real GNP of $1171 billion in constant dollars of

TABLE 3

COMPOSITION OF REAL GROSS OUTPUT IN 1976
(PERCENT OF TOTAL REAL GROSS OUTPUT)

	Simulated with 1972 energy prices	Simulated with actual energy prices
Agriculture, Construction	10.2	10.1
Manufacturing	33.3	33.2
Transportation	4.0	3.9
Services, Trade, Communications	46.6	47.8
Energy	5.9	5.0
Total	100.0	100.0

1972. This corresponds to an energy-GNP ratio of 61.4 (million Btu's per dollar (1972)). In 1976, GNP had increased to $1275 billion in constant dollars but energy use had risen only to 73.7 quadrillion Btu's,[6] giving a significantly reduced energy-GNP ratio. If the 1972 energy-GNP ratio still applied in 1976, the primary energy input required to sustain the actual 1976 GNP would have been 78.3 quadrillion Btu's. Further, if GNP had not been reduced by 3.2 percent as a result of the energy changes, the required energy input would have been 80.8 quadrillion Btu's. In these very aggregative terms, therefore, the changes in energy use patterns and economic structure induced by the rise in energy prices are shown to have resulted in an annual energy reduction of 7.1 quadrillion Btu's by 1976. The mechanisms yielding this energy saving are now outlined.[7]

The composition of real final demand changed significantly between the high and low energy price simulations. These changes were presented above. They imply that the direct energy content of a given total of real final spending is reduced in response to the rise in energy prices. Between the two simulations there is a reduction of 0.45 percent in the share of spending going to energy. When applied to the simulated 1976 total real final spending of $1330 billion in constant dollars, this represents a reduction of $6.0 billion in constant dollars in the demand for energy.

The non-energy component of real final spending accounts for the larger proportion of total final spending in 1976 as a result of higher

6. U.S. primary energy input in 1976 is estimated to be 73.7 quadrillion Btu; see, II ENERGY INFORMATION ADMINISTRATION xx (1978).

7. The role of energy in the current recovery also is discussed in JORGENSON, *The Role of Energy in the U.S. Economy*, NAT'L TAX J. (forthcoming). The impact of energy policy on future U.S. economic growth is considered in HUDSON & JORGENSON, *Energy Policy and U.S. Economic Growth* vol. 68 AMER. ECON. REV. 2 (1978).

energy prices. This shift in itself implies that more energy will be absorbed in satisfying non-energy final demand. Also, composition of spending as between the non-energy types of goods and services is altered. Services absorb a greater part of this spending while the other sectors decline in relative importance. Since services are the least energy-intensive type of production, this corresonds to a shift away from energy-intensive purchases. This shift works to reduce the energy content of final demand. These two types of adjustment work in opposite directions as far as energy use is concerned. The net change in the energy content of non-energy final demand could, therefore, be either positive or negative.

The information needed to calculate the impact of the change in non-energy final demand on energy utilization is presented in Table 4. This table determines the direct energy requirements for 1976 non-energy final demand spending, as well as the energy requirements of the same total spending allocated over commodities in the pattern associated with 1972 energy prices. Under the higher energy prices, there is a reduced requirement for direct energy for agriculture and construction, manufacturing and transportation. In contrast, spending on services is increased and this additional energy demand is sufficient to offset the energy reduction in the other three sectors. The net effect is that the direct energy content of non-energy final spending increases as a consequence of the higher energy prices. The increase is small, about $0.4 billion in constant dollars,

TABLE 4

CHANGE IN DIRECT ENERGY CONTENT OF
1976 REAL NON-ENERGY FINAL DEMAND
(REAL VARIABLES IN BILLION DOLLARS (1972))

	Real Final Demand in Pattern for Prices of:[1]		Energy Input Coefficient:[2]	Energy Content for Spending in Pattern of:[3]		Change in Direct Energy Content:[4]
	1976	1972		1976	1972	
Agriculture, Construction	159.0	163.6	.0219	3.48	3.58	−0.10
Manufacturing	428.4	431.0	.0215	9.21	9.27	−0.06
Transportation	33.1	34.5	.0415	1.37	1.43	−0.06
Services, Trade, Communications	663.5	649.0	.0176	11.68	11.42	0.26
				25.75	25.70	0.04

1. Total real final demand in the 1976 simulation allocated over sectors in the 1976 patterns and in the pattern simulated for 1976, based on 1972 energy prices.
2. Input-output coefficients for energy into each producing sector as simulated for 1976, based on 1972 energy prices.
3. Direct energy input into each of the two sets of final demand.
4. Direct energy content of 1976 non-energy final demand allocated in the pattern corresponding to 1976 energy prices, less direct energy content of this final demand allocated in the pattern corresponding to 1972 energy prices.

but it does work to counter the energy reductions achieved by fewer direct final purchases of energy.

The pattern of inputs into each production sector also changes as a result of the energy price increases; these changes have been analyzed above in terms of adjustments in input-output coefficients. This restructuring of inputs means that the energy content of any set of total sectoral outputs is reduced. The implications of this reduction caused by energy saving are developed in Table 5. This table gives the energy content of the 1976 gross sectoral outputs for input patterns simulated under the 1976 energy prices, as well as the energy content of this output given the input patterns simulated on the basis of the 1972 energy prices. The change in energy content is the energy saving achieved by producing a given set of outputs in a less energy-intensive way. These energy savings are substantial, corresponding to $6.4 billion in contant dollars of 1972. The greatest energy savings are achieved in the manufacturing and the services sectors, reflecting the large size of these sectors and the substantial reductions in unit energy requirements achieved in these sectors.

The final type of energy saving is that due to a reduction in the overall level of economic activity. The rise in energy prices led to a reduction in 1976 real GNP, relative to its simulated level based on 1972 energy prices, of 3.2 percent. This reduction implies a decline of approximately 3.2 percent in energy use, even with no changes in economic structure. This yields an estimated $4.0 billion in constant

TABLE 5

CHANGE IN ENERGY CONTENT OF
1976 PRODUCTION DUE TO INPUT RESTRUCTURING
(REAL VARIABLES IN BILLION DOLLARS (1972))

	Total Output:[1]	Energy Input Coefficients for Energy Prices of:[2]		Energy Content with Coefficients of:[3]		Change in Energy Content:[4]
		1976	1972	1976	1972	
Agriculture, Construction	221	.0204	.0219	4.51	4.84	−0.33
Manufacturing	719	.0181	.0215	13.01	15.46	−2.45
Transportation	86	.0380	.0415	3.27	3.57	−0.30
Services, Trade Communications	1004	.0143	.0176	14.36	17.67	−3.31
				35.15	41.54	−6.39

1. Total real sectoral outputs in the 1976 simulation.
2. Input-output coefficients for energy into the production sectors for the 1976 simulation, and for the simulation of 1976 under 1972 energy prices.
3. Energy content of the given sectoral outputs under the two sets of energy input coefficients.
4. Energy content of 1976 output, given input based on 1976 energy prices less energy content of this output under the coefficients based on 1972 energy prices.

dollars as energy saved from reducing the scale of economic activity.

These changes show the mechanism of economic adjustment to higher energy prices and the resulting energy saving. In brief, there are three general sources of energy saving: the scale of economic activity is reduced, final demand becomes less energy intensive, and methods of production become less energy intensive. Using the approximations that these three types of energy reduction add up to the total estimated 1976 energy saving of 7.1 quadrillion Btu's, and that each constant dollar of energy purchases is equal to the same number of Btu's, we can allocate the total energy saving over its sources. The results are presented in Table 6.

TABLE 6

SOURCES OF ENERGY SAVING IN 1976

	Energy Reduction, Percent of Total		Energy Reduction Quadrillion Btu	
Changes in Final Demand				
Reduction in energy purchases	37.5		2.7	
Restructuring of non-energy purchases	− 2.5		−0.2	
Total		35.0		2.5
Changes in Inputs to Production				
Agriculture, Construction	2.1		0.1	
Manufacturing	15.3		1.1	
Transportation	1.9		0.1	
Services, Trade, Communications	20.7		1.5	
Total		40.0		2.8
Reduction in Economic Activity		25.0		1.8
Total Energy Reduction		100.0		7.1

Final demand changes account for 35 percent of the total saving, and all of this saving is due to redirection of final demand away from energy purchases and towards purchases of non-energy goods and services. Changes in input patterns, as represented by the input-output coefficients, account for 40 percent of the total energy saving. Reductions in energy used in service-oriented activities are the greatest single source of saving, at 21 percent of the total, with energy savings in the manufacturing sector, at 15 percent of the total, also being significant. Energy reduction in agriculture, construction and transportation provides a much smaller volume of saving, about 4 percent of the total. Reduction in the scale of economic activity resulting from higher energy prices yields the final 25 percent of energy saving. In terms of physical units of energy, the total saving of over 7 quadrillion Btu's is achieved by a reduction of 2.5 quads in final demand energy use, a reduction of 1 quad in manufacturing, a decline of 1.5 quads in services, and a decrease of almost 2 quads due to the reduced level of economic activity.

REDUCTION IN CAPITAL STOCK

The adjustments in spending and production patterns that reduce energy utilization relative to GNP also affect capital, labor and other factors of production. Demand for capital is affected as a result of changes in the mix of final demand and changes in the pattern of inputs into each sector. In addition, any effect of the energy changes on the level of real GNP will affect the overall level of demand for capital services as an input to production. Each of these three sources of change in demand for capital services will now be examined and the implications of the energy changes for investment and capacity growth indicated.

The change in the composition of final demand will alter the demand for capital input. For example, a decline in the proportion of spending directed to energy and an increase in spending on services will result in a different overall level of demand for capital services, since the capital requirements of these two types of production are different. The magnitudes of these changes are calculated in Table 7. This table presents the direct capital requirements of the simulated total 1976 real final demand when allocated over sectors in the 1976 patterns, and when allocated over sectors in the patterns corresponding to the 1972 energy prices. As a result of the higher energy prices, spending is directed away from energy and goods and towards services. The capital content of each type of production is held constant at the levels given by the input-output coefficients corresponding to 1972 energy prices. Under these conditions, the change in final demand composition leads to an increase in the direct requirement of capital services input of $1.3 billion in constant 1972 dollars. The central reason for this increase is the shift of spending towards services, which are relatively capital-intensive.

The demand for capital services also changes as a result of adjustments in the pattern of inputs to each producing sector. Specifically, the energy changes are accompanied by shifts in the capital input-output coefficients. In some sectors, production becomes more capital intensive; in other sectors it becomes less intensive. The overall

TABLE 7

CHANGE IN DIRECT CAPITAL INPUT TO 1976 REAL FINAL DEMAND
(REAL VARIABLES IN BILLION DOLLARS (1972))

	Real Final Demand Pattern for Prices of:[1]		Capital Input Coefficient:[2]	Capital Content for Spending in Pattern of:[3]		Change in Direct Capital Content:[4]
	1976	1972		1976	1972	
Agriculture, Construction	159.0	163.6	.2242	35.65	36.68	−1.03
Manufacturing	428.4	431.0	.1059	45.37	45.64	−0.28
Transportation	33.1	34.5	.1777	5.88	6.13	−0.25
Services, Trade Communications	663.5	649.0	.2962	196.53	192.23	4.29
Energy	45.7	51.6	.2396	10.95	12.36	−1.41
Total	1329.7	1329.7		294.38	293.04	1.33

1. Total real final demand in the 1976 simulation allocated over sectors in the 1976 pattern and in the pattern simulated for 1976, based on 1972 energy prices.
2. Input-output coefficients for capital into each producing sector as simulated for 1976, based on 1972 energy prices.
3. Direct capital input into each of the two sets of final demand.
4. Direct capital content of 1976 final demand allocated in the pattern corresponding to 1976 energy prices, less direct capital content of this final demand allocated in the patterns corresponding to 1972 energy prices.

change depends on the size of the shift in each sector and the magnitude of each sector. Estimates of the size of the overall change are presented in Table 8. This table gives the input of capital services needed to sustain the simulated 1976 set of sectoral outputs under two sets of conditions: the 1976 input patterns and the input patterns simulated for 1976 based on 1972 energy prices. The difference in total demand for capital services, a reduction of $0.3 billion in constant dollars of 1972, is due to a change in methods of production. Under higher energy prices manufacturing uses less capital services, while the services sector demands a higher input of capital. These are almost offsetting, resulting in a small overall decline in demand for capital.

In addition, the energy price increases lead to a reduction in the simulated 1976 real GNP below the level estimated on the basis of a continuation of 1972 energy prices. The 1976 real GNP was 3.2 percent less than the level estimated for lower prices. As an approximation, this corresponds to a 3.2 percent reduction in the demand for capital services input. In constant dollars of 1972 this results in a $15.5 billion reduction in demand for capital services purely because the overall level of economic activity has been reduced.

The three types of changes in demand for capital services can now be brought together. Under the first order approximation that these components can be added to find the total change in capital demand, this yields the result that total demand for the input of capital ser-

TABLE 8

CHANGE IN CAPITAL CONTENT OF
1976 PRODUCTION DUE TO INPUT RESTRUCTURING
(REAL VARIABLES IN BILLION DOLLARS (1972))

	Total Output:[1]	Capital Input Coefficients for Energy Prices of:[2]		Capital Content with Coefficients of:[3]		Change in Capital Content:[4]
		1976	1972	1976	1972	
Agriculture, Construction	221	.2222	.2242	49.11	49.55	−0.44
Manufacturing	719	.1015	.1059	72.98	76.14	−3.16
Transportation	86	.1743	.1777	14.99	15.28	−0.29
Services, Trade, Communications	1004	.2995	.2962	300.70	297.38	3.32
Energy	128	.2418	.2396	30.95	30.67	0.28
Total				468.73	469.02	−0.29

1. Total real sectoral outputs in the 1976 simulation.
2. Input-output coefficients for capital services into the production sectors for the 1976 simulation and for the simulation of 1976 under 1972 energy prices.
3. Capital content of the given sectoral outputs under the two sets of input coefficients.
4. Capital content of 1976 output, given input coefficients based on 1976 energy prices less capital content of this output under the coefficients based on 1972 energy prices.

vices in 1976 is reduced by $14.5 billion in constant 1972 dollars, due to the increase in energy prices. Capital services are the effective input services, or the implicit rental value, of capital stock. In any year, each dollar of capital stock provides about $0.14 of capital services. Therefore, this reduction in demand for capital services corresponds to a reduction of $103.3 billion in constant dollars in the desired level of capital stock. The allocation of this reduction over its sources is given in Table 9. The principal sources of change in demand for capital are the restructuring of inputs into manufacturing, which has a $22.4 billion reduction in constant dollars in demand for capital stock, the restructuring of inputs into services, which increases demand for capital stock by $23.5 billion in constant dollars, and the decline in the level of economic activity, which reduces demand for capital stock by $110.7 billion in constant dollars.

These are significant changes in the demand for capital. The overall decrease in demand for capital stock will be reflected by investment levels being lower than they would otherwise have been. If, as an illustration, all the capital adjustments were made in 1976, investment would be $103 billion less in constant dollars than would normally be expected. When this is compared to actual 1976 gross investment of $165 billion in constant dollars, it can be seen that the relative magnitude of the investment adjustment can be substantial.

TABLE 9

SOURCES OF REDUCTION IN CAPITAL STOCK IN 1976

	Capital Reduction, Percent of Total:	Capital Reduction, $(1972) billion:
Changes in Final Demand:	−9.2	−9.5
Changes in Inputs to Production:		
Agriculture, Construction	3.0	3.1
Manufacturing	21.9	22.4
Transportation	2.0	2.0
Services, Trade, Communications	−23.0	−23.5
Energy	− 1.9	− 2.0
Total	2.0	2.1
Reduction in Economic Activity:	107.2	110.7
Total Reduction in Capital Stock:	100.0	103.3

CHANGE IN EMPLOYMENT

Demand for labor and employment is affected by the energy-induced adjustments through a restructuring of final demand spending, a restructuring of the pattern of inputs into production, and a reduction in the overall level of economic activity. Final demand is redirected, as a result of the higher energy prices, away from energy and energy-intensive products. The implications of this adjustment for labor demand are presented in Table 10. The 1976 total real final demand is allocated over sectors in two patterns, one based on the 1976 energy prices, the other based on the lower 1972 energy prices. The direct energy content of these demands is calculated using one set of input-output coefficients. The result of the rise in energy prices is a substantial increase in labor demand. This increase of $2.9 billion in constant dollars of 1972 reflects the shift of final demand towards services and away from energy and goods. Since service activities have a higher labor content than any of these other sectors, the result of the shift is an increase in the labor content of each dollar of real final demand.

A restructuring of input patterns occurs in the producing sectors of the economy. In each sector increased labor input per unit of output results from the higher energy prices, so that the labor input for any given set of production outputs is increased. Table 11 presents the information necessary to make an exact calculation of this change in labor demand. In each sector, the labor input coefficient

TABLE 10

CHANGE IN DIRECT LABOR CONTENT OF 1976 REAL FINAL DEMAND
(REAL VARIABLES IN BILLION DOLLARS (1972))

	Real Final Demand in Pattern for Prices of:[1]		Labor Input Coefficient:[2]	Labor Content for Spending in Pattern of:[3]		Change in Direct Labor Content:[4]
	1976	1972		1976	1972	
Agriculture, Construction	159.0	163.6	.2532	40.26	41.42	−1.16
Manufacturing	428.4	431.0	.2822	120.89	121.63	−0.73
Transportation	33.1	34.5	.4102	13.58	14.15	−0.57
Services, Trade, Communications	663.5	649.0	.4262	282.78	276.60	6.18
Energy	45.7	51.6	.1329	6.07	6.86	−0.78
Total	1329.7	1329.7		463.58	460.66	2.92

1. Total real final demand in the 1976 simulation allocated over sector in the 1976 pattern and in the pattern simulated for 1976, based on 1972 energy prices.
2. Input-output coefficients for labor into each producing sector as simulated for 1976, based on 1972 energy prices.
3. Direct labor input into each of the two sets of final demands.
4. Direct labor content of 1976 final demand allocated in the pattern corresponding to 1976 energy prices, less direct labor content of this final demand allocated in the pattern corresponding to 1972 energy prices.

increases, leading to additional labor demand totaling $16.6 billion in constant dollars of 1972. The largest increases in labor demand occur in services and in manufacturing, although there is also a significant increase in the agriculture and construction sector.

These two structural shifts add substantially to the demand for labor. Together they amount to $19.5 billion in constant dollars of

TABLE 11

CHANGE IN LABOR CONTENT OF
1976 PRODUCTION DUE TO INPUT RESTRUCTING
(REAL VARIABLES IN BILLION DOLLARS (1972))

	Total Output:[1]	Labor Input Coefficients for Energy Prices of:[2]		Labor Content with Coefficients of:[3]		Change in Labor Content:[4]
		1976	1972	1976	1972	
Agriculture, Construction	221	.2591	.2532	57.26	55.96	1.30
Manufacturing	719	.2909	.2822	209.16	202.90	6.26
Transportation	86	.4135	.4102	35.56	35.28	0.28
Services, Trade, Communications	1004	.4347	.4262	436.44	427.90	8.54
Energy	128	.1344	.1329	17.20	17.01	0.19
Total				755.62	739.05	16.57

1. Total real sectoral outputs in the 1976 simulation.
2. Input-output coefficients for labor services into the production sectors for the 1976 simulation and for the simulation for 1976 under 1972 energy prices.
3. Labor content of the given sectoral outputs under the two sets of input coefficients.
4. Labor content of 1976 output, given input coefficients based on 1976 energy prices less labor content of this output under the coefficients based on 1972 energy prices.

1972, or 2.64 percent of the total demand for labor at the lower energy prices. If there had been no change in real GNP as a result of higher energy prices, the adjustment to these higher prices would greatly stimulate the demand for labor. If all of this increase were reflected in an increase in employment, it would imply a 2.6 percent reduction in the rate of unemployment as a result of higher energy prices. In the absence of an increase in energy prices, the rate of unemployment would have been 10.3 percent rather than the actual rate of 7.7 percent. In fact, the increase in energy prices reduced the level of GNP. This decreased the demand for labor and worked against the employment expansion which was resulting from high energy prices.

The estimated real GNP impact of the higher energy prices in 1976 is a reduction of 3.2 percent. This reduces the demand for labor by approximately 3.2 percent. Therefore, the overall impact on labor of the higher energy prices is a decrease in effective demand of 0.6 percent. The GNP decline, then, more than affects the employment increase resulting from the changed economic structure, so the net result in 1976 of the higher energy prices is a slight decline in labor demand and in employment. The structural increase in employment is significant, however, in that it serves to minimize the loss of employment associated with the lower general level of economic activity.

This change represents a reduction of 0.5 million jobs. Table 12 shows the sources of this change in employment. The restructuring of the inputs into production, as labor substitutes for energy input, adds substantially to labor demand. In particular, there are large increases in the manufacturing and services sectors. The change in final demand patterns adds only slightly to labor demand. These increases are more than offset by the effects of the reduced level of economic activity. All told, restructuring of inputs provides about two million more jobs, changed final demand patterns lead to 0.3 million jobs, and the decline in real GNP causes a loss of 2.8 million jobs.

The adjustments of spending and input patterns in response to higher energy prices leads to a substantial increase in the demand for labor. This increase in labor input is beneficial for employment, reducing the loss of jobs in the face of the GNP reduction, but it has an adverse effect on productivity. More labor input per unit of output is equivalent to less output per unit of labor input. These adjustments, therefore, lead to a reduction in the average gross productivity of labor. Specifically, the economic restructuring that occurs between the high and low energy price simulations leads to a 2.57 percent

TABLE 12

SOURCES OF REDUCTION IN EMPLOYMENT IN 1976

	Employment Reduction, Percent of Total:	Employment Reduction, Millions of Jobs:
Changes in Final Demand:	−71.1	0.3
Changes in Inputs to Production:		
Agriculture, Construction	−31.6	0.2
Manufacturing	−152.3	0.8
Transportation	−6.8	0.0
Services, Trade, Communications	−207.8	1.0
Energy	−4.6	0.0
Total	−403.1	2.0
Reduction in Economic Activity:	574.2	−2.8
Total Increase in Employment:	100.0	−0.5

reduction in average labor productivity. To place this change in perspective, it can be noted that the average annual rate of labor productivity increase between 1950 and 1970 was 1.44 percent. Against this norm, the reduction of 2.57 percent corresponds to the loss of two years of productivity improvement.

The decline in productivity growth implies that the rate of growth in real wages will not be as rapid as would otherwise have occurred. To the extent that real wages outstrip the slower growth of productivity, unit labor costs will increase and inflation will be accelerated. Lower productivity leads to slower real growth, slower growth of real wages, and more rapid inflation. It should be noted that these are one-time' effects rather than permanent trends. Once the economy has adjusted to the new labor and productivity conditions, there will be no further energy-induced pressures for further changes. Continued changes will occur only if there is a secondary wave of induced price responses.

CONCLUSIONS

The oil price increases beginning in 1973 have had a significant impact on the U.S. economy. One direct effect of the higher oil prices has been to raise all energy prices and to induce a reduction in the intensity of energy use throughout the economy. This change in energy use patterns is estimated to have reduced 1976 energy input from about 81 quadrillion Btu's, corresponding to historical energy use patterns, to the actual level of about 74 quadrillion Btu's. Analysis of the sources of this energy saving suggests that about one third of the savings came from a redirection of final demand—consumption, investment, government, and export purchases—away from energy and energy-intensive goods and services; that almost half came from a restructuring of patterns of input into production away from energy; and that one fourth came from the reduced scale of economic activity. Four particular facets of these changes stand out: a substantial reduction in direct final demand purchases of energy, an increase in final purchases of services, substantial reductions in energy input to manufacturing, and substantial reductions in energy input to the service industries.

The effects of the energy changes have spread throughout the entire economy. Demand for capital input is reduced as a result of the higher energy prices. This leads to a reduction in investment levels and to a slowing in the rate of growth of capital stock and productive capacity. Equally important is the change in demand for labor input. The adjustment in economic structure, with final spending shifted towards labor intensive services and with labor substituting for energy as an input into production, results in an increase in the demand for labor, largely offsetting the adverse employment impacts of the reduced level of economic activity resulting from the higher energy prices. It is estimated that in 1976 employment under the higher energy price conditions was only 0.6 percent, or 0.5 million jobs less than would have been the case if 1972 energy prices were still in effect.

These structural effects are of interest in themselves, but they are also of great importance in interpreting recent economic developments. Two features of the current economic recovery stand out sharply from the pattern of virtually all previous business cycle upswings. The first feature is that employment has expanded much more rapidly, and unemployment has declined to a greater extent, than would have been anticipated from past cyclical upturns. The second feature is that investment has picked up more slowly than would have been anticipated. But both of these developments tie in closely with the predicted effects of the energy changes. This suggests that the observed changes are due at least in part to structural shifts, permitting adjustment to lower energy use, being superimposed on the normal cyclical patterns of recovery from recession. A related feature of the present economic situation that is at variance with the pattern of previous recoveries is the low level of advance in productivity. But again, at least part of the reason for this result lies in the structural shifts, in particular the greater intensity of labor use, resulting from the energy changes.

Finally, the energy price increases have significant impacts on the level and growth of real GNP. The estimated decline in 1976 real GNP between a situation characterized by 1972 energy prices and the actual present energy price situation is 3.2 percent. This means that the oil price increase amounted for part, though certainly not all, of the recession of the mid-1970's. Further, the entire future economic growth path has been shifted down as a result of the energy changes so that, even if long-term future growth rates are not affected, the level of real GNP will always be less than it would have been in the absence of the oil price increase. The oil price rise has, therefore, imposed a significant and continuing cost on the U.S. economy.

Chapter 14

THE CONTINUING PROBLEM
OF NUCLEAR WASTE

ENVIRONMENTAL LAW–RADIOACTIVE WASTE STORAGE: The Energy Research and Development Administration (ERDA) must prepare site-specific environmental impact statements for the construction of high-level radioactive waste storage tanks in order to comply with the requirements of the National Environmental Policy Act. In addition, ERDA must look at design and safety alternatives in the construction of these tanks. *NRDC v. ERDA*, _____ F. Supp. _____(DDC 1978).

The National Resources Defense Council, Inc. (NRDC) and several other parties brought a three count suit against the Energy Research and Development Administration (ERDA) in the U.S. District Court for the District of Columbia concerning the construction of 22 high-level radioactive waste storage tanks at the Hanford Reservation in Richland, Washington and the Savannah River Plant in Aiden, South Carolina.[1] NRDC challenged ERDA's failure to seek and obtain licensing under section 202(4) of the Energy Reorganization Act of 1974[2] (the Energy Act) for the construction of the tanks. Further, NRDC alleged that the Nuclear Regulatory Commission (NRC) failed to assume jurisdiction and exercise its licensing authority over the tanks under section 202(4) of the Energy Act. The decision on the part of ERDA to not prepare site-specific environmental impact statements (EISs) for the waste tanks under section 102(2)(C) of the National Environmental Policy Act of 1969 (NEPA)[3] was also challenged by NRDC.

The 22 storage tanks in question were authorized by ERDA to be built in 1976 and 1977[4] to replace deteriorating tanks and to provide for storage of additional wastes.[5] The tanks, expected to be completed in 1979 and 1980, would all be double-shell, stress-relieved corbon steel tanks which should prevent leakage such as has occurred in the present single-shell tanks.[6] The existing tanks, as well

---

1. NRDC v. ERDA, _____F. Supp. _____, (D.D.C. 1978).
2. 42 U.S.C. § 5842(4) (Supp. II 1975).
3. 42 U.S.C. § 4332(2)(C) (1970).
4. ERDA projects 76-8-a, 76-8-b, 77-13-c, 77-13-d.
5. Most Government generated high-level radioactive wastes are presently stored at Hanford and Savannah.
6. Some 20 of the present tanks at Hanford and Savannah have leaked 450,000 gallons of high-level radioactive waste into the surrounding soil.

as the new ones, are considered by ERDA to be part of "an interim program" for waste management until a permanent storage program can be implemented.[7] Wastes would be stored in these new tanks for at least 15-20 years, and possibly longer. The licensing issue hinged on whether the new tanks would be for the long-term storage of high-level radioactive wastes, as opposed to short-term storage. NRDC wanted the tanks to be licensed by the NRC in order to have the "environmental, safety, and economic effects and implications" of waste storage in these tanks recognized and evaluated.[8]

ERDA sought a summary judgment on the licensing issue, alleging that the tanks were not licensable within the scope of section 202(4) of the Energy Act. This section states that the NRC shall have licensing authority over "facilities authorized for the express purpose of subsequent long-term storage of high-level radioactive waste."[9] ERDA claimed that these tanks were not for long-term storage. ERDA had told Congress these tanks were part of its "interim, i.e., short-term, storage of waste" and that "long-term storage will be available between 15 .and 20 years after construction of the tanks in question have been completed."[10]

NRDC contended that, in spite of what ERDA claimed, the tanks were facilities for the "express purpose of long-term storage." Therefore, they were licensable under section 202(4) of the Energy Act. Plaintiffs asserted that "long-term" storage meant any storage for more than 20 years. Plaintiffs based this contention upon language from a senate committee report dealing with NRC licensing under 202(4) of the Energy Act, which defined "long-term" as "tens to hundreds of years."[11] The district court, however, did not agree with this interpretation. The court stated any storage over 20 years does not necessarily have to be considered "long-term."

NRDC then claimed that any storage "substantially likely" to be used for more than 20 years was "authorized for the express purpose of long-term storage." The court said that Congress would have used the term "substantially likely" in defining "long-term storage" if they had wanted the statute to cover those situations. Summary judgments in favor of the defendants were therefore granted on the licensing issues.

ERDA denied that they violated section 102(2)(C) of NEPA by

---

7. An ultimate storage program is expected to be selected and implemented sometime between the years 1994 and 2000.
8. Plaintiff's memorandum, April 25, 1977 at 28.
9. *Supra* note 3.
10. S. Rep. No. 94-514, 94th Cong., 1st Sess. 76 (1975).
11. S. Rep. No. 93-980, 93d Cong., 2d Sess. 59 (1974).

not preparing site-specific EISs for the tanks in issue.[12] Such EISs, ERDA claimed, were not required because the 1976 tanks would not have a significant environmental impact[13] and, besides, the effects of all the tanks were analyzed in separate programmatic environmental impact statements (PEIS) for the entire Hanford and Savannah River projects.[14] But NRDC attacked the sufficiency of these PEISs as concerns the construction of the tanks. For NEPA requires, NRDC asserted, ERDA to "analyze design alternatives and alternative safety features for the new tanks and to evaluate the long-term planning and decision-making consequences of the present construction of the (tanks)."[15]

The court recognized that the PEISs for both the Hanford and Savannah River projects were necessary under Section 102(2)(C). But the construction of the new waste tanks, the court stated, might not be analyzed in enough detail in the PEISs to satisfy NEPA requirements.

In considering the PEISs, the court first held that they did not adequately cover design and safety feature alternatives. This was the case in spite of ERDA's argument that NEPA's "rule of reason" did not require an analysis of every conceivable project variation. ERDA had relied upon *Brooks v. Coleman*[16] in making this claim. In *Brooks,* the 9th Circuit held that an adequate EIS did not necessarily have to discuss a particular design alternative.

The D.C. Court limited the application of *Brooks* to its particular facts. In holding the PEISs to be inadequate, the court relied instead on two cases which held that "all reasonable alternatives must be considered even if such alternatives 'do not offer a complete solution to the problem.' "[17] It was noted that ERDA's own regulations require them to analyze reasonable alternatives.[18]

Both NRDC and ARHCO, ERDA's principle contractor at Hanford, had advanced reasonable, "focused and feasible," design and safety alternatives for the tanks in issue.[19] The court stated that

---

12. NEPA requires EISs to cover, among other things, "the environmental impact of (a) proposed action, any environmental effects which cannot be avoided should the proposal be implemented, and alternatives to the proposed action."

13. If this were true, NEPA would not require an EIS on them. This contention was later withdrawn.

14. The PEISs analyzed the overall ongoing waste management operations at Hanford and Savannah River.

15. *Supra* note 1, at _____.

16. 518 F.2d 17 (9th Cir. 1975).

17. NRDC v. Morton, 458 F.2d 827, 836 (DC Cir. 1972) aff'g 337 F. Supp. 165 (D.D.C. 1971); NRDC v. Callaway, 524 F.2d 79, 93 (2nd Cir. 1975).

18. 40 C.F.R. §1500.8(a)(4) (1977).

19. NRDC notified ERDA of these by letter in August 1975.

ERDA should have at least given reasons why the alternatives presented by NRDC should not have been considered further.

The court also found the PEISs were inadequate in discussing the "long-term planning and decision-making implications" of the construction of the tanks in issue. ERDA, in 1975, had been forced to act and to act quickly because of the leakages from some of the existing tanks. Their only choice was to construct some kind of new storage tanks. Within this choice, however, ERDA had had several decisions to make. The method of construction they selected determined both the durability of the tanks and the ease of removing the wastes from these tanks for placement in their ultimate storage place. Durability and ease of removal, in turn, would affect the selection of an ultimate storage program. Hence, the construction of these tanks has long-term planning implications. These were not discussed in the PEISs and so section 102(2)(C) of NEPA's requirements were not met.

The court granted NRDC's summary judgment motion on the NEPA issue. Further, ERDA was given 30 days in which to file a timetable for the preparation of adequate site-specific EISs for the tanks.

This case indicates that the problem of nuclear waste and nuclear waste storage is far from being solved. It is clear that reasonable design and safety alternatives of storage tanks and facilities need to be examined and implemented in dealing with the short-term solution of this problem. Long-term solutions are, however, at a minimum. Hopefully, cases such as this will demonstrate to ERDA that environmental groups will not accept an inadequate solution to the long-term problems associated with nuclear wastes and its storage.

ROBERT MUEHLENWEG

Chapter 15

CLEAN AIR ACT PROVISIONS EXTENDED TO OUTER CONTINENTAL SHELF

ENVIRONMENTAL LAW–CLEAN AIR ACT: EPA rules that provisions of the Clean Air Act are applicable to oil storage and treatment facilities located on the Outer Continental Shelf, although the Act itself is not expressly applicable to such facilities. 43 Fed. Reg. 16, 393 (1978).

"Preservation of the sea is prior to the law of the sea, in urgency as well as logic."[1]

"The future of the world's oil industry lies underwater. . . . Seismic exploration goes much faster on water–it's flat, and there are no obstructions."[2]

Today about one-fifth of the world's oil and gas is coming from offshore sources and the proportion could be half by the turn of the century. Scientists predict that there is far more petroleum to be found under the sea than on land.[3] As the energy squeeze tightens, large oil and mining companies are turning increasingly to developing these potentially richer offshore deposits. But opposition and concern over their efforts are mounting. Environmental and civic groups raise the specter of massive oil spills and other forms of pollution; concern about the inevitable development of large, onshore industries to augment the drilling has also been expressed. Government regulation has often lagged, however–with the hesitancy to be expected in formulating new rules or adapting old ones. A good example is the recent ruling by the Environmental Protection Agency (EPA) which extends its jurisdiction to the Outer Continental Shelf (OCS).[4] EPA debated the action for two years, then issued a bold and unequivocal ruling–one that is surely destined to a stormy, uncertain future.

The ruling requires Exxon Corporation to both comply with the Clean Air Act provisions for its proposed Santa Barbara oil storage and treatment facility and to obtain EPA approval before construct-

---

1. Abrams, *The Environmental Problems of the Oceans: An International Stepchild of National Egotism*, 5 ENVT'L AFF. 3, 30 (1976).
2. Marden, *The Continental Shelf: Man's New Frontier*, 153 NAT'L GEOGRAPHIC 495, 507 (1978).
3. Hudson, *The International Struggle*, BULL. ATOMIC SCIENTISTS (1977).
4. 43 Fed. Reg. 16,393 (1978).

ing this facility in the Santa Barbara Channel.[5] The ruling is not limited to the Exxon facility, but "apply(s) to all activities on the Outer Continental Shelf that can have an adverse effect on air quality over the United States."[6] The determination is the first of its kind and, unless overturned by a court ruling or congressional amendment, could affect all fixed structures on the OCS. The ruling concedes only that the Clean Air Act was intended to protect air quality over the geographical United States and, therefore, should not apply to structures so far from shore that they could not affect national air standards.[7]

The conditions giving rise to the new ruling originated a decade ago. In 1968, Exxon was one of several companies to obtain oil leases in the Santa Barbara Channel. The leases were consolidated and Exxon was named the unit operator.[8] The first tract to be developed was the Hondo field, where a platform was installed in June 1976. Exxon then sought to construct one of two alternate storage and treatment facilities proposed in the original development plan.[9] The first and preferred alternative called for the processing unit to be located on the Santa Barbara coast and connected via pipeline to the Hondo platform. But, as the company had anticipated, it was unable to obtain the necessary approval from state and local authorities to implement this alternative.[10] Undaunted, Exxon resorted to its so-called "offshore alternative."[11] This facility, a converted tanker with processing equipment mounted on its deck, would be moored to the Hondo platform located 3.2 miles from shore, just outside of state jurisdiction. The rather unusual "floating" unit was quickly approved by the Department of Interior.[12]

At this point, EPA opened hearings into Exxon's proposal. The move came as a surprise since the Agency had never before asserted jurisdiction with respect to the hundreds of oil exploration and development facilities that dot the Continental Shelf. But EPA was now buoyed with increased authority: the 1977 Amendments to the Clean Air Act substantially strengthened the provisions on preven-

5. *Id.*
6. *Id.*
7. *Id.* at 16,397.
8. *Id.* at 16,393.
9. Exxon submitted the development plan in 1971. It was approved by the Department of Interior in 1974 after preparation and circulation of a lengthy environmental impact statement.
10. Exxon was unable to obtain approval from the California Coastal Commission on terms acceptable to the company.
11. 43 Fed. Reg. 16,394 (1978).
12. *Id.*

tion of significant deterioration and new source review.[13] EPA
hoped to make it clear that it was willing to flex its muscles and
enforce the new provisions. In making its ruling, EPA interpreted the
law to its four corners, asserted its authority beyond the geographical
U.S., and deftly countered each of Exxon's objections.

Exxon argued that EPA could not assume jurisdiction now when
the agency had not interfered with the initial construction and installation of the Hondo platform. The ruling explains that EPA took no
action previously because it believed that emissions from the platform would be insignificant. But figures revealed a different picture
when, two years later, EPA took notice of the proposed storage and
treatment facility. Estimates by EPA showed that at a minimum
production rate of 30,000 bbl/day[14] the facility would emit enough
hydrocarbons, sulfur dioxide and nitrogen dioxide to classify it,
under the Clean Air Act, as a "major modification" for purposes of
new source review,[15] and a "major emitting facility" for purposes of
prevention of significant deterioration.[16]

The statistics were alarming for southern California. The entire
South Central Coast Air Basin is already classified as a non-attainment area for photochemical oxidants.[17] The Basin includes Santa
Barbara and Ventura Counties, the two areas most likely to be
affected by the Exxon facility. It also encompasses Orange County
and portions of Los Angeles, Riverside and San Bernardino Counties
—all of which are listed as non-attainment areas for several pollutants, including photochemical oxidants.[18] Since these hydrocarbons
can be transported long distances, the focus of regulatory action
must be on the origins of the particulates, not where they are measured.[19] The ruling reasons that "unless regulated, emissions of air
pollutants from sources located on the Outer Continental Shelf will
adversely impact air quality in such areas by adding additional pollu-

---

13. *Id.*

14. The ruling also contains estimates for a production rate of 60,000 bbl/day.

15. The Interpretative Ruling for new source review defines a "major source" as any
structure, building, facility, installation, or operation (or combination thereof) for which
the allowable emission rate of particulate matter, sulfur oxides, nitrogen oxides or non-
methane hydrocarbons is 100 tons per year or more. A "major modification" is any modification to an existing source which increases the allowable emissions to the above levels.

16. The prevention of significant deterioration provisions define a "major emitting
facility" as a stationary source of air pollutants within specified categories of sources,
including petroleum storage and transfer facilities with a capacity exceeding three hundred
thousand barrels, which emit or have the potential to emit, one hundred tons per year of
any air pollutant. 42 U.S.C. §7479(1) (1976).

17. 43 Fed. Reg. 16,394, 16,397 (1978).

18. *Id.*

19. *Id.*

tants to areas where air quality is worse than national ambient air quality standards."[20] Similarly, where air quality onshore is better than national standards, state and federal regulations should apply in order to prevent significant deterioration.

Having found a justification for its action, EPA then outlined its authority by law. The ruling concedes that the Clean Air Act is not expressly applicable to facilities located on the OCS. But it explains that the Act can be extended to the Shelf by virtue of the Outer Continental Shelf Lands Act (the OCS Lands Act) which extends the Constitution, laws and jurisdiction of the United States to "the subsoil and seabed of the Outer Continental Shelf and to all artificial islands and fixed structures which may be erected thereon for the purpose of exploring for, developing, removing and transporting resources therefrom."[21] No problem is raised, the ruling states, by the fact that the OCS Lands Act was enacted several years prior to the Clean Air Act. EPA explains that the intent of Congress in passing the OCS Lands Act was to extend all the laws, present and future,[22] of the United States to the seabed. Moreover, it is only by asserting this jurisdiction that EPA can fulfill the very goals of the Clean Air Act: the attainment and maintenance of national ambient air quality standards.[23]

The ruling also states that Exxon's acquisition of a leasehold interest does not exempt the company from "reasonable" regulation. Exxon had argued that EPA's jurisdiction over its facilities would be contrary to its development and production rights as a lessee of the Santa Barbara tract. But EPA, relying on two cases from the 9th Circuit Court of Appeals,[24] stated: "It is only where regulation amounts to a taking of the lessee's property rights without compensation that regulation becomes unconstitutional."[25]

Finally, the ruling refutes Exxon's contention that EPA is without authority to regulate OCS facilities. The company had argued that the OCS Lands Act confers exclusive authority upon the Secretary of

---

20. *Id.*
21. 43 U.S.C. §§ 1331-1343 (1970).
22. 43 Fed. Reg. 16,394, 16,397 (1978).
23. To this end, it is necessary that State Implementation Plans (SIPs) also be applicable. As required by the Clean Air Act Amendments of 1970, all states must formulate their own plans to implement the provisions of the Clean Air Act. SIPs are the basic mechanisms for achieving nationwide air quality. Fortunately, the OCS Lands Act also adopts as "the law of the United States," for application to the OCS, the "civil and criminal laws of each adjacent State" to the extent that such laws "are applicable" and "not inconsistent with the Act or other Federal laws and regulations. . . ." 43 U.S.C. § 1333(a)(2) (Supp. V 1975).
24. Gulf Oil Corp. v. Morton, 493 F.2d 141 (9th Cir. 1974); Union Oil Co. v. Morton, 512 F.2d 743 (9th Cir. 1975).
25. 43 Fed. Reg. 16,394, 16,398 (1978).

Interior to administer OCS leases and to prescribe rules and regulations in that regard.[26] EPA, however, points out that the OCS Lands Act also includes the provision that applicable state laws "shall be administered and enforced by the appropriate officers and courts of the United States."[27] Since the Clean Air Act is administered by EPA, it is apparent that EPA is the proper agency to enforce its provisions. It is also "equally apparent" that the Secretary of Interior would not be the "appropriate" official, even with respect to facilities on the OCS, since the Secretary does not presently have any responsibility for administration of the Clean Air Act.[28]

EPA's interpretation of the OCS Lands Act may be considered superficial at best by some observers. The ruling ignores that section of the Act which clearly states that the Secretary of Interior shall "prescribe and amend such rules and regulations as he determines to be necessary and proper in order to provide for the prevention of waste and conservation of the natural resources of the Outer Continental Shelf. . . ."[29] The section also states that "in the enforcement of conservation laws, rules, and regulations the Secretary is authorized to cooperate with the conservation agencies of the adjacent state."[30] Congress apparently envisioned a working relationship between the Interior Department and the appropriate conservation agencies, a possibility which EPA does not address to the obvious consternation of officials at the Interior Department. "Unless they're willing to put the resources into this area, they have bitten off more than they can handle," remarked a dubious attorney in the Department's solicitor's office.[31] The Department is understandably reluctant to relinquish any of its authority over the OCS leases. It is lobbying for an amendment to the OCS Lands Act which would make the Interior Secretary responsible for applying national ambient air quality standards, under the Clean Air Act, to the OCS lease tracts.[32]

Exxon has not decided yet whether to appeal this ruling. It is possible that the company is waiting to see what action Congress will take on proposals to amend the OCS Lands Act. This case points up the need to either amend or interpret the 20-year-old law to fit the realities of ever-increasing, modern-day offshore exploration and

---

26. 43 U.S.C. § 1334 (1970).
27. 43 Fed. Reg. 16,394, 16,398 (1978).
28. *Id.*
29. 43 U.S.C. § 1334(a)(1) (1970).
30. *Id.*
31. Current Developments, ENVIR. REP. (BNA) 1989, 1990 (1978).
32. *Id.*

development activities. This is, perhaps, the most significant aspect of the EPA determination. Apart from the inevitable tug-of-war between EPA and the Interior Department, and whatever the eventual outcome, this ruling is important for what it may herald. Our eagerness to exploit the sea is in fact compelled by a growing population on the one hand and dwindling resources on the other. A whole new frontier is opening for development and, with it, a new era in the law of the sea and regulations pertaining to its use. The EPA ruling is a cautious step into this new frontier and, as such, it may represent a bold leap forward.

FRANCES BASSETT

Chapter 16

NEW STANDARDS FOR STRIP MINING:
SOCIAL, ECONOMIC AND
ENVIRONMENTAL COSTS NOW CONSIDERED

ENVIRONMENTAL LAW–SURFACE MINING CONTROL AND RECLAMATION ACT: District Court for the District of Columbia upheld regulations promulgated to protect the environment from the adverse effects of strip mining, which had been challenged on both procedural and substantive grounds. U.S. Court of Appeals for the District of Columbia affirmed without opinion the district court's decision generally upholding the Department of Interior's interim stripmining regulatons. *Surface Mining Regulation Litigation,* 11 E.R.C. 1593 (1978).

The policy behind the Surface Mining and Reclmation Act of 1977,[1] as stated by Congress, is to balance the nation's need for coal as a source of energy against the growing necessity of protecting the environment and preserving agricultural productivity.[2] Although coal is necessary to fulfill the nation's energy requirements, the impact from unreclaimed, mined areas results in heavy social and economic costs, as well as impairment of environmental quality. In addition, coal mining often results in a diminution of the potential post-mining uses of the land. But technological developments in the areas of surface mining and reclamation have progressed to the point where it has become appropriate to minimize these adverse effects of surface mining.[3]

Implementation of the Surface Mining and Reclamation Act (Act) was to occur in two stages. Nine months after the date of enactment, mine operators were to begin complying with eight subsections of the Act. This is the interim program. The purpose of this initial regulatory program is to phase in the full standards and procedures of the permanent program in a way that is consistent with the intent of Congress. The standards of the interim program do not implement the provisions of the entire Act. Rather, the full range of standards and procedures required by the Act is covered in the permanent program. Development of the permanent program is supposed to depend on the requirements of the Act and the experience gained during the initial program.[4] The interim regulations provide for, *inter*

---

1. 30 U.S.C. § § 1201-1328 (1977).
2. 30 U.S.C. § 1202 (1977).
3. 30 U.S.C. § 1201 (1977).
4. 42 Fed. Reg. 62,641 (1977).

alia: land restoration after mining, preservation of top soil and the hydrologic balance, revegetation, disposal of wastes and the use of explosives.[5] New operations commencing on or after February 3, 1978 must comply with the interim regulations. Operations which commenced before February 3, 1978, with exceptions, must comply with the interim regulations by May 3, 1978.[6]

Twenty-two challenges to the Act were consolidated for review in the U.S. District Court for the District of Columbia.[7] Industrial plaintiffs' motions[8] dealt with both the manner of promulgation of the regulations and substantive challenges to the regulations themselves.[9] Environmental plaintiffs[10] raised one substantive issue: whether the Secretary of the Department of Interior (Secretary) exceeded his authority in allowing extensions to the compliance deadline for pre-existing, non-conforming structures or facilities.[11] In general, the industrial plaintiffs joined in each other's motions for a preliminary injunction; the environmental plaintiffs moved for summary judgment.[12]

Section 1252(c) of the Act set up the interim program which required compliance with eight subsections of the Act nine months after the date of enactment. Industrial plaintiffs' substantive challenges alleged that five of the provisions to be included in the permanent program were improperly included in the interim program.[13] The five provisions in dispute dealt with surface effects of underground mining, mining on prime farmlands and in alluvial valley floors, and spoil and waste disposal.[14] Plaintiffs noted the absence of citation to these five provisions in section 1252(c) as the basis of their challenge. The federal defendant[15] argued that these provisions were necessary to preserve the hydrologic balance of the mined lands and to prevent water pollution, as required by a regulation[16] that was incorporated into the interim program via section 1252(c). The court held that regulation in these areas was necessary in the interim program period, and for the reasons stated by defendant, plaintiffs' motion was denied.

---

5. Surface Mining Regulation Litigation, 11 E.R.C. 1593, 1594 (1978); 30 U.S.C. § 1265(b)(2), (b)(3), (b)(5), (b)(10), (b)(13), (b)(15), (b)(19), (d) (1978).

6. 30 U.S.C. § 1252(c) (1977).

7. Surface Mining Regulation Litigation, 11 E.R.C. 1593 (1978).

8. Industrial plaintiffs included coal mine operators and trade associations.

9. ,Surface Mining Regulation Litigation, 11 E.R.C. 1593, 1595 (1978).

10. National Wildlife Federation and other environmental groups.

11. Surface Mining Regulation Litigation, 11 E.R.C. 1593, 1606 (1978).

12. *Id.* at 1594.

13. *Id.* at 1595.

14. *Id.* at 1597-99.

15. The federal defendant is the Department of the Interior.

16. 30 U.S.C. § 1265(b)(10)(F) (1977).

Plaintiffs also asserted that the interim regulations as a whole were invalid because the Secretary failed to provide adequate exemption and variance procedures.[17] In deciding this issue, the district court cited to *E. I. duPont de Nemours and Co. v. Train.*[18] In that case the Supreme Court stated:

> The question, however, is not what a court thinks is generally appropriate to the regulatory process; it is what Congress intended for *these* regulations. It is clear that Congress intended these regulations to be absolute prohibitions. (97 S. Ct. at 980).

"In the statutory scheme before the court, Congress continually rejected broad exemption provisions."[19] One reason for rejection is that "to provide for unlimited exemptions would render the bill meaningless."[20] Congress was willing to allow limited variance, but only where such variances would result in equal or better protection to the environment and would result in higher post-mining land use.

Two sections provide for variances: section 1301 which concerns experimental practices and section 1265(b)(16) which deals with combined surface and underground mining. The only exemption under the Act is for small operators in section 1252(c).

Congress has made it clear that mine operators have two alternatives: to comply with the regulations or to cease operation.[21] For this reason, the court stated, plaintiffs' claim that variance and exemption granting procedures are necessary is without merit. Plaintiffs' motions were denied.[22]

The regulations were upheld where the federal defendant demonstrated that the regulation under attack was a proper implementation of a section properly within the interim program or that the Secretary in promulgating the regulations had not acted arbitrarily, capriciously or inconsistently with law. Regulations dealing with topsoil standards, blasting limitations, valley fills and third party commitments were upheld, by the court, as constituting a reasonable exercise of agency discretion under the Act. In regard to the small operator's exemption, the court found that Congress intended that the exemption should apply only to genuinely small operators. This regulation, as promulgated by the Secretary, ensures that the exemption cannot be exploited by large producers.

The industrial plaintiffs prevailed on those motions where they

---

17. Surface Mining Regulation Litigation, 11 E.R.C. 1593, 1599 (1978).
18. 430 U.S. 112 (1977).
19. Surface Mining Regulation Litigation, 11 E.R.C. 1593, 1600 (1978).
20. *Id.*
21. *Id.*
22. *Id.*

demonstrated that the Secretary, in promulgating the regulations, had: imposed standards on operations exempt from those requirements—scope of grandfather exemption and waste impoundments; not promulgated "final" rules which had the effect of imposing procedural restraints on plaintiffs' ability to obtain judicial review—sedimentation ponds; had superceded Federal Water Pollution Control Act[23] standards contrary to the Act—effluent limitations; and had regulated retrospectively without the required explicit statement in the statute—pre-existing structures and facilities.

The environmental plaintiffs moved for summary judgment on the sole issue in their complaint: whether the Secretary had exceeded his authority in allowing limited time extensions for compliance with performance standards for pre-existing, non-conforming structures or facilities. These limited extensions, the environmental plaintiffs argued, violated the mandates of the Act. The court held, however, that the Secretary had the power to grant limited variances. The motion for summary judgment on this issue was denied.[24]

One of the underlying policies of the Act is "to ensure a fair and generally applicable set of standards for all mining operations. . . ."[25] Although fear has been expressed that overly strict regulations will force many mining operations to close, these regulations reflect the intent of Congress and the Act.[26] They are necessary if environmental and social harm is to be kept to a minimum. By upholding the regulations the District Court of the District of Columbia and the D.C. Circuit Court of Appeals have ensured the protection of the environment and of agricultural productivity—both national necessities.

LINDA BONNEFOY

[*Editor's Note: In the second portion of its review, on August 24, 1978, the court upheld most of the contested regulations. Remanded to the Department of the Interior for further consideration were certain regulations regarding valley and head-of hollow spoil, disposal, prime farmlands, stream buffer zones, and waste dam construction. This decision, as with the first, was the result of the consolidation of 24 suits by industry, state, and environmental plaintiffs challenging the regulations. 11 ERC 2078.*]

---

23. Federal Water Pollution Control Act, 33 U.S.C.A. § § 1251-1361 (1977 Supp.).
24. Surface Mining Regulation Litigation, 11 E.R.C. 1593, 1606 (1978).
25. 42 Fed. Reg. 62,640 (1977).
26. 42 Fed. Reg. 62,640 (1977).

NOTES

TENNESSEE VALLEY AUTHORITY v. HILL: PROTECTION OF ENDANGERED SPECIES UNDER SECTION 7 OF THE ENDANGERED SPECIES ACT OF 1973

ENVIRONMENTAL LAW—ENDANGERED SPECIES ACT: The United States Supreme Court upholds the Sixth Circuit Court of Appeals decision construing the Endangered Species Act of 1973. The Court holds that the Act prohibits completion of the Tellico Dam since completion of the dam would jeopardize the continued existence of the snail darter, an endangered species. *Tennessee Valley Authority v. Hill*, 98 S. Ct. 2279 (1978).

On June 15, 1978, the United States Supreme Court decided *Tennessee Valley Authority v. Hill*,[1] the much-publicized case involving the multimillion dollar Tellico Dam, the snail darter, and Section 7 of the Endangered Species Act of 1973.[2] The decision is significant in three fundamental respects. First, the decision provides the long-awaited judicial interpretation of several key aspects of Section 7.[3] Second, the decision may prompt amendment of the Act, thus posing the possibility that much of the judicial interpretation of it to date could be rendered moot. Finally, the Supreme Court's resolution of the Section 7 issue invites consideration of the broader question: to what extent is the federal government willing to commit itself to the protection of vanishing species? This note considers these aspects of the decision. Also, as background to this consideration, the mandate of the Act in general, and that of Section 7 in particular, is discussed.

THE ENDANGERED SPECIES ACT AND SECTION 7

The Endangered Species Act of 1973 presents a broad endangered species preservation mandate to the entire federal government, not merely to those federal agencies traditionally associated with wildlife management. The policy statement of the Act provides that "all Federal departments and agencies shall seek to conserve endangered species and threatened species and shall utilize their authorities in furtherance of the purposes of this Act."[4] This affirmative mandate

---

1. 98 S. Ct. 2279 (1978).
2. 16 U.S.C. § § 1531-1543 (1973).
3. 16 U.S.C. § 1536 (1973).
4. 16 U.S.C. § 1531(c) (1973).

is buttressed by the unqualified definition of "conserve": "to use all methods and procedures which are necessary to bring any endangered or threatened species to the point at which measures provided pursuant to this act are no longer necessary."[5] The substantive basis for insuring that this mandate is carried out is provided by Section 7.

Section 7, the section of the Act that deals specifically with interagency cooperation, is perhaps the most controversial and potentially far-reaching section of the Act. It states:

> All federal departments and agencies shall, in consultation with, and with the assistance of the Secretary . . . (take) such action necessary to insure that actions authorized, funded, or carried out by them do not jeopardize the continued existence of such endangered and threatened species, or result in the destruction or modification of habitat of such species which is determined by the Secretary, after consultation as appropriate with the affected states, to be critical.[6]

The significant aspects of this section are that (1) no provisions exist for balancing of factors: federal actions cannot destroy or modify critical habitat or jeopardize the continued existence of a species; (2) all federal agencies shall consult with the Secretary[7] regarding the effect of their activities upon critical habitat; and (3) the Secretary is responsible for the all-important designation of critical habitat.[8] These aspects of the section have resulted in its being labeled "nondiscretionary" by some. Indeed, the strict language of the section might lead to this conclusion. The Secretary is to designate critical habitat; the action-taking agency cannot destroy or modify critical

---

5. 16 U.S.C. § 1532(2) (1973).
6. 16 U.S.C. § 1536 (1973).
7. The Office of Endangered Species in the Fish and Wildlife Service of the Department of the Interior is responsible for the consultation process regarding land-dwelling species. The National Marine Fisheries Service in the Department of Commerce administers the consultation process for marine species. Throughout this note, rather than refer specifically to the relevant endangered species offices in both the Department of the Interior and the Department of Commerce, we use the term Secretary (as does the Act itself) unless more specific usage is needed. 16 U.S.C. § 1532(10) (1973).
8. The Act does not define "critical habitat"; however, the Secretary of the Interior has construed the term:
> Critical habitat means any air, land, or water area (exclusive of those existing manmade structures or settlements which are not necessary to the survival or recovery of a listed species) and constituent elements thereof, the loss of which would appreciably decrease the likelihood of the survival and recovery of a listed species or a distinct segment of its population. The constituent elements of critical habitat include, but are not limited to: physical structures and topography, biota, climate, human activity, and the quality and chemical content of land, water and air. Critical habitat may represent any portion of the present habitat of a listed species and may include additional areas for reasonable population expansion. 43 Fed. Reg. 874 (1978) (to be codified as 50 C.F.R. § 402.02).

habitat; and the action-taking agency must consult with the Secretary to insure that its projects will not destroy or modify critical habitat. In certain circumstances Section 7, in fact, leaves very little discretion in the action-taking agency. *Tennessee Valley Authority v. Hill* provides a classic example of such a situation. However, to appreciate the context of *Tennessee Valley Authority,* it is helpful to first consider the circumstances in which substantial discretion may be left with the action-taking agency.

Although Section 7 requires that critical habitat not be destroyed or modified and provides for an interagency consultation process to insure that it is not, the final decision as to whether a project will modify critical habitat is left with the action-taking agency. The consultation process is implemented pursuant to Guidelines on Interagency Cooperation, which provide primarily procedural guidance.[9] They require that each federal agency consult with the Fish and Wildlife Service in the Department of the Interior.[10] After consultation, the Service is to issue an opinion regarding the effect of the project on critical habit.[11] Procedural guideposts for the process are presented by the guidelines. Yet, the substantive basis upon which a decision as to any given project is to be made is not provided by the guidelines and probably cannot be provided. Consequently, Section 7 can potentially leave much discretion in the action-taking agency. When the opinions of Fish and Wildlife Service and the action-taking agency differ, the fundamental consideration is not whether consultation is mandatory, or whether the language of Section 7 states that agencies "shall not" modify or destroy critical habitat. The important consideration is, rather, who makes the final decision as to whether a given action will jeopardize the continued existence of a species or will destroy or modify critical habitat. That decision is made by the action-taking agency. Since, under the guidelines, it is the perogative of the Fish and Wildlife Service only to advise, an agency may well decide to proceed with a project against the recommendation of the Fish and Wildlife Service. If an agency so decides, the ultimate resolution of the conflict may be in the judicial process.

TENNESSEE VALLEY AUTHORITY v. HILL

Under the citizen suit provision of the Endangered Species Act, anyone may sue to (1) enjoin any violator of the Act (including the action-taking agencies of the U.S. Government) or (2) compel the

---

9. 43 Fed. Reg. 870 (1978) (to be codified in 50 C.F.R. §402).
10. 43 Fed. Reg. 875 (1978) (to be codified in 50 C.F.R. §402.04).
11. 43 Fed. Reg. 875-876 (1978) (to be codified in 50 C.F.R. §402.04).

administering agencies to enforce the prohibitions of the Act or to take certain actions pursuant to administrative authority.[12] The provision regarding the second type of suit limits the otherwise broad discretion of the Secretary. Challenge to the discretion of the Secretary under this provision provides substantial potential for suit under the Act, but the most noted type of suit is that listed first above—suits challenging the discretion of action-taking agencies in their project decisions regarding destruction or modification of critical habitat.

Any action taken by any federal agency that under Section 7, might jeopardize the continued existence of a species or contribute to the destruction of critical habitat may be subject to suit. We have alluded to suit as a means of resolving a dispute involving conflicting opinions of the Fish and Wildlife Service and the action-taking agencies. Such suits involve the questions of what judicial deference is to be given a Fish and Wildlife opinion and whether critical habitat will be destroyed or modified.[13] Although these questions are quite significant in the overall interpretation of Section 7, they are not raised by *Tennessee Valley Authority v. Hill,* and they are not analyzed in this note. In *Tennessee Valley Authority,* the question is not whether critical habitat will be destroyed or modified if the project were completed; all parties agree that it would.[14] The question is whether other considerations justify the potential destruction or modification of critical habitat.

In *Hill v. Tennessee Valley Authority,* the Association of Southeastern Biologists and certain other parties sought to enjoin the completion of the Tellico Dam and impoundment of the Little Tennessee River pursuant to the Endangered Species Act. After much of the dam had been completed, a species of fish, the snail darter, was discovered in the Little Tennessee. The snail darter is a small, tannish-colored fish which feeds on snails and thrives in the stretch of the river that would be impounded by the dam. This stretch is the only known habitat in the world where the darter exists naturally.[15] Consequently, the snail darter was listed as an endangered species.[16] The snail darter requires high levels of oxygen in the waters it inhabits and derives the necessary oxygen from the flowing waters of the Little Tennessee. It also requires a gravel substrate, like that found on the bottom of the Little Tennessee, to reproduce. The

12. 16 U.S.C. § 1533(g)(1) (1973).
13. See *Sierra Club v. Froehlke,* 534 F.2d 1289 (8th Cir. 1976); *National Wildlife Federation v. Coleman,* 529 F.2d 359 (5th Cir. 1976).
14. 98 S. Ct. 2290 (1978).
15. 40 Fed. Reg. 47,505-47,506 (1975).
16. *Id.*

impoundment of the river by the Tellico Dam would effectively cease the oxygen-producing flow of the river and cause heavy siltation of the gravel stream bed. Impoundment would also eliminate the snail darter's primary food source; snail populations would most likely not survive in the reservoir. It is clear the critical habitat of the snail darter would be modified by the project.[17] For these reasons the respondent sought to enjoin the project under Section 7 of the Act.

The Eastern District Court of Tennessee heard the issues of whether the project would jeopardize the continued existence of the snail darter, and whether injunctive relief would be appropriate to force compliance with the Act if it were found that the project would jeopardize the species' survival.[18] The court found that "the preponderance of the evidence demonstrates that closure of the Tellico Dam ... will result in the adverse modification, if not complete destruction, of the snail darter's critical habitat."[19] Yet, despite this finding, the court denied injunctive relief.[20]

The court was obviously swayed by the fact that over $35 million had already been spent on the project when the Endangered Species Act was enacted:

> The case must be viewed in the context of its particular facts and circumstances. We go no further than to hold that the Act does not operate in such a manner as to halt the completion of this particular project. A far different situation would be presented if the project were capable of reasonable modifications that would insure compliance with the Act or if the project had not been underway for nearly a decade.
>
> If plaintiff's argument [that given the Courts' first finding it has little discretion regarding the issuance of an injunction] were taken to its logical extreme, the Act would require a court to halt impoundment of water behind a fully completed dam if an endangered species were discovered in the river on the day before such impoundment was scheduled to take place. We cannot conceive Congress intended that result.[21]

Despite the court's conception of congressional intent, there is no indication in the language of Section 7 that the degree of a project's completion should be a relevant consideration once it is determined that critical habitat will be adversely modified.

---

17. 98 S. Ct. 2290 (1978).
18. *Hill v. Tennessee Valley Authority*, 419 F. Supp. 753 (E.D. Tenn. 1976).
19. *Id.* at 760.
20. *Id.* at 763.
21. *Id.*

In overruling the district court, the Sixth Circuit Court of Appeals recognized the seeming inappropriateness of the district court's balancing of equities and consideration of project status:

> Were we to deem the extent of project completion relevant in determining the coverage of the Act, we would effectively defeat responsible review in those cases in which the alternatives are most sharply drawn and the required analysis most complex. ... Courts are ill-equipped to calculate how many dollars must be invested before the value of a dam exceeds that of the endangered species.[22]

The appeals court viewed its role conservatively, as a guardian of "the status quo where endangered species are threatened, thereby guaranteeing the legislative or executive branch sufficient opportunity to grapple with the alternatives."[23] Further, the court was not persuaded by the argument that Congress did not intend the Act to apply to this project because appropriations measures for the project continued to be passed by Congress even after the darter was discovered.[24]

The court recognized the good faith effort of the Tennessee Valley Authority (TVA) to preserve the snail darter by transplanting populations into areas of river that would not be modified by the Tellico Dam project and that appear to be suitable to the continued existence of the darter.[25] Yet, such a good faith effort does not per se meet the requirements of the Act. The court recognized that as long as the snail darter is listed as endangered by the Department of the Interior, efforts by TVA to compensate for the destruction or modification of the snail darter's habitat should not have a bearing on the court's decision: "Nowhere in the Act are courts authorized to override the Secretary by arbitrarily 'reading' species out of the endangered list or by redefining the boundaries of existing critical habitats on a case by case basis."[26] TVA claimed that it had done everything possible to save the snail darter, short of abandoning work on the dam. Yet, abandoning work on the dam is not an unreasonable alternative under the Act. Rather, it seems to be the only means available to "insure" the continued existence of the snail darter. The court recognized that the abandonment of past expenditures in favor of an endangered species is within the spirit of the Act.[27]

The appeals court was sympathetic to the district court's recogni-

---

22. *Hill v. Tennessee Valley Authority*, 549 F.2d 1064, 1070 (1977).
23. *Id.* at 1071.
24. *Id.* at 1072.
25. *Id.* at 1074.
26. *Id.*
27. *Id.*

tion of the equitable factors involved in the Tellico case, although it noted the impropriety of the lower court's weighing of these factors in reaching its decision.[28] The court suggested that were it not for its conception of the judicial function in strictly upholding the language of the Act, the equitable considerations might have been persuasive:

> ... only Congress or the Secretary of the Interior can properly exempt Tellico from compliance with the Act. The separation of powers doctrine is too fundamental a thread in our constitutional fabric for us to be tempted to preempt Congressional action in the name of equity or expediency ... [29]

Later in the analysis, we discuss the possibility of legislative or administrative action influencing not merely the Tellico Dam controversy but the Act itself.

In its decision of June 15, 1978 the Supreme Court affirmed the opinion of the Sixth Circuit Court of Appeals.[30] Like the district court and court of appeals, the Supreme Court began its analysis with the premise that the completion of the Tellico Dam would eradicate the snail darter population in the Little Tennessee or destroy its critical habitat. Given this premise, the Court discussed two issues. First, the Court asked whether TVA would be in violation of the Act if the Tellico Dam were completed and operated as planned. Second, the Court queries whether an injunction would be an appropriate remedy if indeed TVA's actions would violate the Act.[31]

The Court looked to the "ordinary meaning of the plain language" of the statute to determine that completion and operation of the dam would violate the Act:

> One would be hard pressed to find a statutory provision whose terms were any plainer than those in §7 of the Endangered Species Act. Its very words affirmatively command all federal agencies "to insure that actions authorized, *funded*, or *carried out* by them do not *jeopardize* the continued 'existence' of an endangered species or 'result in the destruction or modification of habitat of such species'" (court's emphasis). This language admits no exception.[32]

In affirming the court of appeals decision, the Supreme Court recognized what the district court did not; the Act does not provide for the balancing of benefits between dam and darter. Once a court determines that an action would destroy critical habitat of an endan-

28. *Id.*
29. *Id.*
30. *Tennessee Valley Authority v. Hill,* 96 S. Ct. 2279 (1978).
31. *Id.* at 2290.
32. *Id.* at 2291.

gered species, the action-taking agency would be in violation of the Act if the project is completed. At this point, the Act is indeed nondiscretionary. The past expenditures on the project or the benefits foregone by its abandonment are not to be considered. In this regard, the Court stated that "[i]t may seem curious to some that the survival of a relatively small number of three inch fish among all the countless millions of species extant would require the permanent halting of a virtually completed dam for which Congress has expended more than $100 million."[33] Nonetheless, the Court concluded that the explicit provisions of the Endangered Species Act require precisely that result. It recognized that Congress viewed the value of endangered species as "incalculable."[34]

It was argued by TVA that Congress did not intend the Act to stop a project such as the Tellico Dam; millions had been spent on the project before the snail darter was discovered and it was virtually complete at the time the Supreme Court heard the case. The Court looked to the legislative history as well as the words of the statute to reject TVA's contention. The Court, in interpreting the legislative history, concluded that the "plain intent of Congress in enacting this statute was to halt and reverse the trend toward species extinction, whatever the cost."[35] Also, TVA argued once again that because appropriation measures funding continued work on the Tellico Dam passed subsequent to both the passage of the Act and discovery of the snail darter, Congress intended that the project be allowed to proceed in spite of the Act's provisions. The majority opinion was not persuaded by TVA's arguments in this regard and held that "(t)o find a repeal of the Endangered Species Act under these circumstances would surely do violence to the 'cardinal rule . . . that repeals by implication are not favored.' "[36] Since the claim for repeal rests only with an appropriations act, the Court discerned all the more reason to reject the TVA appropriation argument. Finally, the Court rejected TVA's argument that there should be an exception to the rule of implied repealers in circumstnaces, such as those of this case, where appropriations committees expressly stated their understanding that earlier legislation would not prohibit the proposed expenditure on the dam.[37]

---

33. *Id.*
34. *Id.* at 2298.
35. *Id.* at 2297.
36. *Id.* at 2299.
37. It should be noted that the dissenting opinion, of Justices Powell and Blackmun, relies on the "subsequent appropriations" argument as an important element of its conclusion that the Act should not be applied to the Tellico Dam project. 98 S. Ct. 2279, 2309.

Having decided that completion and operation of the dam would constitute a violation of Section 7 of the Act, the Court then considered whether an injunction would be the appropriate remedy. The Court recognized that "a Federal judge sitting as a chancellor is not mechanically obligated to grant an injunction for every violation of the law,"[38] yet it views its role conservatively in fashioning a remedy. In granting an injunction the Court stated:

> Our individual appraisal of the wisdom or unwisdom of a particular course consciously selected by Congress is to be put aside in the process of interpreting the statute. Once the meaning of an enactment is discerned and its constitutionality determined, the judicial process comes to an end. We do not sit as a committee of review, nor are we vested with the power of veto.[39]

In so construing its function, the Court precluded judicially created modification of or flexibility with regard to Section 7.

In sum, the *Tennessee Valley Authority* decision clarifies two aspects of Section 7. First, it confirms that Section 7 does not allow for balancing of considerations in deciding whether to proceed with an action that will destroy or modify critical habitat or that will jeopardize the continued existence of a species. Endangered species are to be given undeniable priority over such action, regardless of the seeming insignificance of the species or the significance of the project. The stage of the project's completion or the appropriations of Congress regarding the action should not provide justification for continuing a project that will violate the Act. Second, just as a balancing of considerations cannot be used to justify proceeding with a project that will jeopardize the continued existence of an endangered species, so is it improper for the courts to balance the equities of a case arising under Section 7 in fashioning a remedy to achieve a result that it, as a court, considers to be fair. Congress has made the determination that once a project is found to be in violation of the Act, it should not proceed; flexibility in the statutory mandate will come, if at all, not from the courts, but from the administrators of the Act or Congress itself.

IMPLICATIONS OF THE SUPREME COURT DECISION

As a result of the *Tennessee Valley Authority* decision a number of amendments to the Act have been proposed. Indeed, this effect of the decision may be its greatest significance. The general thrust of

---

38. *Id.* at 2301.
39. *Id.* at 2302.

the amendments proposed is to lessen the rigidity of the Section 7 mandate. The means by which this general objective can be accomplished vary from use of the administrative process in providing for more consideration of traditional factors in decision-making to strict legislative or administrative exclusion of projects or species from the Act's coverage.[40] Whatever the form a potential amendment of the Act may take, the process of modifying the Endangered Species Act necessitates a reconsideration of national priorities with regard to endangered species protection.

Although balancing of competing factors is contrary to the language, legislative history, and policy of the Act, the value of such a procedure should not be discarded. It represents what is perhaps a pragmatic approach the problem. The provisions of the Endangered Species Act notwithstanding, is it really a desirable allocation of resources to halt construction of a dam that is virtually completed so that the snail darter can continue to thrive in the waters of the Little Tennessee?[41] In the eyes of many it is not, and consequently, the result of *Tennessee Valley Authority* casts a questioning shadow upon the Act.

The Tellico Dam controversy highlights the extremes of the Act's provisions. It involves a project, the planning and construction of which is so far advanced that the project itself cannot be modified to avoid destruction of critical habitat. It involves a species that, absent its symbolic significance, has attracted little national concern; the

40. At the time this note goes to press, amendment of the Act seems likely. Because the precise substance of the potential amendment cannot be predicted with accuracy, we discuss the possible amendments in no greater detail than to mention the proposed legislation here. The Senate has passed a bill (S 2899) that would provide funding for the Act through 1981. The bill amends the Endangered Species Act of 1973 so that a seven-member cabinet-level committee would be created to decide cases in which there exists irreconcilable conflict as to whether a given project should be exempt from the Act. The House has not yet taken any similar actions. Greater flexibility in the administrative consultation process may also provide action-taking agencies with a greater range of potential alternatives than was exercised by TVA prior to the Supreme Court decision. For example, the Department of the Interior has recommended a conservation program pursuant to the consultation process with the Corps of Engineers that would allow co-existence of the Dickey-Lincoln School Lakes Dams and the endangered plant species, the Furbish lousewort (1978) 9 Envir. Rep. (BNA) 446-447.

41. The benefits lost by abandonment of the Tellico Dam project may not be as substantial as dam expenditures and stage of completion might indicate. Testifying before a House subcommittee on June 23, 1978 TVA Chairman, S. David Freeman stated that "the real waste of the taxpayers' money may be in flooding the land." (1978) 9 Envir. Rep. (BNA) 364. TVA's reevaluation of traditional cost benefit analysis used in the original planning of the project may lead to the conclusion that the benefits produced by the dam may, in fact, be minimal. The utility of the dam, of course, is not a relevant consideration under the Court's reading of Section 7. Moreover, the fact that the actual benefits of the dam may not be substantial should not minimize the significance of the Tennessee Valley Authority case as an illustration of the potential for conflict under the Act.

snail darter hardly generates the wide-spread sympathy or enthusiasm aroused for such "glamorous" species as the whooping crane, the peregrin falcon, or the grizzly bear. It is a situation such as that surrounding the *Tennessee Valley Authority* case that can precipitate efforts to weaken the Act so that the traditional values that rank dams above darters can govern once again. Through the Endangered Species Act, Congress has determined the management priorities of federal agencies with regard to endangered species. The wisdom of this sweeping decision may be questioned not only for the result it dictates in certain projects, but also for its restriction of administrative authority of action-taking agencies to set priorities and make decisions.

On the other hand, it is important to recognize that it was the failure of traditional decision-making values to protect endangered species adequately that led to passage of the Endangered Species Act of 1973. Therefore, something more is needed than a mere grant of authority to federal agencies to consider endangered species protection in decision-making. Traditional resource management perspectives focus on benefit/cost analysis, utilitarian concepts of the greatest good for the greatest number for the longest period of time, and more recently, environmental protection considerations. The worth of endangered species is not easily measured by such criteria. To a degree, endangered species protection is contemplated by established environmental protection considerations; when the species diversity of an ecosystem is significantly reduced, as can occur with the extinction of a key species, the dynamic balance of the ecosystem can be severely altered. Yet, the probability of causing substantial ecological harm by the elimination of certain endangered species is at worst unknowable, and in many instances may be slight. Absent some specific endangered species mandate, more visible aspects of environmental protection or resource management may consistently receive administrative priority over endangered species. Consequently, even a general environmental protection mandate is likely not sufficient to assure significant administrative progress in endangered species protection.

The failure of the equation of traditional management objectives to yield satisfactory protection of endangered species does not indicate unworthiness of the endangered species protection objective. Rather, it illustrates the fact that something more than traditional management perspectives must be considered in the protective efforts. Perhaps more than anything else, conservation of endangered species is an ethical responsibility. Concern for protection of endangered species can exist even if their extinction might not have severe ecological or environmental consequences. It has been estimated that during the past 150 years, the rate of extinction of mammals has increased 55-fold, and the activities of man are the cause of this increase.[42] The sense of ethical responsibility elicited by this situation is fundamental to the effort to protect endangered species and to the realization that there is something more that inspires the protection of endangered species than their potential material benefit to man. Because the particular bases for a general ethical standard can and do vary, legislation that addresses a general ethical concern may not be consistent with all these various bases for that concern. Legislation or administrative action based upon ethical value preferences can be imprecise and prone to pleasing few in the effort to please many.

Despite the fact that a fundamental philosophy of endangered species conservation is to value species using indicia other than the species' utility for man, and despite the ideological incompatibility of benefit/cost and endangered species, it may be necessary in some situations to allow a project to continue despite its potential modification or destruction of critical habitat. The ethical considerations that precipitate endangered species protection efforts may not always require that these efforts be carried out to the exclusion of all other interests. Just as certain other resource policies with scientific or economic justifications may sometimes be altered by competing factors, so it is that the ethical basis for endangered species conservation may not always be determinative of the endangered species issue. The important consideration is that all components, including the ethical component, of endangered species protection be recognized as viable factors to be used in giving endangered species substantial priority, although not necessarily paramount priority, in federal decisions.

LARRY AUSHERMAN

*Editor's Note—Passed on October 15, 1978, HR 14104 amends the Endangered Species Act of 1973. The amendment establishes a seven-member interagency committee to review disputed projects involving endangered species. The committee is to review the Supreme Court decision in *Tennessee Valley Authority v. Hill.* If the committee does not make a final decision within 90 days, the Tellico Dam project would be exempted from the Act. The interagency review committee may also review other controversial projects after initial review by a three-member review board. The reviewing bodies are to balance economic considerations against environmental goals in making their decisions. Consequently, the "nondiscretionary" aspects of Section 7 are weakened substantially by the recent amendment.

---

42. L. R. REGENSTEIN, THE POLITICS OF EXTINCTION (1975).

Chapter 18

COMMERCE CLAUSE LIMITATIONS ON A STATE'S REGULATION OF WASTE DISPOSAL

CONSTITUTIONAL LAW–THE NEW JERSEY WASTE CONTROL ACT–In holding that a state may not isolate itself from a national problem by closing its landfills to waste from outside the state, the Supreme Court may have been looking ahead to more serious conflicts over nuclear disposal. *City of Philadelphia v. New Jersey,* 98 S.Ct. 2531 (1978).

The New Jersey Waste Control Act[1] was designed to prohibit the disposal in New Jersey landfills of waste originating outside that state. After having been twice sustained by the New Jersey Supreme Court against constitutional attacks, it was recently struck down by the Supreme Court of the United States as an impermissible regulation of interstate commerce.

In the early 1970's the State of New Jersey found itself running out of land to use for the disposal of waste. In 1973, the state legislature found a threat to the quality of the environment and declared "that the public, health, safety and welfare require that the treatment and disposal within this State of all wastes generated outside of the State be prohibited."[2] The Waste Control Act was enacted to achieve that end.

Operators of private landfills in New Jersey, along with several cities in other states that had agreements with the operators for waste disposal suffered an immediate adverse effect. Two actions were brought against New Jersey and its Department of Environmental Protection in state court.[3] The trial courts declared that the law was unconstitutional because it discriminated against interstate commerce. On appeal[4] the New Jersey Supreme Court consolidated these cases and considered the constitutionality of the Waste Control Act.

The New Jersey Court took pains to point out the dire nature of

---

1. N.J. Stat. Ann. § § 13:11-1 et seq. (Supp. 1978).

2. *Id.* § 13:11-9.

3. Hackensack Meadowlands Dev. Comm. v. Municipal Sanitary Landfill Auth., 127 N.J. Super. 160, 316 A.2d 711 (ch. div. 1974); In the other case judgment was rendered on an oral opinion. See Hackensack Meadowlands Dev. Comm. v. Municipal Sanitary Landfill Auth., 68 N.J. 451, 348 A.2d 506, 507 (1975).

4. Hackensack Meadowlands Dev. Comm. v. Municipal Sanitary Landfill Auth., 68 N.J. 451, 348 A.2d 506 (1975).

the problem faced by the state. Several studies had been made and all predicted that the state would run out of sites for landfill disposal operations in the near future. In the court's opinion, the problem had reached "crisis proportions."[5] Viewing the problem in this light, the court proceeded to examine the constitutional issues raised by the Waste Control Act and its accompanying regulations.

As a preliminary step the court addressed New Jersey's argument that the Act presented no issues under the commerce clause of the constitution. This argument was based on the theory that the waste involved was valueless and therefore its movement was not commerce within the meaning of the constitution. The United States Supreme Court has long recognized the theory that interstate movement of objects harmful to the general public falls outside of the scope of the Commerce Clause.[6] But the New Jersey court found that theory, and the state's argument slightly beside the point, because some of the regulations designed to enforce the Waste Control Act were broad enough to prohibit importation of waste that could have some economic value—for instance, recyclable waste. In any event, the court assumed for purposes of its decision that the mere transportation and disposal of valueless waste between states is interstate commerce for constitutional purposes.[7]

This brought the court to the issue of preemption—whether or not the United States Congress had the exclusive right to legislate. Congress had taken action in the form of the Solid Waste Disposal Act of 1965,[8] but the court found a clear intention not to pre-empt state action. In fact, the court found that Congress had intended to encourage state action.

The next question was whether the Waste Control Act was a constitutionally impermissible regulation of interstate commerce. The court expressed the opinion that there are two ways of defining commerce for the purposes of applying the commerce clause. Accordingly, when the clause is used to support some exertion of federal control or regulation—an affirmative application—the clause has been given a sweeping interpretation by the U.S. Supreme Court. On the other hand, when the clause is used to strike down or restrict state legislation this is a negative application, and the reach of the clause is much more confined. The current attempt, then, to use the

---

5. *Id.* 348 A.2d at 509.
6. *Id.* 348 A.2d at 512.
7. *Id.* 348 A.2d at 514.
8. Solid Waste Disposal Act of 1965, 42 U.S.C. § § 3251 et seq. (1970) (current version at 42 U.S.C.A. § § 6901 et seq. (West 1977)).

commerce clause to invalidate New Jersey's Waste Control Act would be a negative application.

Relying on a 40 year-old Supreme Court opinion[9] and a more recent treatise,[10] the court arrived at criteria to use in testing a state law under the "negative implications" of the commerce clause. The court's test contained four questions. 1) Did the state legislature act within its province? 2) Were the means of regulation reasonably adapted to the end sought? 3) Does the legislation discriminate against interstate commerce? 4) Is the burden on interstate commerce outweighed by the benefit to the state?[11]

The court found that the legislature had properly acted: there being no federal pre-emption, the state was free to act. And the legislation was a proper exercise of the state's police power because the preservation of the environment and protection of ecological values for the purpose of protecting the public health are primary objectives of that power.[12] Due to the serious nature of the problem, the court had no trouble finding that the means were reasonably adapted to these objectives. In the court's words, "Less than total exclusion of solid waste generated outside New Jersey would have been to no avail."[13]

The court was less than critical in its analysis of the discrimination question. It concluded that because the legislature had had no intent to impose economic barriers or create commercial restrictions, there was in fact no economic discrimination against interstate commerce. The court also observed that the ban on bringing garbage into the state applied equally to refuse collectors both from New Jersey and from out of state, and that out of state residents remained free to collect and dump within the state. Therefore, concluded the court, the Waste Control Act was not discriminatory.

Finally, the court found that the burden on interstate commerce imposed by the Waste Control Act was "slight indeed" compared with the benefit to the state of averting danger to the public health and environment.[14] Alternative methods and places of disposal were found by the court to be available to neighboring states at little cost. The court concluded that "where the effect upon trade and commerce is relatively slight, as is here the case, and where at the same time the values sought to be protected by the state legislation are as

9. South Carolina State Highway Dept. v. Barnwell Bros., 303 U.S. 177 (1938).
10. Engdahl, Constitutional Power: Federal and State § 11.03, at 272 (1974).
11. Hackensack Meadowlands Dev. Comm., 348 A.2d at 517.
12. *Id.* 348 A.2d at 516.
13. *Id.* 348 A.2d at 517.
14. *Id.* 348 A.2d at 518.

crucial to the welfare of its citizens as is here true, we have no hesitancy in sustaining the state action."[15]

This decision was appealed to the United States Supreme Court. Probable jurisdiction was noted April 5, 1976.[16] Shortly before the case was argued the Resource Conservation and Recovery Act of 1976 (RCRA)[17] was signed into law by President Ford. For this reason, the judgment of the New Jersey court was vacated and the case remanded. On remand the question for the N.J. court to decide was "whether or to what extent the Resource Conservation and Recovery Act of 1976 pre-empts the New Jersey [Waste Control Act]."[18]

In June 1977, the N.J. Supreme Court announced its decision.[19] It expressed the belief that the United States Supreme Court had been "especially reluctant to find an intent to pre-empt where state legislation has been enacted to serve local environmental interests."[20] And it found that although the RCRA called for waste disposal guidelines to be established by the federal government, Congress intended to leave to each state the decision as to whether or not to accept recommendations set forth in the guidelines.[21] Thus the previous decision of the N.J. court was affirmed, and the case was appealed again to the United States Supreme Court.

On June 23, 1978 Justice Stewart delivered the opinion of the Court. The Court briefly agreed with the New Jersey court that the Waste Control Act had not been pre-empted. It then turned to the weightier constitutional question.

The Court criticized the N.J. court's belief that the definition of commerce varies according to the purpose to which the Commerce Clause is being put. The Supreme Court majority held that all objects of interstate trade, including garbage, merit Commerce Clause protection, with none being excluded by definition. A state cannot escape constitutional scrutiny when it bans out of state waste, merely by labeling the waste "valueless."[22]

The Court then summarized its past decisions defining permissible and impermissible state regulation of interstate commerce. A virtually per se rule of invalidity has prevailed when the object of state

---

15. *Id.* 348 A.2d at 519.
16. Hackensack Meadowlands Dev. Comm., probable jurisdiction noted sub nom. City of Philadelphia v. N.J., 425 U.S. 910 (1976).
17. Pub. L. No. 94580, 42 U.S.C.A. § §6901 et seq.
18. City of Philadelphia v. N.J., 430 U.S. 141, 142 (1977).
19. City of Philadelphia v. State, 73 N.J. 562, 376 A.2d 888 (1977).
20. *Id.* 376 A.2d at 891.
21. *Id.* 376 A.2d at 893.
22. City of Philadelphia v. N.J., 98 S. Ct. 2531, 2535 (1978).

regulation has been simple economic protectionism.[23] However, "incidental burdens" on interstate commerce have been allowed when they seemed to be an unavoidable result of state legislation designed to protect the health and safety of people in the state.[24] Legislation of this sort, which evenhandedly serves a legitimate local purpose and only incidentally affects interstate commerce, will be upheld unless the burden imposed on interstate commerce is clearly excessive in relation to the putative local benefits.[25] The Court found the crucial question to be whether the Waste Control Act was simply a protectionist measure or a law directed to legitimate local concerns with only incidental effect upon interstate commerce.[26]

Contrary to the N.J. court, the Supreme Court found it not particularly helpful to make a determination of what it called the ultimate legislative purpose of the Waste Control Act. The "evil of protectionism" can lurk in the means of legislation as well as in the ends. Whether the legislature intended to reduce disposal costs to N.J. residents or to protect the environment, the Court assumed the state could have achieved either purpose by slowing the flow of all waste into the remaining landfill sites, even though interstate commerce would be incidentally affected. But discrimination against articles of commerce coming from outside the state, without some reason apart from the origin of the articles to treat them differently, is not a permissible way to achieve the state purpose, regardless of the purpose. The Court held "Both on its face and in its plain effect, the [Waste Control act] violates this principle of nondiscrimination."[27]

In two cases decided early in this century,[28] the Supreme Court held that a state may not accord its own citizens a preferred right of access to natural resources within the state, to the disadvantage of out of state consumers. These cases both involved state imposed restrictions on transporting natural gas to other states. In the present case the natural resource—landfill space—sought to be preserved for the citizens of New Jersey at the expense of out of state citizens is not an article of commerce, as had been the situation in the previous natural resources cases. The Court found this difference inconsequential:

> It does not matter that the State has shut the article of commerce

---

23. *Id.*
24. *Id.*
25. *Id.*
26. *Id.*
27. *Id.* at 2537.
28. Oklahoma v. Kansas Natural Gas Co., 221 U.S. 229 (1911); Pennsylvania v. West Virginia, 262 U.S. 553 (1923).

inside the State in one case and outside the State in the other. What
is crucial is the attempt by one State to isolate itself from a problem
common to many by erecting a barrier against the movement of
interstate trade.[29]

Even if the law was found to be discriminatory, New Jersey asked
the Court to consider it to be a quarantine law. Such laws have been
repeatedly upheld even though they appeared to single out interstate
commerce for special treatment.[30] The Court has said that the states
"have power to ... prevent the introduction into the States of
articles of trade, which, on account of their existing condition,
would bring in and spread disease, pestilence, and death."[31] The
quarantine laws that have been upheld, however, did not discriminate
against interstate commerce as such, but simply prevented traffic in
noxious articles, whatever their origin.[32]

Accordingly, the Waste Control Act was found not to be a quarantine law. No claim has been made that waste from within New Jersey
was any less harmful to the life expectancy of landfill sites than
waste from outside the state. Because of this the Court found that
New Jersey's attempt to ban out of state waste while leaving landfill
sites open to in state waste was an obvious effort to saddle those
outside with the entire burden of making the remaining sites last
longer. The Court stated that "legislative effort is clearly impermissible under the Commerce Clause of the Constitution." A state may
not isolate itself in the stream of interstate commerce from a problem shared by all.[33]

In his dissent, Justice Rehnquist focused attention on the asserted
health hazards presented by current state-of-the-art waste disposal.
He characterized the majority decision as offering New Jersey a Hob-
son's choice of either prohibiting all landfill operations in the state or
accepting waste from every portion of the United States. In his
words: "The physical fact of life that New Jersey must somehow
dispose of its own noxious items does not mean that it must serve as
a depository for those of every other State ... New Jersey should be
free under our past precedents to prohibit the importation of solid
waste because of the health and safety problems that such waste
poses to its citizens."[34]

29. City of Philadelphia v. N.J., 98 S.Ct. at 2538.
30. *Id.*
31. Bowman v. Chicago and N.W. Ry. Co., 125 U.S. 465, 489 (1888).
32. City of Philadelphia v. N.J., 98 S. Ct. at 2538.
33. *Id.* at 4805.
34. *Id.*

CONCLUSION

It is probably significant that the court gave so little credence to New Jersey's claims of the health hazards posed by the extra volume of waste from out of the state. The court was much more impressed with the fact that waste disposal is a problem shared by all of the states, and it implicitly decided that all states must therefore share in the solution. Also of note is the fact that the court's decision means no state can prevent others from sharing its natural resource of waste disposal sites, even though it is a resource which does not move in interstate commerce.

Apparently, any state faced with a similar problem in the future—the disposal of nuclear waste, for instance—will have to choose either to ban all disposal or allow disposal of wastes from other states. Although the Court implies that a claim that movement of a particular substance is hazardous might possibley lead to a different result,[35] this is little solace. That the Court would uphold a state's outright ban against nuclear disposal is unlikely for two reasons. First, if one state could impose such a ban, all could, and the problem would be aggravated rather than solved. Second, as technology makes it increasingly safe to transport nuclear waste, the significant problem remains the problem of permanent disposal. This is a national problem, and, as the court says, "What is crucial is the attempt by one State to isolate itself from a problem common to many by erecting a barrier against the movement of interstate trade."[36]

CHARLES L. McELWEE

---

35. *Id.* at 4804.
36. *Id.*

Chapter 19

PROPOSED RULES FOR ADMINISTERING THE ACREAGE LIMITATION OF RECLAMATION LAW

RECLAMATION LAW—Recent litigation, resulting from a history of non-enforcement, has caused the Bureau of Reclamation to propose regulations relating primarily to the disposition of excess lands.

INTRODUCTION

In a recent Ninth Circuit opinion, the limitation on the amount of land an individual may own within an irrigation district receiving federal reclamation water was applied to California's Imperial Irrigation District.[1] The limitation had long been part of the reclamation law, but had not been enforced. The decision of the Ninth Circuit and other recent litigation have forced the Bureau of Reclamation to promulgate new rules for present-day administration of the reclamation laws. This note will examine the history of reclamation law, case law developments and the resulting proposed regulations.

BACKGROUND

The Reclamation Act of 1902[2] was passed in response to a need for federally funded irrigation works. Before the Act was passed, attempts at irrigation in the West had been inadequate because of the need for costly dams and works.[3] The Act provided for construction costs of such irrigation dams, advanced without interest. It also provided that public lands irrigated with reclamation water were to be distributed into small units and that private lands were to receive a limited supply of water.[4]

The policy behind the Act required that benefits from the reclamation program be available to the largest possible number of people. This was accomplished by limiting the quantity of land in a single ownership to which project waters were supplied.[5] Such an acreage limitation, or "excess land law," was clear evidence that the

---

1. United States v. Imperial Irrigation District, 559 F.2d 509 (9th Cir. 1977).
2. 43 U.S.C. § 372 et seq. (1970).
3. Warne, *The Bureau of Reclamation,* Praeger Publishers (1973), p. 6.
4. Taylor, *The Excess Land Law: Execution of a Public Policy,* 64 Yale L.J. 477, 479 (1955).
5. Ivanhoe Irrigation District v. McCracken, 357 U.S. 275, 292 (1958).

sponsors of the Act intended that it prevent a monopoly of water on reclaimed public land and break up existing monopolies on private lands.[6] Thus, "the restriction on the size of land ownerships that would be permitted to use water from federal irrigation facilities became the keystone of the federal policy."[7]

The Reclamation Act was amended in 1911 by the Warren Act[8] which expanded the provision on excess land to include water already in private ownership when stored or carried by federal works.[9] An additional amendment was passed in 1912[10] which has resulted in confusion over the enforcement of the excess land provisions.[11] It is unclear whether the wording in section 3 of that amendment was intended to mean that in no case shall a person own irrigable land in excess of 160 acres or if it was to mean that in no case shall a person own in excess of 160 acres of irrigable land before final payment of building charges for the excess.[12] The acceptance of the second interpretation led to the practice of permitting excess landowners to pay cash rather than dispose of excess lands.[13]

The current acreage limitation rule was adopted in the 1926 Omnibus Adjustment Act, Section 46.[14] It was passed primarily to correct the problem of land speculation.[15] Section 46 bars delivery of reclamation water to private lands in excess of 160 acres in one ownership unless the owner executes a recordable contract with the Secretary of the Interior and thus becomes obligated to sell the excess at a price excluding the incremental value resulting from the existence of the project. Section 46 also requires that water delivery contracts be entered into only with public irrigation districts organized under state law.[16] No contracts with individuals may be made.

HISTORY OF NON-ENFORCEMENT

Before the enactment of the reclamation law, national land policy was breaking down in the West, especially in the Central Valley of California. Land was acquired in huge tracts from which were created

---

6. Taylor, at 484.
7. Warne, at 8.
8. Act of Feb. 21, 1911, 36 Stat. 925, 43 U.S.C. §524 (1952).
9. Taylor, at 487.
10. 37 Stat. 266 (1912), 43 U.S.C. §543, 544 (1952).
11. Taylor, at 487.
12. *Id.*
13. *Id.* at 487-488.
14. Omnibus Adjustment Act of May 25, 1926, section 46 as amended, 43 U.S.C. §423e.
15. Warne, at 72-73.
16. United States v. Tulare Lake Canal Company, 535, F.2d 1093, 1094 (9th Cir. 1976).

large-scale agricultural and livestock operations.[17] Obviously, a national policy of water distribution that would bring about redistribution of land was not favored.

When acreage limitations were passed, Congressional exemptions were sought by landowners. As an alternative pressure was put on the administrator not to enforce the requirements,[18] and when non-enforcement was achieved, it was used as a precedent against any future enforcement.[19] In addition, a letter from the Solicitor of the Interior Cohen to the Commissioner of Reclamation in 1947 contained the opinion that the 1912 amendment meant that full and final payment of construction charges against excess lands would free the lands of the acreage provisions, and that where payment of charges was not available officials should press for reasonably prompt disposal of excess lands.[20] Cohen's opinion added to the confusion.

The restrictions on land have consequently not been uniformly or diligently enforced. Recent action in the courts, however, has forced the Bureau to change this practice.

RECENT LITIGATION

Recently, the trend in litigation has been aimed at enforcement of the provisions of the Omnibus Act. In *United States v. Tulare Lake Canal Co.,*[21] the United States brought an action to determine the application of reclamation law to private lands receiving irrigation benefits from the Pine Flat Dam on the Kings River. Opposition came from large landowners in the Tulare Lake Basin who argued that Pine Flats was exempt because of the Flood Control Act of 1944 and that they were released from the limitation by repayment of construction charges.[22] The court looked to Section 8 of the Flood Control Act and its legislative history, finding that the Pine Flat project was to be operated under reclamation law and particularly in conformity with the acreage provisions.[23]

The important issue in the case was whether by repaying construction charges, owners of excess lands may avoid the obligation of executing recordable contracts providing for the sale of excess lands at ex-project prices.[24] The court found the theory was not sup-

17. Taylor, at 501.
18. *Id.* at 502.
19. *Id.* at 503.
20. *Id.* at 505-506.
21. 535 F.2d 1093 (9th Cir. 1976).
22. *Supra,* note 16, at 1118.
23. *Id.* at 1119.
24. *Id.* at 1118.

ported by the language of Section 46, the purpose and legislative history of the section, or the administrative practice of the Department of the Interior.[25] There was nothing in the wording of the act to suggest the option of paying construction charges. Moreover, the goals of the reclamation laws were to create family-sized farms in areas irrigated by federal projects, to break up and redistribute large private land holdings, to have wide distribution of the subsidy involved and to limit speculative gains. Since users of project water for irrigation were only charged with the project costs attributable to irrigation and not to navigation, flood control and other uses, the benefits from the project often would exceed the costs landowners would have to pay. The court therefore rejected that interpretation of the 1912 Act. If landowners were allowed to pay off construction costs and keep the enhanced value of the land they would be defeating the purpose of the Act.[26]

Finally, the court found that the administrative practice for the most part had been inferentially or expressly contrary to the "payout" policy. The Cohen letter had at times been used to justify that policy, but the opinion in the letter was wrong and its authority limited. The court concluded that the general scheme of enforcement of the acreage limitation provided no basis for the construction charge exception.[27] The outcome was that landowners in the project must execute recordable contracts to sell excess land at ex-project prices in compliance with Section 46 in order to receive project water for excess lands, even if construction costs are repaid.[28]

United States v. Imperial Irrigation District, 559 F.2d 509 (9th Cir. 1977), concerned the application of the excess land provision of Section 46 to the Imperial Irrigation District.[29] The argument against enforcement was based on the past interpretation of a letter from the Secretary of the Interior Wilbur and on the lack of department enforcement. The landowners claimed it would be unfair to enforce the excess lands provision because of individual landowners' reliance on the letter and on the past non-enforcement of the 160 acre limit.[30] The letter in question was sent in 1933 from the Secretary of Interior to the Imperial Irrigation District.[31] It stated that

---

25. *Id.*

26. *Id.* at 1119-1135.

27. *Id.* at 1143.

28. *Id.* at 1143.

29. *See* Recent Development: *Reclamation Act of 1902: After 75 Years 160 Acre Limitation Held Valid,* 17 N.R.J. 673.

30. *Supra* note 1, at 536.

31. *Id.*

the limitation did not apply to lands "now cultivated and having a present water right,"[32] thus providing for recognition of vested water rights for areas larger than 160 acres and permitting delivery of water to satisfy vested water rights in ownerships of more than 160 acres.

In considering the circumstances surrounding the letter, the court concluded that it could not be given any weight.[33] The court also considered the fact that in practice the department did not enforce the 160 acre limit on land in the district, because of the Wilbur letter and because of previous non-enforcement. However, the court held that neither the letter nor the administrative inaction could be considered administrative determinations to which the court should defer.[34] The court added that although individual landowners might be entitled to compensation for any impairment to property caused by Section 46, such a possibility could not prevent enforcement.[35] Therefore, in the absence of any express Congressional exemption for the Imperial Irrigation District, the district's land fell under the excess land provisions of reclamation law.

In *National Land for People, Inc. v. Bureau of Reclamation,* 417 F. Supp. 449 (1976) (U.S.D.C.), a non-profit membership organization brought action against the Bureau of Reclamation to require the adoption of rules and regulations, in accordance with the Administrative Procedure Act, with respect to the approval of sales of private lands in federally subsidized water projects. The court found the group had demonstrated the likelihood of prevailing on the merits and issued a preliminary injunction restraining land sales pending the formal adoption of rules.

The organization included many small farmers who had been unsuccessful at finding land available in 160 acre tracts at a price that excluded the enhancement from federal subsidy. Other members had offered to buy excess land and had their offers rejected.[36] There had been no formal rulemaking with regard to the Bureau's criteria for approving private sales. Because the organization had shown harm to an interest protected by the Act due to the Bureau's failure, the injunction was granted.[37]

---

32. *Id.* at 537.
33. *Id.*
34. *Id.* at 540.
35. *Id.* at 541.
36. National Land for People, Inc. v. Bureau of Reclamation, 417 F. Supp. 449, 452 (U.S.D.C. 1976).
37. *Id.* at 453.

PROPOSED REGULATIONS

Pursuant to the court order in *National Land For People,* the Bureau has proposed rules for the enforcement of the 160 acre limitation and other conditions of the Reclamation Act.[38] The proposed rules re-state the purposes of the Act's limiting the area of land for which water is to be supplied and requiring landowners to reside on or in the neighborhood of the land. These purposes are (a) to provide for a maximum number of farmers, (b) to widely distribute the benefits, (c) to promote family-size owner-operated farms and (d) to preclude speculation.

The following changes in the administration of the limitation have been proposed. First, although these rules do not address the residency requirement, they define an eligible non-excess owner as being a person residing on or in the neighborhood of the land, so all sales of excess land will be to residents of the area.[39] In addition, excess lands will only be sold to multiple ownerships—joint tenancies, partnerships, corporations, trusts—when there exists a family relationship among all of the persons, and each person involved must qualify as an eligible non-excess owner.[40]

The most important change, at least for purposes of enabling a wider distribution of irrigated land, is the method of disposition of excess lands. Excess lands may only receive water if the owner executes a valid recordable contract for the sale of that land. The recordable contract must provide that the excess owner will dispose of the land within five years.[41] For the excess lands to be eligible to receive project water, they must be disposed of to an eligible non-excess owner at a price approved by the Secretary based on the value without reference to enhancement by the project.[42] The excess landowner is to divide the land under the recordable contract into parcels of no more than 160 acres, or the district or the Secretary will so divide it.

After the execution of a recordable contract, the Secretary will publish a notice of availability. Prospective eligible purchasers are then to file a formal expression of interest with the Regional Director. At the time of sale, the Bureau is to select by lottery or other impartial means a purchaser at the approved price.[43] This is a depar-

---

38. 42 Fed. Reg. 43044 (1977) (proposed; to be codified in 43 C.F.R. sec. 426). *See* Ellis & Dumars, *The Two Tiered Market in Western Water,* 57 Neb. L. Rev. 333 (1978).
    39. 42 Fed. Reg. 43046 (1977) (proposed; to be codified in 43 C.F.R. §426.4(1)).
    40. 42 Fed. Reg. 43047 (1977) (proposed; to be codified in 43 C.F.R. §426.7).
    41. 42 Fed. Reg. 43046 (1977) (proposed; to be codified in 43 C.F.R. §426.10).
    42. 42 Fed. Reg. 43048 (1977) (proposed; to be codified in 43 C.F.R. §426.10).
    43. *Id.*

ture from the past practice of allowing an excess land seller to privately arrange sale. A person in a family relationship with the excess land seller will, however, still have a preference to buy the land offered.[44] In addition, the seller is not permitted to lease the land back from the purchaser.[45]

A further restriction which will promote small farm operations by the actual owners is that no person will be entitled to lease more than 160 acres of land served by federal water under reclamation law.[46] Each lease must be filed with the District which is to keep a file and report to the Department annually.

One other significant change is that the Secretary is authorized to monitor resales of land. Non-excess land acquired from excess status for an approved price must be sold at a price approved by the Secretary as not reflecting project benefits if resold within 10 years. The Secretary will also monitor resales after 10 years until one-half of the construction costs have been paid to prevent unreasonable profit from accruing to the seller.[47] This provision is intended to reverse the current practice of allowing an excess land purchaser to realize windfall profits by immediate resale.[48]

The proposed rules could have many positive effects. The goals of promoting family owner-occupied farms, and providing a maximum number of farms and widely distributed benefits would be furthered by the provisions in the rules for actual enforcement of the acreage limitation. Tightening of criteria for eligible purchasers, impartially selecting purchasers and restricting leasing all serve these goals. And the rule that sale prices and resale prices will be subject to approval should work to end speculative gain.

On the other hand, because of the widespread non-conformance with the limitations, enforcement will meet serious opposition and could disrupt agricultural operations. To cope with this problem, the rules provide that a period of adjustment will be given to allow those who do not live on or near their land time to bring themselves into compliance.[49] Additionally, owners of excess lands are given five years in which to dispose of them under recordable contracts. However, the rules do not provide any other means of easing the transition period. Such a change in land-use patterns may not be feasible for present farming methods. If the 160 acre dream is no longer

---

44. 42 Fed. Reg. 43044, and 42 Fed. Reg. 43048, *supra.*
45. 42 Fed. Reg. 43048, *supra.*
46. 42 Fed. Reg. 43047 (1977) (proposed; to be codified in 43 C.F.R. § 426.8).
47. 42 Fed. Reg. 43047-43048 (1977) (proposed; to be codified in 43 C.F.R. § 426.9).
48. 42 Fed. Reg. 43044 (1977).
49. *Id.*

238

possible, it is up to Congress to declare a new policy for reclamation law and new land use goals.

NANCY JONES

COMMENT

GROUND AND SURFACE WATER IN NEW MEXICO: ARE THEY PROTECTED AGAINST URANIUM MINING AND MILLING?

UNANSWERED QUESTIONS ABOUT THE ENFORCEMENT AND INTERPRETATION OF BOTH STATE AND FEDERAL WATER POLLUTION STATUTES LEAVE AN APPARENT VOID IN THE CONTROL OF THE URANIUM INDUSTRY IN NEW MEXICO.

New Mexico is important to the uranium industry: 49.5% of all domestic uranium is in New Mexico.[1] That supply, located in the "Grants Mineral Belt" has an estimated worth of four billion dollars.[2] Uranium mining is a lucrative business. In one year United Nuclear's net profits increased 39%, and it plans to do even better. On the basis of mining and milling costs of $20 per pound it estimates its reserves as of March 31, 1977 at 100 million pounds. If United Nuclear is able to sell the ore at the current price of $43 a pound, its plan of continued success should be easily realized.[3]

It is not so clear how important this industry is to New Mexico. Within the "Mineral Belt" are rivers, streams and aquifers on which New Mexico farmers depend for irrigation and watering their livestock. These same aquifers are the major source of water for domestic and industrial users in the region.[4] The uranium companies' methods of mining, milling and waste disposal affect both the surface and ground waters. While few people contend, as does Henry Zeller

---

1. Testimony of P. Howard, Rio Grande Chapter of the Sierra Club, Transcript of the Proceedings of the Application of Kerr-McGee Nuclear Corp. for NPDES Permits 59 (November 26, 1974) (hereafter cited as *Kerr-McGee Transcript*).

NPDES is the National Pollution Discharge Elimination System. No pollutant can be discharged into a "navigable body of water" without permission from EPA in the form of an NPDES permit. 33 U.S.C. § 1342 (Supp. 1975).

2. *Fuel Shortages Trigger a New Uranium Rush in N.M.,* Vol. 26, No. 8, Mining Engineering (August 1974) (a publication of the Society of Mining Engineers of the American Institute of Mining, Metallurgical and Petroleum Engineers).

3. "Earnings for 1978 fiscal year rose 48% to $31,800,000 . . . these outstanding results reflect both higher uranium production and an increase in the average price United Nuclear Corporation received for uranium delivered to customers." UNITED NUCLEAR ANNUAL REPORT (1978).

4. U.S. ENVIRONMENTAL PROTECTION AGENCY, *Water Quality Impacts of Uranium Mining and Milling Activities in the Grants Mineral Belt, New Mexico* (Dallas, TX: U.S. EPA, Region VI, Sept. 1975, EPA doc. no. 906/9-75-902 4). Also personal conversation with Maxine Goad, Water Quality Division, New Mexico Environmental Improvement Division (EID) (August, 1978).

of the Sierra Club, that "water is a possibly more valuable resource than uranium,"[5] both federal and state legislatures have enacted statutes, the Federal Water Pollution Control Act[6] and the N.M. Water Quality Act,[7] intended to balance the need to protect water with the need to produce uranium.[8]

As of July, 1978 the balance has tilted in favor of uranium production. Only one company has a facility which is subject to effective federal control over its operations.[9] Five companies have succeeded, since 1974, in having federal controls stayed as to them, while they are in adjudicatory hearings challenging the Environmental Protection Agency's (EPA) jurisdiction under the Federal Act.[10] And it is unlikely that many of the New Mexico uranium mines and mills in operation as of June 1977 will be subject to discharge plans required by regulations enacted pursuant to N.M. Water Quality Act. It is even possible that the regulations themselves will be declared inoperative by the N.M. Supreme Court. Nine uranium companies are presently objecting to their legality.[11] This comment, then, examines the effectiveness of the FWPCA and New Mexico's regulations in protecting both ground and surface water in the "Grant's Mineral Belt."

GRANTS MINERAL BELT

I. DESCRIPTION OF THE AREA

The "Grant's Mineral Belt" is a thirty mile wide strip extending from a point slightly north of Albuquerque west towards Gallup. Four mining districts predominate: Churchrock which is about 15 miles north of Gallup, Ambrosia Lake about 20 miles north of Milan, Paquate Jackpile about 10 miles north of Laguna and thirty miles

---

5. *Kerr-McGee Transcript, supra* note 1, at 51.

6. Federal Water Pollution Control Act, Act of Oct. 18, 1972, Pub. L. 92-500 §101, 86 Stat. 816, amending 33 U.S.C. §1151 (1970) and codified at 33 U.S.C. §1251 (Supp. 1975) (hereafter cited as *FWPCA* or *The Act*).

7. New Mexico Water Quality Act, N.M. STAT. ANN. §75-39-1 to 12 (Repl. 1968) (hereafter cited as *Water Quality Act* or *state act*).

8. §3-110, N.M. Water Qual. Control Comm'n Regs. (Jan. 1, 1977) (hereinafter *Regs.*) allows the EID to grant a variance for non-health contaminants to a discharger if the EID believes the "discharge plan demonstrates the maximum use of technology within the economic capability of the discharger . . . [or] that there is no reasonable relationship between the economic and social costs and benefits to be obtained." *Id.*

9. Only United Nuclear's Churchrock facility is subject to an effective NPDES permit.

10. 9(a)0 Fed. Reg. § 125.35(d)(2).

11. The companies who have challenged the regulations are: Bokum Resources Corp., Continental Oil Co., Gulf Oil Corp., Kerr-McGee Nuclear Corp., Phillips Petroleum Co., Rancher's Exploration and Development Corp., United Nuclear Corporation, United Nuclear Homestake Partners, and Union Carbide Corporation. They are doing so in a case entitled Bokum Resources, et al. v. New Mexico Water Quality Commission, No. 2869 (Ct. App. field Feb. 17, 1977).

west of Albuquerque, and Crownpoint about 16 miles north of Thoreau. Although groundwater is the principal source of water in the area, supplying the municipalities of both Grants and Gallup,[12] surface water is also important. Both the Puerco River, which is the receiving water of many of the mines in the Churchrock area, as well as the San Mateo Creek and its tributary, the Arroyo del Puerto, which are the receiving waters of the mines and mills in the Ambrosia Lake area, are used for irrigation of range land and for livestock watering.[13] Both are subject to New Mexico's general stream standards.

The water in the Ambrosia Lake area has already been affected. Discharges from Kerr-McGee's ion exchange plant and their mines, and from United Nuclear's ion-exchange plant have resulted in radium concentrations in Arroyo del Puerto which exceed New Mexico water quality criteria.[14] The increased concentrations of selenium and vanadium has rendered the stream unfit for irrigation, livestock watering and human consumption according to 1972 EPA Water Quality Criteria. Selenium contamination has also been found in the groundwater downgradient from the United Nuclear Homestake Partners mill.[15]

Still most company officials contend that humans have not been harmed. In fact, as of 1975 the Gallup, Grants, Milan and Bluewater water supplies had not been found to contain contaminants in excess of the proscribed limits.[16] However, not only is the data incomplete,[17] but New Mexico is confronted with the probability of great growth in the uranium industry in the next 40 years,[18] and the certainty that each company will have more waste to dispose of than it currently discharges. Consequently it is unreasonable to suppose that there is no problem yet since the lethal level is a measure of the density of the same kind and quality of radioactive particles already present in the water and unable to disappear before one million years.

One company promised that it would not oppose the 3.3 pCi/l limit[19] because

---

12. *EPA report, supra* note 4, at 2.

13. *Kerr-McGee transcript, supra* note 1, at 54.

14. *EPA report, supra* note 4, at 4.

15. *Id.*

16. *Id.* at 2.

17. Perkins, *Summary of Data Publicly Available for Uranium Industry,* EID Grants Mineral Belt file (January 1978).

18. DEPARTMENT OF ENERGY (DOE) GJO 100 (71) Statistical Data on the Uranium Industry.

19. pCi=picucurie. A picucurie is a measure of radioactive disintegration per unit time. The rate of radioactive disintegration depends on the particular chemical.

> [I] t was cognizant of the concerns of the New Mexico Environ-
> mental Improvement Agency and of the need to insure (pure water).
> Kerr-McGee will take all steps to reach the lowest picucurie limit
> consistent with the best practicable control technology available.
> Accordingly we will do all in our power to seek and achieve the 3.3
> limitation.[20]

But, Kerr-McGee, as other companies under only a moral obligation
to comply, has not done so. In fact, an EID survey conducted in
October, 1977 found that the Kerr-McGee facility was exceeding 3.3
pCi/l limit by 27 times and was emitting 89 pCi/l of radium 226.[21]
Apparently even a willing spirit needs the law's coercion.

In spite of this gross violation of the EPA "guidelines," Kerr-
McGee need not reduce its effluent because it is in the process of
challenging EPA's jurisdiction under the Federal Water Pollution
Control Act Amendments of 1972.[22] Whether its objection is valid is
the question which must be answered.

II. THE FEDERAL WATER POLLUTION CONTROL ACT AMENDMENTS OF 1972

In 1972 the U.S. Senate and the House of Representatives over-
whelmingly passed the amendments to the Federal Water Pollution
Control Act (the Act) over President Nixon's veto: 247-160 in the
House, 52-12 in the Senate.[23] The vote demonstrates Congress's
determination to safeguard water supplies for both present and
future generations. In an important step, Congress rejected the view
of previous congresses that industry could use water for waste disposal as long as it did not interfere with other uses of that water. The
Act's focus on polluters rather than on the pollution's effect on
water is specially significant in the Grant's Mineral Belt where, due to
inadequate monitoring and the often unknown effects and delayed
disease etiology of many of the discharged chemicals, it is hard to
accurately evaluate the harm done. Yet the legislative scheme forbids
justification of pollution on the grounds that "no one is being hurt."

The regulatory scheme of the Act is relatively simple. Basically,

---

20. James Cleveland (Superintendent of Environmental Control Individual Hygiene
Dept., Kerr-McGee Nuclear Corp.) *Kerr-McGee Transcript, supra* note 1, at 25.

21. Intra-office compilation of data by the Water Quality Division at EID.

22. It is not clear that EPA has the authority to waive limitations prior to final decision.
FWPCA, supra note 6, §1311 states that "except as in compliance with this section and
sections 302, 307, 318, 402 and 404 of this act, the discharge of any pollutant completed
by any person shall be unlawful." *Id.* None of these sections allow for waiver.

23. 118 CONG. REC. S 18554 (daily ed. Oct. 17, 1972); *Id.* H. 10272 (daily ed. Oct. 17,
1972).

any facility which discharges pollutants into "waters of the U.S." from a point source must obtain a permit issued by the EPA.[24] A permit requires a discharger to demonstrate that it is using, by 1977, the best practicable control technology (BPT) currently available and by 1983 the best available technology (BAT) economically achievable. Guidelines for BPT and BAT are established by EPA in terms of effluent limitations for the entire industry.[25] The state may, if it meets certain criteria, issue the permits instead of the EPA, subject to EPA approval.[26] Even if the state does not issue permits, it can require that provisions of state law necessary for the protection for water within the state, be included within the permits.[27] The Act provides both civil and criminal penalty provisions[28] as well as provisions for citizen suits.[29]

The crux of the problem concerning EPA's ability to control a company's discharges and the one remaining workable objection[30] raised by the companies in their challenge is the meaning of the words "waters of the United States." The Act prohibits discharges of pollutants to "navigable water." "Navigable waters" are defined as "waters of the United States and its territorial seas." EPA's jurisdic-

---

24. *FWPCA, supra* note 6, § 301(a) provides that "except in compliance with this section and sections 302, 306, 307, 318, 402, and 404, the discharge of any pollutant by any person shall be unlawful." 33 U.S.C. § 1362(12) (Supp. 1975) provides that "the term discharge of pollutant . . . means (A) any addition of any pollutant to navigable waters from any point source. . . ." *Id.* § 502(7) defines navigable waters as "water of the United States. . . ." *Id.*

25. 33 U.S.C. § 1314 (Supp. 1975) directs the EPA to publish "guidelines for effluent limitations" within a year of the Act's effective date. *Id.* It suggests that the EPA consult with appropriate state and federal agencies and other interested persons and lists the factors that the agency should consider in establishing BPT and BAT. The guidelines provide the general standard on which to base the specific limits in the permits.

26. 33 U.S.C. § 1342 (Supp. 1975). Twenty-seven states have already done so; New Mexico has not.

27. 33 U.S.C. § 1341 (Supp. 1975).

28. 33 U.S.C. § 1319 (Supp. 1975).

29. 33 U.S.C. § 1365 (Supp. 1975).

30. Between 1976 and 1977, five uranium companies applied for permits under protest contending that 1) the limitations imposed by the permit could not be achieved by July 1, 1977 using BPT, 2) EPA did not have the authority to impose discharge limits in the absence of EPA's promulgation of appropriate national effluent guidelines and standards of performance, 3) the state conditions imposed by the state certification go beyond federal law i.e. indirect discharges, discharge limits and monitoring techniques, and 4) their discharges were not into navigable waters. Issues raised in memo accompanying Kerr-McGee's request for an Adjudicatory Hearing, January 10, 1975, pursuant to 40 C.F.R. § 125, 36(b)(2).

Since the July 1, 1977 deadline is passed, the BPT issue is moot. And, since as of July 11, 1978, 1978 guidelines have been promulgated, the guideline issue is moot, at least as to these particular companies. As to the third objection, *see* notes 94-100 *infra,* and accompanying test.

tion depends on whether the discharges from the mines, mills and ion-exchange plants are discharges into "waters of the U.S." Since the facts concerning the discharges are in dispute, and the meaning of "waters of the U.S." is "shrouded in ambiguity," EPA's jurisdiction is a question both of fact and law.

A description of the hydraulic situation is helpful in understanding the legal issue. Four of the challenges concern discharges into San Mateo Creek in the Ambrosia Lake area, while the fifth involves a discharge into the Rio Puerco in the Churchrock area.[31] At Ambrosia Lake, the mines and mills discharge into unnamed arroyos which flow into either the San Mateo Creek or the Arroyo del Puerto which then flows into the San Mateo. Under normal circumstances the "discharge" in Kerr-McGee words, "goes down an arroyo (San Mateo Creek) 5-10 miles where it then disappears into the ground."[32] However, EPA in asserting jurisdiction is interested not in the present-day normal flow but in the unusual flow, and in past and future flows. EPA contends that thirty years ago the San Mateo reached the Rio San Jose, a tributary of the Rio Grande. It also claims that during severe storms the San Mateo once again reaches the San Jose, carrying enough water to flood two trailer parks. The EPA also offers proof that cows eventually sold out of state, drink from the Creek. Furthermore, the EPA asserts that once the Creek disappears from view, it in fact joins a groundwater flow part of which ends up in Milan water supply, albeit not for 145 years. That part of the "Creek" which is not used by Milan, could continue downgradient for another nine years where it would resurface at Horace Springs, and then join the Rio San Jose, a navigable stream.[33] The uranium companies dispute most of the EPA's factual contentions.[34] Presumably they will also dispute their legal significances.

---

31. The following is a list of the companies in adjudicatory hearings with a description of the receiving waters as appears on the permit.
    (1) Kerr-McGee Nuclear Corp.: natural watercourse into Arroyo del Puerto to San Mateo Creek (Actually Kerr-McGee alleges that its discharges from certain mines never reach the Arroyo del Puerto.); natural watercourse into the Puerco River.
    (2) Gulf Oil Corp.: unnamed arroyo tributary to San Mateo Creek.
    (3) Ranchero-Exploration and Development Company: San Mateo Creek.
    (4) United Nuclear Homestake Partners: Arroyo del Puerto tributary to San Mateo Creek.
32. Cleveland, *Kerr-McGee Transcript, supra* note 20, at 24.
33. Testimony of Charlie Nylander, Water Quality Division, EID, prepared for Adjudicatory Hearing on NPDES permit for Kerr-McGee Nuclear Corp. (July 11, 1978) (hereafter cited as *Nylander, adjudicatory hearing testimony*).
34. Testimony of Dr. William Gannis, expert witness for Kerr-McGee, hearing on NPDES permit for Kerr-McGee Nuclear Corp. (July 11, 1978) (hereafter cited as *Gannis, adjudicatory hearing testimony*).

Kerr-McGee Nuclear Corporation has a mine in the Churchrock area whose discharge is also the subject of an adjudicatory hearing. EPA contends that the discharge flows into an unnamed tributary of the Puerco River which joins an unnamed drainage system of the Puerco River which then flows into a stem of the Puerco River, through the City of Gallup into Arizona.[35] Kerr-McGee thinks it significant that there is no flow in the unnamed arroyo "upstream" from its plant and that the flow downstream is not always continuous.[36] The significance of EPA's factual contentions of course depends on the interpretation of "waters of the U.S."

III. EPA'S JURISDICTIONAL DISPUTE

At the outset it is important to determine whether groundwater is encompassed within "waters of the U.S." for if so there is no issue as to EPA's jurisdiction. A literal reading of "waters of the U.S." would cover groundwaters since aquifers are certainly part of the United States. However, an amendment to include groundwaters within the regulatory scheme of the Act was defeated.[37] That defeat has been treated as indicative of Congress's intent to exclude discharges into groundwater.[38]

However, legislative intent not to regulate groundwater per se should not preclude regulation of discharges which first flow to the surface and then percolate into the ground. Congress rejected the amendment thinking that the federal government did not have the "vast store of knowledge essential to full protection of subsurface"[39] waters and that therefore it should not interfere with or displace "the complex and varied state jurisdiction over groundwater."[40] The amendment was defeated not because groundwater was thought unimportant[41] but because Congress feared that the EPA lacked the expertise to determine BPT and BAT. But what was

35. *Nylander, adjudicatory hearing testimony, supra* note 33.

36. *Gannis, adjudicatory hearing testimony, supra* note 34.

37. The Senate defeated the groundwater amendment by a vote of 86 to 34. A LEGISLATIVE HISTORY OF THE FEDERAL WATER POLLUTION CONTROL ACT AMENDMENTS OF 1972, at 597, Senate Committee on Public Works (1973) (hereafter cited as *Legis. History*).

38. *See* Train v. Colorado Public Interest Research Group, No. 74-1270, slip op. filed 16 June 1, 1976; United States v. GAF, 389 F. Supp. 1379 (D.S.D. 1975); and Exxon Corp. v. Train, 554 F.2d 1310 (5th Cir. 1977).

39. 118 CONG. REC. H2642 (daily ed. March 28, 1972).

40. S. Rep. No. 414, 2 *Legis. History, supra* note 37, at 1491.

41. In fact, even a cursory glance at *The Act, supra* note 6, shows concern for groundwater: §102(a) (Comprehensive Programs for Water Pollution Controls) states "The Administration shall, after careful investigation, and in cooperation with other federal agencies, interstate agencies, and the municipalities and industries involved, prepare and develop comprehensive programs for preventing, reducing or eliminating the pollution of navigable

really meant to be excluded from regulation was the deep well injection process of *United States v. GAF*[42] and *Exxon Corp. v. Train*[43] not the sort of discharges made by the uranium companies which may reach groundwater. In the case of the uranium companies' waste, the fear of complicated technology is unjustified. The technology is the same whether the effluent ends up in a stream or in the groundwater. It is not logical that under an act which uses technology as the regulating criteria mere happenstance of the terrain should determine EPA's jurisdiction.

Knowing that the legislative history neither mandates regulation of discharges to groundwater nor precludes their control does not resolve the issue of EPA's jurisdiction. The crucial question then is the significance of the Congressional omission of the word "navigable" from the definition of protected waters. "Navigable waters of the United States" is the term used in previous acts to define the extent of federal control over maritime commerce. The term encompasses two distinct concepts:

> First the waters had to be navigable, this meant any water that was or had been capable of sustaining maritime commerce or could be given such capability through reasonable public works. Second they had to be navigable "waters of the United States." This meant that they form in their ordinary condition by themselves or by uniting with other water, a continual highway over which commerce is or may be carried on with other states.[44]

Because many in Congress thought that navigable waters as defined in the *Daniel Ball* too narrowly restricted the scope of federal jurisdiction, "navigable" was amended to read "waters of the United States." Although there is general agreement that the omission was intentional, the uranium companies and the EPA dispute its new meaning.

Not surprisingly EPA interprets the omission as giving it broad jurisdiction. Simply put, the EPA through its interdepartmental memos and decisions of counsel defines its limits over any water of the United States in terms of whether "pollution of the waters" affects interstate commerce.[45] However, until the Supreme Court

---

waters and *groundwaters*, and improving the sanitary condition of surface and *underground waters."* *Id.* (emphasis added). For further evidence of interest in pollution control of groundwaters *see The Act, supra* note 6, §104(5), §106(e)(1), §212(a), §208(b)(2)(k), §304(a)(1)(A) & (B), §304(e), and §402(b)(1)(d).

42. 389 F. Supp. 1379 (Tex. 1975).

43. 554 F.2d 1310 (5th Cir. 1977).

44. The Daniel Ball, 77 U.S. 557, 563 (1870).

45. John Quarles, Assistant Administrator for Enforcement and General Counsel issued a memo on February 6, 1973, which after defining "navigable water of the U.S." as 1)

rules on the meaning of "navigable waters" for purposes of the Act, one must examine the legislative history and developing case law. For even if the EPA asserts jurisdiction it may be overturned.

A case which, if accepted as controlling, would be dispositive of the issue is *United States v. Phelps-Dodge*.[46] There the court held that discharges to normally dry arroyos could be controlled if they end up in groundwater in which there is some public interest. It states:

> For the purposes of this Act to be effectively carried into realistic achievement, the scope of its control must extend to all pollutants which are discharged into *any waterway* including normally dry arroyos, where any water which might flow therein might reasonably end up in any body of water, to which or in which there is some public interest, including underground waters.[47]

Since there is "some" public interest in New Mexico's groundwater, under this court's rationale permits in both Ambrosia Lake and Churchrock would be required.

Phelps-Dodge has not been appealed and it has been cited as good law.[48] Perhaps a court hearing the appeal will follow it unquestioningly. However, that is unlikely. Other than policy reasons there is little support for a broad assertion of jurisdiction. Its reference to groundwater seems contradicted by legislative history.[49] It is worthwhile, therefore, to examine what congress intended in its definition of navigable waters and how those words have been treated by courts.

The term "navigable waters" has been rarely discussed in Congress. The most quoted and the most significant is the comment of the House Conference Committee. It reads: "The conferees fully intend that the term 'navigable waters' be given the broadest possible constitutional interpretation unencumbered by agency determinations which have been made or may be made for administrative purposes."[50] That language tracks the language in the House Report,[51] and has given rise to the statement that Congress intended

---

navigable in fact and 2) capable of being used in interstate commerce, reasons that the omission of "navigable" means that the only remaining requirement, then, is that the pollution of the waters must be capable of affecting interstate commerce.

46. 391 F. Supp. 1181 (D. Ariz. 1975).

47. *Id.* at 1187.

48. Comm. of Puerto Rico v. Alexander, 438 F. Supp. 90 (D.D.C. 1977); Wyoming v. Hoffman, 437 F. Supp. 114 (D. Wyo. 1977).

49. *See* discussion *supra* note 37-39.

50. Committee of Conference H.R. Rep. 92-1465, 92nd Congress, 2nd sess. 144 (1972).

51. H.R. Rep. No. 92-911, 92nd Congress, 2nd sess. 335 (1975) (hereafter cited as *House Report*).

for the EPA to assert jurisdiction "to the maximum extent permissible under the commerce clause of the Constitution." *Natural Resources Defense Fund v. Calloway.*[52] If that were the only comment in the legislative history then presumably the District of Columbia court's statement and EPA's interpretation of its authority would be correct. However, there are other references. The report of the Senate Committee on Public Works,[53] and even the House Report[54] placed in context do not show a Congress determined to bestow upon EPA jurisdiction to the maximum extent of the Commerce Clause.

These reports indicate a much more modest intent. They are concerned that the EPA not be limited to controlling discharges into waters which were navigable-in-fact and capable of being used in interstate commerce—that is the *Daniel Ball* definition of navigable waters. They show their approval of recent court decisions, all of which involve water which has the potential for use "in the stream of commerce between the states." These reports seek to contrast the new meaning with the narrow coverage of previous acts which failed to recognize waters not part of a navigable-in-fact interstate highway. Aware that water moves in hydraulic circles and it is essential that discharges be controlled at the source, they wanted the EPA to control discharges into streams which although they themselves weren't navigable-in-fact might enter navigable-in-fact streams.

The facts in a leading and widely quoted case reflect just such a situation. *United States v. Ashland Oil and Transportation Co.*[55] involved a company's discharge "into the waters of a small tributary of Little Cypress Creek . . . (which) is a tributary to Cypress Creek, which is a tributary to Pond River, which is a tributary to Green

---

52. 392 F. Supp. 685 (D.D.C. 1975).

53. The control strategy of the Act extends to navigable waters. The definition of this term means the navigable waters of the United States, portions thereof, tributaries thereof, and includes the territorial seas and the Great Lakes. Through a narrow interpretation of the definition of interstate waters the implementation of the 1965 Act was severely limited. Water moves in hydrologic cycles and it is essential that discharge of pollutants be controlled at the source. Therefore, reference to the control requirement must be made to the navigable waters, portions thereof and their tributaries. Senate Committee on Public Works, S. Rep. No. 92-414, 92nd Congress, 1st sess. 77 (1975).

Obviously, the Senate was concerned that the waters which flow into navigable waters be regulated. However, it does not refer at all to regulating waters that are used in ways other than in navigation.

54. When the House Report stated that "navigable waters" be given the broadest possible constitutional interpretation, "navigable waters" had not yet been re-defined as "waters of the United States." That occurred later in the Conference Committee. Thus, when the House Report says that navigable waters should be broadly defined, it still retains a notion that *navigable* waters and *not* waters of the United States should be so broadly defined.

55. 504 F.2d 1317 (6th Cir. 1974).

River . . . only Green River is actually navigable 'in fact' in terms of water-borne commerce."[56] The court decided that Congress intended this tributary of a navigable river to be covered. In fact that is exactly what the Senate Report recommended.

What is interesting about *Ashland* however is not merely the decision to require a permit, but the language that the court used to reach that decision and the subsequent use of that language by other courts. In justifying Congress's constitutional powers to control pollution the court stated: "We believe . . . that Congress was convinced that uncontrolled pollution of the nation's waterways is a threat to the health and welfare of the country, as well as a threat to interstate commerce."[57] It then listed irrigation, fishing, boating, swimming and the dislocation of industry as examples of uses of water which can affect commerce. In so doing it went far beyond what had been mentioned by Senate or House reports and started a trend in which courts, as in *Phelps-Dodge,* have looked to "the *intention of congress* . . . to eliminate or reduce as much as possible all water pollution throughout the United States both surface and underground," (emphasis added)[58] rather than on the statutory scheme devised.

For example, in *United States v. Holland,*[59] a case involving the periodic inundations of wetlands, the court held that the EPA could control defendant's activities above the mid-high tide water mark, the line which had marked the boundary of federal jurisdiction under previous acts. Although it ostensibly justified its decision on the grounds that any pollution which might reach navigable waters should be controlled at its source, the court referred to the effect of defendant's activities on the eco-system. The implication is that if a facility's discharge touches the eco-system, as all do, then EPA has jurisdiction.[60] As congressman James C. Wright of Texas observed . . . "the court now says that Congress meant the permit program to apply literally to every pond and puddle in the U.S.[61] Although the puddle case has yet to appear it is difficult to find any court which

---

56. *Id.* at 1320.
57. *Id.* at 1325.
58. United States v. Phelps-Dodge, 391 F. Supp. 1181, 1187 (D. Ariz. 1975).
59. 373 F. Supp. 665 (M.D. Fla. 1974).
60. "The inclusion of ecological factors in the determination of whether the corporations should grant a construction permit allows for the denial of a permit *on purely ecological, rather than on navigational grounds"* (emphasis added). Properties Inc. v. Train, 399 F. Supp. 1370, 1381 (D.D.C. 1975).
61. CURRENT DEVELOPMENTS, Envt'l Rep. 1758 (Feb. 13, 1976). Congressman Wright is a member of the House Public Works and Transportation Committee having jurisdiction over water pollution control legislation.

has rejected EPA's assertion of jurisdiction over a discharge to surface water.[62]

The language used by the courts then, implies agreement with EPA's "affecting commerce" assertion of jurisdiction. Thus the discharges of the uranium companies would be subject to NPDES permits. Admittedly this interpretation is more in line with the goal of "water quality which provides for the protection and propagation of fish, shellfish and wildlife and provides for recreation both in and on the water,"[63] without encouraging industry dislocation since it is mere coincidence that wildlife and fish use water that are part of the "stream of commerce."

However, even with the narrowest construction of navigable waters, EPA may be able to assert jurisdiction if it shows that occasionally the discharges into San Mateo Creek reach the Rio San Jose and that discharges at Churchrock flow into the Rio Puerco, because they both flow into interstate streams. A court may also be convinced by the argument that because at one time the discharges from the San Mateo flowed into the Rio San Jose, the San Mateo should be treated as a navigable water. *Puente de Reynosa, S.A. v. City of McAllen*[64] held that a portion of the Rio Grande could be considered navigable because evidence of prior use would raise a presumption that navigability could be restored.

The importance of a stream occasionally flooding a couple of trailer parks and being used by cows depends on how closely the courts stick to a notion of navigability. The dicta of the *Ashland* and *Holland* courts would require that a permit be obtained.

The fact that the discharge reaches Milan's water supply or Horace Springs will probably be more significant if it gets there within 150 years rather than 1000 years as Kerr-McGee contends. One hundred and fifty years is a conceivable time frame while a court may decide that the consequences of uranium or radium contamination 1000

---

62. For examples of court approval of EPA assertion of jurisdiction see: PFZ Properties Inc., v. Train, 393 F. Supp. 1370, 1381 (D.D.C. 1975); Wyoming v. Hoffman, 437 F. Supp. 114, 145 (D. Wyo. 1977); Comm. of Puerto Rico v. Alexander, 438 F. Supp. 90, 92 (D.D.C. 1977); Conservation Council of North Carolina v. Train, 398 F. Supp. 653, 673-4 (E.D.N.C. 1975); Leslie Salt Co. v. Froelke, 403 F. Supp. 1292 (N.D. Cal. 1974); Sun Enterprises Limited v. Train, 394 F. Supp. 211 (S.D.N.Y. 1975); Minnesota v. Hoffman, 543 F.2d 1198, 1200 (8th Cir. 1976); Sierra Club v. Lynn, 502 F.2d 43 (5th Cir. 1974).

63. 33 U.S.C. §1251(a)(2) (Supp. 1975). The court in United States v. GAF Corp. 389 F. Supp. 1379 (S.D. Tex. 1975), stated that a discharge into underground waters could be regulated under the FWPCA, provided that it could be shown that the underground waters flow into or otherwise affect surface waters. *See also* Sierra Club v. Lynn, 502 F.2d 43, 64 (8th Cir. 1974): If a ranch is discovered to be polluting the underground water supply (of the municipality) the developer has the legally enforceable duty to remedy the situation.

64. 347 F.2d 43 (5th Cir. 1966).

years hence is too speculative. However, even if EPA can prove that the discharge will reach Milan in 100 years, the uranium companies may argue that in essence this constitutes a discharge to groundwater. It is excluded from the Act's regulatory scheme because it is the type of discharge that congress intended to be left to the states to control.

IV. STATE GROUNDWATER REGULATIONS

EPA's inability to regulate the uranium company's discharges in the Ambrosia Lake and the Churchrock may provide the impetus needed to implement the "congressional plan . . . to leave control over subsurface pollution to the states."[65] In fact, Congress's belief that the states know best reflects the attitude of some members of the New Mexico Environmental Improvement Division (EID), which is charged with implementing the state act. The practicability of that attitude, however, depends upon the companies' success in avoiding New Mexico's groundwater regulations.

Under authority granted it by the New Mexico Water Quality Act,[66] the Water Quality Control Commission is authorized to adopt standards and regulations to protect New Mexico's waters. However, not until ten years after the Act was passed, on January 11, 1977, did the commission adopt standards and regulations governing groundwater.[67] In brief, the regulations require every person whose discharge affects groundwater to submit a plan to EID which demonstrates that the discharge will not result in concentration of pollutants in the water in excess of New Mexico's water quality standards. Some exemptions are provided for, such as those contaminants in particular discharges already covered by an NPDES permit.

However, the regulations distinguish between facilities before and after so that only the latter *must* submit a discharge plan. Facilities presently operating as of June 18, 1977 need not submit a plan unless EID specifically requests them to do so. As of July 1, 1978, of all the uranium mines and mills in operation before June 1977, only Anacanda has been asked to submit a plan.[68]

---

65. Exxon Corp. v. Train, 554 F.2d 1310 (5th Cir. 1977).
66. N.M. STAT. ANN. § 75-39-4(c) (Repl. 1968); § 73-39-4 (Repl. 1968).
67. The standards and regulations were amended on June 14, 1977 and on November 8, 1977.
68. Plants in operation before June, 1977 but which modify their operations are subject to regulations applicable to new facilities. Rancher's Exploration and Development Corp., Gulf Mineral Resources, United Nuclear Corp. and United Nuclear Homestake Partners have been required to submit discharge plans for existing discharges which are being modified. Personal conversations with Maxine Goad, New Mexico Water Quality Division, EID (August 1978).

As of August 4, 1978 EID has sent notification of discharge requirements to 21 uranium mines and mills who started operation after June 18, 1977. Eight discharge plans have been received and two have been approved.[69] Yet, even these may be declared inoperative if the nine uranium companies now challenging the regulations are successful.[70]

The state act differs from the FWPCA in ways which reflect both differences in philosophy and available expertise. Unlike FWPCA which operates under the premise that no one has the right to discharge pollutants, and sets effluent limitations in accordance with available technology,[71] the state act sets water quality standards in terms of use, and prohibits discharges which would result in higher concentrations of contaminants than "use" allows.[72] And unlike the federal act which is directed at improving the nation's waters, the state act allows water to be polluted up to a certain level. Moreover, it provides that if the water, due to previous pollution, contains levels of pollutants above the statutory standard, the higher contaminated level will be the standard.

In part, New Mexico's approach reflects the fact that it has limited funds. The state does not have the resources to set effluent limits for each industry and apply them to each discharge. Instead it places the burden on the discharger to prove that its effluent does not unduly pollute the states' waters.[73]

The regulations do have some advantages. First, they definitely cover discharges to groundwater. Second, because the exemption for the NPDES permit is operable only if the permit is "effective and enforceable," and only for those constituents included, the discharges to San Mateo Creek could be covered.[74] Moreover unlike the permits, the regulations have not been suspended. And the companies' appeal is moving more rapidly than the adjudicatory hearing.

In their challenge the companies have alleged a number of defi-

69. Report on progress of compliance with groundwater regulations, compiled by Bruce Garber, attorney with EID. One additional plan has been approved as of June 16, 1978.

70. See note 11.

71. See 40 CFR 130.17 (1977); 33 U.S.C. § 1313(c); 303(C)(20) (1977).

72. Regs., supra note 8, § 3-103 sets three uses: human health, domestic water supply, and irrigation.

73. Steve Reynolds, New Mexico State Engineer, thought the Commission should put the burden of proof where it belongs, namely on the discharger. He should prove that his discharge would not impair any other use of the groundwater. This would parallel state water law where a permit cannot be granted except with a finding that other rights will not be impaired. Minutes of Commission Consideration for Adoption of Proposed Regulations Governing Discharges to Ground Water (Dec. 14, 15, 16, 1976). Adopted by the Commission Jan. 26, 1977. 2 RECORD OF BOKUM RESOURCES, et al. 29 (hereafter cited as Minutes).

74. Regs., supra note 8, § 3-105.

ciencies in the regulatory scheme. Three issues merit brief discussion: 1) whether the Water Quality Commission gave sufficient reasons for the adoption of the regulations; 2) whether the commission has statutory authority to regulate leachate; and 3) whether the toxicity standard is too vague.

1) *Reasons*

The New Mexico courts require that an administrative agency explain why it adopts regulations for "some very practical reasons." In *City of Roswell v. N.M. Water Quality Commission*,[75] the court incorporated Davis's elucidation of the reason's requirement:

> The reasons have to do with facilitating judicial review, avoiding judicial usurpation of administrative functions, assuring more careful administrative consideration, helping parties plan their cases for rehearings and judicial review, and keeping agencies within their jurisdiction. 2 Davis, Administrative Law Treatise 16.05 (1958).[76]

In this case where the record reveals only the notice of public hearing, the testimony of various experts, and others, some exhibits and the regulations, the court held that "it could not effectively perform the review."[77] The New Mexico courts require reasons primarily in order to "know what [they] might review."[78] Clearly then an agency must provide a minimal record.

The type of record required is suggested by the court in *New Mexico Municipal League v. New Mexico Environmental Board*.[79] There under the authority granted it by the Environmental Improvement Act, the EIA issued regulations relating to the collection and transportation of solid waste. The EIA explained the purpose of the regulation in 12 reasons.[80]

The regulations were challenged under the same statute which the uranium companies now challenge the groundwater regulations.[81]

---

75. 84 N.M. 561 505 P.2d 1237 (Ct. App. 1972).
76. *Id.* at 565.
77. *Id.*
78. SCHWARTZ, ADMINISTRATIVE LAW 421 (1976).
79. 88 N.M. 201, 539 P.2d 221 (Ct. App. 1975).
80. The reasons speak in general terms and track the statutory language concerning EID's responsibility for environmental protection. Some of the reasons are that no regulations concerning solid waste disposal have been adopted previously, that testimony shows both that existing procedures impinge on public health and that new procedures will not place an unreasonable economic burden on the state, and that these new regulations are necessary to protect the health of New Mexico's citizens.
81. Both the appellants in the groundwater regulations and appellants in City of Roswell appealed under N.M. STAT. ANN. § 75-39-6 (Repl. 1968, Supp. 1975). It states that "the regulations shall be set aside only if found to be: (1) arbitrary, capricious, or an abuse of discretion; (2) not supported by substantial evidence in the record or reasonably related to the prevention or abatement of water pollution; or (3) otherwise not in accordance with law."

The *Municipal League* court found the reasons to be adequate stating that the "Environmental Improvement Board, here has given us sufficient indication of its reasoning and of the basis upon which it adopted these regulations."[82] The court also stated that "in its brief the Board amply demonstrated that each of the 12 reasons for adopting the regulations were founded upon evidence and testimony it had accumulated during several meetings it had on the proposed regulations."[83] Interestingly enough, in order to sustain the regulations the court was willing to accept the *post hoc* rationalizations of a lawyer's brief.

Under the *Municipal League* test therefore, the court should uphold the groundwater regulations. The reasons adopted by the Water Quality Commission are similar to those approved in *Municipal League*. Moreoever, in the groundwater appeal the record also consists of 16 pages of minutes which, with only a few exceptions, explain the basis of the Board's adoption of each standard and regulation.[84] Finally the brief submitted by the Water Quality Commission further details the reasons for certain standards.

To say that the *Municipal League* criteria has been met does not resolve the issue of adequate reasons. A second important purpose of the reason requirement is to assure more careful administrative consideration. The *Municipal League* court's acceptance of the lawyer's brief as a source of reasons indicates that it was more concerned with its ability to review. However, if a court is alerted to other purposes of the reason requirements, such as assuring that an agency has engaged in careful deliberations, then it may require an agency to meet a stricter standard than that permitted in *Municipal League*.

Even with the stricter standard applied, the regulations should be approved. The minutes provide just the precise picture of the Commission's reasoning that is desirable. For example, they adopted the standard for uranium of 5 mg/1 rather than the 2 mg/1 suggested by their staff because "2 mg/1 would probably cause an economic hardship and 5 mg/1 appeared safe enough at the time."[85] However gaps do exist in the minutes. For example, the Commission accepted the selenium standard suggested by the staff without explaining why.[86] Because the selenium standard was objected to by the companies, the

---

82. New Mexico Municipal League v. New Mexico Environment Board, 88 N.M. 201, 539 P.2d 221 (Ct. App. 1975).
83. *Id.* at 204.
84. *Minutes, supra* note 73, at 28-44.
85. *Minutes, supra* note 73, at 5.
86. *Id.* at 4.

brief submitted by the Water Quality Commission explains quite succinctly the danger of selenium and the need for its control. However, a court interested in forcing an agency to be careful in its reasoning may be dissatisfied with a brief alone.

In sum, up till now the New Mexico courts have required reasons primarily to help them perform their reviewing function. If they continue to be interested only in that, the record presented by the Water Quality Commission should suffice. However, if they want to assure "more careful administrative consideration" then the court should demand a fuller record for those regulations where the Commission unquestioningly accepted its staff's recommendation. Of course a desire that the Commission articulate the reasons for its decisions should not be translated into a requirement that any decision that it make be correct "beyond any reasonable doubt." The court should not require documented evidence of death and disease before it declares a substance dangerous. Any margin of error should lie on the side of health and safety.

The reasons issue raises significant questions as to the type of record that an agency should make. The two remaining issues show how the uranium companies, through their lawyers, are able to raise issues which irritating at best, at worst show a real disregard for the health of the people of New Mexico.

2) *Leachate*

One of the questions presented by the uranium companies is whether the Commission has the authority to regulate leachate.[87] The issue can arise for uranium companies in two ways. First, uranium companies may emit water which itself meets the groundwater standards but in the course of reaching groundwater, leaches out pollutants which cause it to exceed New Mexico groundwater standards.[88] Second, a company may construct a tailings pond which,

---

87. Leachate is the liquid that has percolated through soil or other medium. *Regs., supra* note 8, §3-104 provides that a discharge place is required for leachate, but exemptions are allowed. §3-105 exempts leachate which conforms to §3-103 standards, has a total nitrogen concentration of 10 mg/l or less and does not contain toxic pollutants. And, even if not exempted under §3-105, if it leaches undisturbed into natural material it is exempted unless a hazard to public health results. *Id.* §3-109(D). Rainwater leachate is also exempted unless a hazard to public health results. *Id.* §3-105(H).

88. In their brief, the uranium companies describe a situation in which a farmer who uses mineral-rich land would be required to have a discharge plan if it rains on the land and leaches out material which would cause the water to be a hazard to public health. Although a sympathetic scenario, it exists only in a lawyer's mind. Rain would not leach out such minerals in levels high enough to create a hazard to public health.

when rained upon, emits contaminants which pose a "hazard to public health."[89]

Whether the Commission has the authority to regulate depends on an interpretation of section 75-39-4.1(A) of the New Mexico statutes[90] which reads: "By regulation the commission may require persons to obtain from a constituent agency designated by the commission a permit for the *discharge of any water contaminant either directly or indirectly into water*" (emphasis added).

The issue centers on the meaning of "discharge of contaminants." The companies interpret this as being the action of its mines and mills in emptying effluent; however, such a reading ignores the phrase "into water." If the focus of the regulations were on the chemical makeup of the water emitted then neither the rain nor the "clean" water that is discharged would require a permit. Such would be the case if the regulating mechanism was effluent limitations. However, it is not. Because the thrust of the regulations is to preserve water quality the focus of the regulations has been on the receiving water, not the water emitted.[91]

Besides objecting to the definition of "discharge," the companies object to the regulation of leachate as unfair, portraying such regulation as forcing them into being responsible for something over which they have no control such as water which has already been emitted from their mines or mills, or rain that happens to fall on their lands. The objection is disingenuous. The "clean" water emitted from the mines and mills will become dangerous only if it travels through dangerous materials. It will be the uranium companies who have discharged the dangerous materials on the ground, and the uranium companies who will have constructed tailings piles through which the rainwater and "clean" water will seep.

3) *Definition of Toxic Pollutants*

The uranium companies also object to the definition of toxic pollutants as being unconstitutionally vague, and to the meaning of "hazard to public health." The apparent problem is the requirement

---

89. *Regs., supra* note 8, § 1-101(N) states that a hazard to public health exists when water which is used or is reasonably expected to be used in the future as a human drinking water supply exceeds at the time and place of such use, one or more of the numerical standards of § 3-103(A), or the naturally-occurring concentrations, whichever is higher, or if a toxic pollutant affecting human health is present in the water. In determining whether a discharge would cause a hazard to public health, the director shall investigate and consider the purification and dilution reasonably expected to occur from the time and place of discharge to the time and place of withdrawal for use as human drinking water.

90. N.M. STAT. ANN. § 75-39-4.1(A) (Repl. 1968, Supp. 1975).

91. *See* discussion *supra* notes 71 and 72 and accompanying text.

that any facility which discharges toxic pollutants must have a discharge plan. Theoretically a facility may not know that it is discharging toxic pollutants, not get a plan and then be held both civilly and criminally liable. However, it is not likely that this would ever happen to any uranium company. A facility that discharges toxic pollutants is probably discharging substances which are subject to control under the regulations, and would therefore require a discharge plan. Obviously all uranium mines and mills will be required to have a discharge plan. The mechanics of getting a plan approved are such that once a facility has an approved discharge plan and is abiding by it, it cannot be held either civilly or criminally liable for the discharge of any pollutants unless it has first been told what pollutants it cannot emit. Therefore it is impossible that a uranium company would be forced to guess at whether a pollutant is toxic.

The test for whether a regulation is unconstitutionally vague is whether someone of common intelligence must guess at its meaning.[92] Since the uranium companies never will have to guess the issues is obviously frivolous.

The fact that the uranium companies could raise the leachate and vagueness issues demonstrates how little they care that the effluent from their mines and mills will pollute the waters of the "Grants Mineral Area" causing people living in the area to suffer serious physical harm. It is possible, of course, that the pollutants may not affect the inhabitants of the "Grants Mineral Belt." However, where, as here, the cost of pollution control is minimal—$520,000 a facility compared to a company's net income of $21 million[93]—and the value of healthy citizens inestimable, their objections seem not only petty, but malevolent.

State Certification

As stated above, the state can incorporate provision of its statutes concerned with water quality into a NPDES permit.[94] The advantages for New Mexico would be twofold. First, the state's limited resources could be conserved since the federal government would enforce the state's standard. Second, such an incorporation would trigger the citizen suit provision of the federal act. Here, too, state resources could be conserved. New Mexico's goal of clean water

---

92. State v. Orzen, 83 N.M. 458, 493 P.2d 768 (Ct. App. 1972).

93. In 1974, United Nuclear estimated that the cost of pollution control would be $520,000 for its Churchrock plant. Transcript of Proceedings before the EPA concerning NPDES permit for United Nuclear Corp., Churchrock Mine (21) (Nov. 26, 1974) (hereafter cited as *United Nuclear Transcript*). *See* note 3 *supra.*

94. 33 U.S.C. §1341 (Supp. 1975).

might be better achieved if watchdogs with federal enforcement powers were encouraged.

Although the Water Quality Commission and EID have considered including state water quality regulations in the NPDES, this has not yet been done. The reasons are not entirely clear. During deliberation of groundwater regulations the Water Quality Commission discussed the possibility of incorporating parameters controlled solely by the Water Quality regulations with the NPDES permit.[95] In March, 1977, the EID asked EPA if they were willing to regulate these parameters as well as discharges that occur upstream from the EPA measuring point (NPDES outfall) in the permit. The request raised interesting legal issues.

First, since New Mexico regulates by water quality standards rather than by effluent limitations, there was a question as to whether standards should be directly included in a permit and, if not, whether either the EPA or EID should translate the standards into effluent limitations. Second, since discharges upstream from the NPDES outfall are not from a point source, and are to be regulated only in order to protect groundwater,[96] this request posed the question as to whether EPA could control discharges from non-point sources to groundwater under state certification. In its answer, EPA did not address the second issue. It merely said that only "effluent limitations" would be appropriate.

Section 401(d) of the FWPCA states that any "certification provision under this section shall set forth effluent limitations and other limitation . . . (and) any other *appropriate requirement of state law* . . . (emphasis added)."[97] EPA understood "appropriate" to refer to effluent limitation. Effluent limitations are obviously much easier to enforce than water quality standards. Because EID has never pursued its request, the question of control of groundwater has not been answered, and EPA's position concerning the meaning of "appropriate" has not been challenged.

Whether EPA's position accurately reflects Congressional intent is unclear. As was stated by the Office of Management and Budget (OMB) and the EPA in their joint comments on the bill, "the scope of the catchall phrase is not defined."[98] Various comments through-

---

95. *Minutes, supra* note 73, at 9.

96. By discharges upstream from a NPDES outfall, the EID was referring to seepage from a tailings pond which could reach surface or groundwater, and seepage from a stream that occurs after the stream leaves the tailings pond but before it reaches the NPDES outfall point.

97. 33 U.S.C. §1341 (Supp. 1975).

98. *Legislative History, supra* note 37, at 853.

out the legislative history show Congress's intent to respect a state's perogative to set more stringent limitations.[99] However, the comments do not say that the EPA must translate state water quality standards into effluent limitations. In fact, comments on Section 303 water quality standards and implementation plans indicate that the Congress, recognizing the difficulty and cost that determining effluent limitation in terms of water quality standards would entail, delegated the task to "secondary priority."[100] Thus, even if EPA is responsible, it can probably excuse itself on the grounds that more vital issues need be dealt with first.

CONCLUSION

The reluctance of EPA to incorporate New Mexico's groundwater regulations and grant the request that discharges upstream from the NPDES outfall be controlled, exemplifies one of the major difficulties in controlling uranium companies, namely, lack of resources. Limited funds mean that New Mexico does not have adequate data to determine whether certain elements such as molybdenum, vanadium, and selenium should be controlled in the permit.[101] The state can only request that monitoring be done. More seriously, although it has the authority to do so, EID cannot demand discharge plans from many of the uranium mines and mills already in operation.[102]

Lack of resources is not the only problem. The uranium companies through their lawyers can prolong the adjudicatory hearing for many years, and may successfully thwart the state's groundwater regulation. If the New Mexico court is swayed by the companies' argument, it may be another five years until discharges to groundwater will be controlled.[103] The lack of a citizen suit provision in the state statute means that the New Mexico Citizens for Clean Air and Water must, as amicus curiae, support the EID against the com-

---

99. § 301(b)(c)(1) of the *FWPCA, supra* note 6, specifically allows for compliance with a state's stricter standards.

100. *Legislative History, supra* note 37, at 171.

101. *United Nuclear Transcript, supra* note 93, at 36.

102. EID can't request that certain elements be controlled because they don't have the data to support the requests. However, the EID can request that the EPA monitor the elements and provide the data to EID. EID has done precisely that. Personal conversation with Maxine Good, New Mexico Water Quality Division, EID (July, 1978).

See discussion in Exxon Corp. v. Train, 554 F.2d 1310 (5th Cir. 1977), in which the court concluded that Congress intended to have the EPA provide "the states with information needed to operate their own groundwater pollution programs the establishment of which 402(a) was designed to encourage." *Id.* at 1326.

103. EID fears that if the regulations are declared illegal, the Water Quality Act will have to be amended and new regulations declared.

pany's challenge rather than assert a position more in line with its own concerns.

Finally, both the federal act and the state regulations should be much stronger. Discharges to groundwater should be controlled by the FWPCA. The issue of EPA's jurisdiction should not have been allowed to prolong regulation so many months. It is senseless in an act that is concerned with technological limits, to allow the happenstance of terrain determine that New Mexico's waters will be polluted.

KATHLEEN KENNEDY TOWNSEND

FUTURE STRATEGIES FOR ENERGY DEVELOPMENT—A QUESTION OF SCALE

Proceedings of a Conference at
Oak Ridge, Tennessee, October 20 and 21, 1976
Oak Ridge Associated Universities
1977. Pp. 297. $9.00, s.c.

This volume contains nine papers which discuss various aspects of energy strategy. They may be regarded as addressing some aspects of the "soft vs. hard energy paths" debate. Indeed, the essay by Amory Lovins which launched this debate, "Energy Strategy: The Road not Taken," is reprinted in this volume. This remarkable article which first appeared in the October 1976 issue of *Foreign Affairs* single-handedly reoriented the discussion of national energy strategy and policy.

Soft energy alternatives are those that rely on dispersed small scale energy sources, rather than large, centralized sources such as nuclear electric stations. Persons conversant with energy policy will be familiar with Lovins' views, which are now also held by many others. I will not try to summarize them because they depend on a fairly complex argument; a brief summary would necessarily turn out to be a parody.

To me the other most interesting papers in the volume are one by Alvin Weinberg, "Can We Do Without Uranium" and one by Sam Schurr and Joel Darmstadter, "Some Observations on Energy and Economic Growth."

Weinberg approaches future energy strategies from an "asymptotic" perspective, looking very far into the future to a time when fossil fuels are gone and humankind must rely on the various forms of solar power or nuclear reactions for energy. He finds that an "all solar future is almost surely a low energy future unless man is prepared to pay a much higher share of his total income for energy than he now pays." If this remote future is to be nuclear, then it must be in a type of world in which effective and socially acceptable systems exist to deal with some ten tons of plutonium each day. Weinberg says of nuclear ". . . if it is indeed to become the dominant energy system (its price), may be an attention to detail, and a dedication of the nuclear cadre that goes much beyond what other technologies have demanded." Such exercises are very fascinating, but it is somewhat difficult to see what, if anything, they mean for our behavior and thinking today except to warn us that if there is a panacea for ultimate energy problems, we have not found it yet.

It is sometimes asserted, especially by advocates of rapid development of hard technologies, that economic growth as measured by rising GNP marches in lock step with energy use. Schurr and Darmstadter examine this relationship and find reason to believe that it is not, or at least does not have to be, as rigid as all that. The structure of the economy affects it, changing prices affect it, and conservation efforts can affect it. Their conclusion is supported by the fact that the energy content of GNP in the United States has dropped substantially in the last few years.

That the soft vs. hard energy strategy debate is a genuine thing was brought home strongly to me recently when I participated in a conference "California's Energy Future" sponsored by the California Energy Resources Commission. Quite serious proposals were put forward to make Calfornia a demonstration state to show that an economy can be prosperous while undergoing a transition to soft technologies. Among participants were a number of representatives from the energy industries and utilities who appeared to be taking the whole thing quite seriously. The seed which Amory Lovins planted has grown into a flourishing tree.

I will close on a note of mild criticism of the volume under review. While I cannot claim to be an energy expert, I have had far more opportunity to read about, hear about, and consider the energy issues than many potential readers of this book. Nevertheless, I have had great difficulty in forming a satisfying and coherent view of appropriate energy strategy. A rich complex of technological, geological, economic, social, and ethical issues must be considered. In my opinion the volume would have been greatly improved if the papers were accompanied by probing comments. We have not seen the chief participants in the energy strategy debate challenge each other enough in print. Adopting this format would help draw out the controversial and debatable points and assist the reader in understanding where he stands.

ALLEN V. KNEESE*

*Dr. Kneese is with Resources for the Future.

THE POLITICAL ECONOMY
OF THE OIL IMPORT QUOTA

YORAM BARZEL and CHRISTOPHER D. HALL
Stanford, California, Hoover Institution
Press, 1977. Pp. 96, $8.95.

This book is the first of a series of studies of public issues sponsored by the Domestic Studies Program of the Hoover Institution. It comes well recommended; the praises for the book from a list of distinguished scholars (Cootner, Dam, Tullock, Stigler) quoted on the dust jacket and in the Preface are almost intimidating to the reviewer. It must be admitted, however, that their evaluations are justified by the text, which sets a high standard for future volumes in the series.

The subject is not an unfamiliar one. The oil import quota system has been studied before, and it is the subject of a recently published treatise from Resources for the Future.[1] Those interested in energy policy will find the Barzel and Hall volume to be a useful compendium of facts, including some that have not been noticed in other studies. Its chief contribution, however, is its analysis of the interaction of government regulation and the private economy. The analysis is set in the context of the particular policy of import control, but it uses analytical economics and some emerging theoretical insights of political economy.

Of course, in some respects oil import control policy is a sitting duck. Like the more recent incarnation of energy policy, the quota system of 1959 to 1973 was a notable example of inept administration, confused objectives, inappropriate instruments, unanticipated effects, and general policy disintegration. Barzel and Hall point out, often with wry humor, the manifestations of those problems. Their analysis of these aspects (such as the effects of the overland restriction, the special treatment of the West Coast, and the special treatment of Puerto Rico and the Virgin Islands) is sharp and incisive. Their discussion of the petrochemical problem and their analysis of the brokerage and distribution of the rents that import restrictions generated are especially good.

This reviewer's only complaint, apart from a few instances of careless editing and proofreading, is that the authors' introduction gives a somewhat misleading impression of the thrust of the book. The introduction concentrates almost entirely on a single point: that oil

---

1. DOUGLAS R. BOHI & MILTON RUSSELL, LIMITING OIL IMPORTS: AN ECONOMIC HISTORY AND ANALYSIS (1978).

is not a homogeneous commodity, and a regulatory system which assumes that it is homogeneous (as the Mandatory Oil Import Program did, in effect) will create difficulties and distortions in its pricing and allocation. The remainder of the book does indeed address that problem, and shows that the program produced a bias toward high-priced, high-value imports which affected the whole subsequent product structure. But this problem is one among many elements of the program that the book discusses.

What the book shows is that the regulations did not and probably could not integrate this highly complex market into a system of control consistent with the ostensible ends of the program. They did not anticipate or direct the reactions of the multitude of firms and other interested parties to the control system. They could not withstand counter-pressures. Regulations and allocations not only failed to solve any problems, they also made two or three new ones grow from the stalk of every old one. Barzel and Hall obviously intended to develop a rich and animated picture of the interactions between public regulation and private enterprise in a dynamic mode, accenting the object lessons for those who would make elementary static economic models the basis for a simply conceived and statically oriented regulatory policy. In this aim they have succeeded brilliantly.

JAMES W. McKIE*

---

*Professor of Economics, University of Texas at Austin.

COAL IN THE U.S. ENERGY MARKET

RICHARD L. GORDON
Lexington: D.C. Heath and Company, 1978.
Pp. 225

The purpose of this book is to survey the history and prospects of the coal industry in the United States. Coal accounted for more than 70 percent of all U.S. fuel consumption during the period 1900 to 1920, but its share decreased to less than 20 percent by the 1970's. In recent years rising costs and decreasing availability of oil and gas have led national policy makers to suggest that a shift toward greater reliance on coal may be both desirable and imminent. The major objective of the book is to appraise the outlook for coal in various segments of the U.S. energy market.

The book includes an evaluation of the present situation and future outlook with respect to the costs of mining and transporting coal as well as an assessment of the prospects for coal use in major consuming sectors. Historic patterns of coal production and consumption are reviewed, and a number of recent coal consumption forecasts are summarized and compared. In addition, the author devotes a complete chapter to review of recent public policy decisions which have major effects on the outlook for coal.

Because of the pervasive influence of public policy on coal production and use, energy policy is treated in the first chapter. Examination of recent policy decisions indicates that their effect has been to place severe restrictions on coal production and use. The critical policy areas affecting coal production have been underground mine health and safety, strip mine reclamation, and leasing of federal and Indian lands. Air pollution regulation has been the dominant influence on coal use. The author concludes that: "These controls promise to equal or exceed those created for nuclear power."

Historic patterns of coal production and use indicate that electric utilities have assumed an increasing importance in coal consumption. The electric utilities' share of total coal consumption rose from 13 percent in 1947 to 42 percent in 1960 and 70 percent in 1976. Today, the industrial sector is the only other major user of coal; coal consumption by the household, commercial, and transportation sectors has declined to negligible levels. Thus, it appears that the prospects for coal in the near future will depend primarily on fuel choice decisions by electric utilities and, to a lesser extent, by the industrial sector.

A review of coal production and transportation cost analyses indicates that ". . . the competitive position of coal is far more uncertain than the publicists contend." The author concludes that present coal reserve data and mining cost analyses provide only a limited basis for coal supply analysis. Three recent coal supply studies are reviewed. These studies indicate that the availability of low cost coal, particularly east of the Mississippi, may be considerably less than is often suggested. All three studies show that efficient coal supply expansion will involve significant increases in the share of national output produced by the western mining areas because of the more elastic supply of coal in the West compared to the East. Transportation costs have a major influence on the competitive position of coal. A review of studies aimed at estimating costs of expanded coal transportation via unit trains and slurry pipelines is undertaken.

Analysis of factors affecting coal utilization includes presentation of alternative projections. These projections are based on various assumptions regarding future trends in capital and operating costs of both nuclear power plants and electric generating facilities fired by eastern and western coal. The author concludes that, while the uncertainties in this area are substantial and a wide range of outcomes is plausible, nuclear power may pose a considerable threat to coal. Regarding the relative position of eastern and western coal, the author offers his opinion that ". . . western coal will indeed increase its market share even in the face of the best available technology approach to air pollution control."

In conclusion, this is an excellent book which deserves serious attention. It provides a thorough review of the factors affecting coal use through the mid-1970's and identifies the critical parameters affecting future production and consumption patterns. A number of major energy policy analyses have been completed over the last few years, and the book serves a very useful role in interpreting and integrating these studies. In addition, the author presents substantial original analysis in the area of utility fuel choice. Although much of the analysis is based on complex econometric models, the results are presented in a manner suitable for the general reader. The wealth of data will be useful to many, and the insights regarding data limitations will be valuable to all serious students of U.S. energy policy. Readers will appreciate the bibliography and fine job of indexing which enhance the book's usefulness as a reference.

F. LARRY LEISTRITZ*

*Visiting Professor of Agricultural Economics, Texas A&M University.

WHERE WE AGREE—
A REPORT OF THE NATIONAL
COAL POLICY PROJECT

Edited by FRANCIS X. MURRAY
Boulder, Colorado, Westview Press, 1978

This two-volume report of the work of the National Coal Policy Project culminates a noble and surprisingly successful attempt to narrow the policy differences separating environmentalists from the producers and consumers of coal. Given the perceived needs of environmentalists and the nature of the production and consumption processes involving coal, conflict was bound to occur. In fact it has occurred throughout coal's turbulent history.

Gerald L. Decker, formerly with Dow Chemical, a heavy coal user, saw the need to reduce the areas of disagreements among the competing factions surrounding the coal industry. He was instrumental in forming a group of coal producers, coal users, and environmentalists who in one year, with financial aid from foundations and industry, hammered out a "consensus on important national policy issues related to the use of coal in an environmentally and economically acceptable manner." A measure of their success is the record of the Mining Task Force composed equally of industry and environmental representatives. This group agreed on over 150 recommendations concerning future coal production and failed to agree on only two major issues. The batting average was lower in other areas studied. Indeed, this report is quick to acknowledge the areas of outright disagreement and partial agreement, as well as issue areas that remain unresolved due to a lack of time or resources to study them thoroughly.

The project was organized into five major areas, each of which was the responsibility of a task force composed of industry and environmental members. The groups include Mining, Air Pollution, Conservation and Fuel Utilization, Transportation, and Energy Pricing. Volume one covers the last four areas (plus a short report on the work of an Ad Hoc Emission Charge Task Force), and the second volume is devoted solely to the Mining Task Force report.

Some of the task force reports are more complete than others. The Mining Task Force report is excellent. It covers a wide range of issues including reclamation, impact of coal mining on water quality, socioeconomic impacts of coal development, and regulation standards. It also approaches the issues from another dimension by making regional assessments of the impact of coal mining on the environment and by recognizing correctly that conditions in the coal industry vary sufficiently from one region to another to warrant a geographical orientation.

Weaknesses appear in the report of the Transportation Task Force where some issues get superficial treatment. In addition one wonders why the study focuses on *energy* pricing when the investigation is supposedly centered on coal. The discussions of marginal versus full cost pricing for electricity are not unique to coal-based electric power. A discussion of the effect on pricing of the existing industry structure and of the government's coal leasing policy might have enriched this section.

An overall assessment of this ambitious project leaves one with mixed feelings. The progress made in narrowing differences between traditionally antagonistic groups is admirable. The project is effective in demonstrating the possibilities for substituting negotiation and explanation for the adversarial process as a means of conflict resolution. One suspects that the parties agreed on many issues because, for the first time, they listened to what the other side had to say. Since the project remains in existence, its leaders might try to find a way to marshall support in Washington and in the state capitals for implementation of their recommendations.

What misgivings does the report foster? First is the concern that coal industry representation on the Task Force may have been inadequate and not representative of the entire industry. "Industry" representatives sometimes took positions affecting coal production without the concurrence of coal operators, the industry members being coal *consumer* representatives. Thus, in the chapter on "Fuel Utilization and Conservation" the report concludes that "use of coal should be viewed as an intermediate step toward the use of long-term, sustainable resources." It is hard to imagine a coal operator agreeing with that conclusion, and in fact, making of the recommendation by the Task Force was devoid of coal industry representation.

The second major area of concern in an assessment of the overall project is the question of the durability of the Task Force recommendations. Each member of the study group represented himself or herself and did not represent the organization with which he or she was affiliated. Would the same problems addressed at a later date by different representatives of the same interest groups be resolved as they were by the members of the National Coal Policy Project.

These are not trivial objections. Nonetheless, they should not obscure the enormous value of this pioneering study. These volumes can serve as a ready reference for the reader interested in learning the status of the environmental conditions surrounding coal in the late 1970s. Useful bibliographies and glossaries accompanying many sections aid both the lay and professional reader. This work's greatest value, however, is not necessarily its informational content. Rather, it is perhaps most important for its delineation and sharpening of issues separating environmentalists and industry representatives and for its creation of a model for conflict resolution, the adoption of which could profit other adversarial groups.

REED MOYER*

*Professor, University of California, School of Business Administration.